A
TIME
for EVERY
PURPOSE
UNDER HEAVEN

❧

A
TIME
for EVERY
PURPOSE
UNDER HEAVEN

The Jewish Life-Spiral as a
Spiritual Path

Arthur Ocean Waskow ❧ Phyllis Ocean Berman

Farrar, Straus and Giroux

New York

Farrar, Straus and Giroux

19 Union Square West, New York 10003

Distributed in Canada by Douglas & McIntyre Ltd.

Printed in the United States of America

First edition, 2002

Library of Congress Cataloging-in-Publication Data

Waskow, Arthur Ocean, 1933–

    A time for every purpose under heaven : the Jewish life-spiral as a spiritual

path / by Arthur Ocean Waskow and Phyllis Ocean Berman.

      p.   cm.

    Includes bibliographical references and index.

    ISBN 0-374-27779-6 (alk. paper)

     1. Judaism—Customs and practices.   2. Life cycle, Human—Religious aspects—

Judaism.   *3. Spiritual life—Judaism.   4. Jewish way of life.   I. Berman, Phyllis*

Ocean, 1942–   II. Title.

BM700 .W37 2002

296.4'4—dc21

                            2002017078

Designed by Abby Kagan

www.fsgbooks.com

1 3 5 7 9 10 8 6 4 2

To ev'ry thing (turn, turn, turn)
There is a season (turn, turn, turn)
And a time for ev'ry purpose under heaven.

A time to be born, a time to die;
A time to plant, a time to reap;
A time to kill, a time to heal;
A time to laugh, a time to weep.
A time to build up, a time to break down;
A time to dance, a time to mourn . . .

A time for ev'ry purpose under heaven.

©   —*Kohelet* (Ecclesiastes) 3:1–4,
according to Pete Seeger

Contents

Three Prefaces

A Time for each and both of us, to set forth a purpose under Heaven.

Arthur's Preface

Twenty-some years ago, I published a book—*Seasons of Our Joy*—on the flow of the Jewish festivals as a spiritual path, from the renewal of the year in autumn to the burn-out of scorching summer, and beyond the burn-out to begin again.

Ever since, I have thought it would be desirable to write a book about that other great spiral of Jewish life and ceremony—the life-cycle from birth through death, and beyond. But I have felt unready, unable, to do so—until now.

In 1980, I was not yet fifty years old. As I write in 2001, I am climbing toward seventy, that marker that the Bible tells us is a reasonable life-span. By now I have had the chance, as I had not in 1980, to undertake the transformations of middle age: to begin and move deeply into a new marriage, to change my career path, to watch my children grow into adulthood, begin their marriages, and themselves have children, to greet my first grandchildren, to understand and speak to God in a new way, with new images and metaphors.

Even more important, perhaps, I have begun to taste the age after "middle age." Oddly, when I make comparisons with macro-history I look upon "middle age" as less like the "Middle Ages" than like "Modernity." For "middle age"—at least my own—felt like that burst of Doing, Achieving, Making that we see in the Modern Age of the human race. And this time that follows after my own "middle age" feels like the time for contemplation, reflection, reassessment. Time to see the successes that sprouted from my failures, the failures that flowered from my successes, time to see the limits of what I have achieved, time to turn all that into the stories that can help give birth to others' achievements. And this seemed like at least a sip of the savor of "maturity," the next age and the one that must be experienced if one is to offer a decent teaching of the cycle of a life as a journey with the Spirit.

Then came two more steps.

In May 2000, my first grandchild—a granddaughter—was born. As I stood to bless her in the *B'rit Bat* ceremony that her mother and father had woven, I recalled that thirty-three years before, when her mother was born, my own mother said with urgency that I must arrange to name her in a Jewish way. But then I could not fathom what to do. For I knew of no such ceremony, and there was no synagogue or other Jewish community to which I felt any call at all. So the moment passed, and I did nothing.

But here I was, standing at my daughter's daughter's side and there *was* a ceremony. Not just a naming, but an entry into covenant. An entire generation of women had made sure there would be such a ceremony. My own daughter had made sure there would be. And there was a man to stand beside her who helped shape this rejoicing, and now a father who could see the next spiral of parenting begin to climb on its own curving path.

Indeed, I myself had helped create a Jewish community that could take delight in these new possibilities. And now there were congregations that did call out to me.

Sweet. And painful. And a welling-up of Thanks.

Then, just five months later, my newborn grandson, my son's son, entered the covenant in the most ancient way, through circumcision. I sat in the *sandek*'s chair and the *mohel* told me to grasp the two legs of my grandson. "Hold tight!" said the *mohel* as he lifted the knife. I did. And I felt something very like an electric charge as the knife swooped and the foreskin fell away.

These two births gave birth to a new I, and to my share in this writing.

In short, till now I was not ready to essay this book. Please God that now I am.

Phyllis' Preface

For more than half a century, I have attended, participated in, created, and led Jewish life-cycle rituals. While each occasion has been significant to the people involved, in only some of the ceremonies did I feel the palpable presence of G!d.

When women ask each other about where and when we feel the presence of G!d, most of us talk about birthing, about nursing, about loving, about intimate conversations with beloved friends (and occasionally strangers), about bedrooms and bathrooms and kitchens and walks in the woods. Rarely do I hear about G!d's presence in prayer, in ritual, in synagogue, in public.

So I have asked myself: What is it that gets lost when we bifurcate our worlds into private and public? And how can we integrate the essential elements of each—G!d's presence, intimacy with others, self-understanding and revelation, and public acknowledgment—into the other?

It seems apparent why we should want G!d's presence, intimacy with others, self-understanding and revelation, as integral parts of our public rituals. Without those elements, such ceremonies lose their potential value for us, become empty and devoid of meaning. But why *is* public acknowledgment so important, why not just have a rich emotional life in private? This is the question that has dominated my thinking for the last decade.

Reb Zalman Schachter-Shalomi speaks of the paradigm shifts that have transformed Judaism from the biblical period to the rabbinic period to this renewal/holistic period. We can only dimly glimpse what life was like for the Western Semitic tribes before the paradigm shift that gave us Biblical Israel. For those of us, especially women, who have lived within the myths of such books as Marion Zimmer Bradley's *The Mists of Avalon* or Anita Diamant's *The Red Tent*, we can taste within ourselves a time before recorded history when women lived in a public arena that was not dominated by men. Whether these imaginings bear any relation to actual history, we may never know.

What we do know is that such imaginings arise from and in turn give rise to our shaping of the next Jewish paradigm. For we live today in a time of liberation, in a time of feminism, in a time when women are rabbis and organization presidents and company CEOs. At the same time, we continue to do these deeds and play these roles in male-constructed contexts, fitting ourselves into a design we had no hand in drawing.

Our ritual life marks the many transitions in what we pray will be a long lifetime. It poses the possibility of integrating our inner experiences with the wisdom of the outer world. It hints at others to whom we can honestly turn for witness, for support, for comfort, for advice, for appreciation, for companionship along the unknown path ahead. And for generations people have been able to find some of this essential contact with an individual or a small group of friends.

However, when that human turning toward one another can only happen in private, in secret, the potential for wholeness (which is G!d's presence in the world) is shattered. We then reduce the public encounters to emptiness, rote recitations of meaningless formulas. And, even more tragic, we feel ourselves separated from that wholeness of the universe because, for most of us, men and women alike, we accept such public occasions as determining what is speakable in public. Though we may be satisfied by the warmth of private connection, when we are real about our lives and our struggles we are left to feel that there is something wrong with us when our deepest concerns do not make for acceptable conversation in the public domain. Or, instead of dismissing ourselves as empty, we may dismiss these public occasions as meaningless, since the issues that burn most strongly within us cannot be talked about in public.

Ashamed, or alienated. Either way, we are a house divided.

But we do not have to live this way. We can draw from the flow of our life-cycle moments of powerful transition that we welcome in the presence of our chosen community. We can shape an ever-growing number of moments when we truly "come of age" by transforming the parts of ourselves that have been divided into private or public beings, emotional or intellectual beings, feminine or masculine beings, real or rote beings, into the whole and holy beings that we are.

May this book, at once a private and a public encounter, be such an opportunity for inviting the presence of that wholeness.

A Preface from the Two of Us Together

One form of midlife transformation is the transformation of a marriage, from the old terms of an old covenant to new terms for a renewed covenant.

To our surprise—we did not plan it that way—this book itself became an important part of the transformation of our marriage in midlife. You might almost say that the writing of this book became the midlife ceremony of our marriage.

For a marriage lives through a life-cycle of its own as an individual does. Indeed, the marriage's life-cycle is likely to be more complex because it is made of two different life-cycles spinning on their own trajectories, sometimes in rhythm with each other and sometimes not. In a marriage, if one of the two partners births a new identity, that joggles the marriage itself into another place. That "place" is not a stable one—it is a time of crisis/transformation, when the new identity and the old covenant confront one another. The question then is whether the marriage can give birth to a new self, a shared self, rooted in a new covenant that is different from the one the partners originally agreed to. If the two partners can create a new covenant with each other, the marriage as a partnership has made a new covenant with the Other, the Divine Other. Then the marriage, as well as the partners, can go forward into a new harvesting of the renewed life.

Most of these transformations within the life-cycle of a marriage are not made known through public ritual. Since society has taught most of us not to show our dirty linen in public, there are few opportunities for camaraderie on the difficult path of partnering. But most relationships undergo such cycles, even though only our most intimate friends may know when this is happening.

At such a moment, many marriages collapse, unable and unwilling to change the terms of engagement.

At such a moment, the desire to honor the love behind the covenant, and to expand it to make room for the new identity, can make miraculous openings in what we may have feared were static boundaries.

In the fifteenth year of our own marriage, we reached such a moment in our lives when the world stood still for us. Assumptions we had made, behaviors we had lived with, expected points of view—all suddenly disintegrated as silent identities within us took on new voices.

As the two of us began to address the question of whether we could make a new covenant embodying different assumptions and behaviors, what seemed at first the utterly separate question of this book arose.

We had a contract to write it. But we also had many other urgent things to do. And the "we" that had agreed to write it was suddenly shaken by an earthquake. Should just one of us actually write it? Or should we write it together after all?

Against all "reasonable" good sense, we decided to dance in the earthquake, to write the book together. At the time we thought we were making this choice for intellectual and practical reasons, not for the sake of an emotional or spiritual renewal.

Yet once we entered into the process, we found ourselves bound together in new ways: As we set to work on the specific chapters on marriage and on intimate friendships, we found ourselves reflecting on our own lives, weaving our own transformations into the book and the book into our own transformations. And throughout our labors on the book, we were learning Torah together, weaving our thoughts together, even weaving our thoughts into separate patterns of our own selves, within the larger pattern.

We bound ourselves together in a new and deeper loving in our marriage.

And we bound the book together, in new and unexpected ways. This was our process: For some chapters, Arthur wrote a first draft, Phyllis and he discussed it in detail, Arthur redrafted it, and the two of us worked out a final version. For other chapters, it was Phyllis who wrote the first draft and the same steps followed. And there were also moments when the life-experience of one or the other of us seemed so distinctive that we decided the book should speak for that passage in one voice alone. Three of these had to do with major ceremonies that Phyllis had crafted for her own life-path, and these essays are specially marked off. About four-fifths of the book, then, is what we wove together in the most intimate ways; and the rest is embroidered so as to expand and enrich the whole and become an integral part of it while remaining visibly distinctive. We preserved and made visible what was "I," what was "Thou," and what was "I-Thou."

Out of the process came not only a new book, different from the work that either of us had ever done before, but also a new marriage, different from what either of us had ever lived before. So this book is not *about* the ceremonies of the spiraling life-cycle, it actually *is* the ceremony we unknowingly created, for making a new turn on the spiral of our own lives.

Introduction

B Y SAYING THIS MUCH OF OUR OWN LIVES, we have of course already begun to hint at our sense of how to walk a Jewish path through the decades of our living. But to rely on our own specific life-paths as the sole source of this pointing toward a Jewish path of life would be sheer chutzpah. To do this well, we need also to draw on the accumulated wisdom of the Jewish people in its long history.

In that "life-path" of the people as a whole, the celebrations and observances of the markers of an individual Jewish life-cycle have themselves been changed as the Jewish people achieved its own pinnacles of Achievement and its own times of Reassessment, Reflection, and Renewal.

In times of reassessment—like the present—some Jews have persevered in giving older practices new richness; some have drawn upon the tradition to shape new possibilities; and some have felt disconnected from any version of the tradition. This book offers guideposts and trail-markers for those who are walking any of these life-paths.

The Great Life-Cycle, Millennia Long

Somewhere between the era we remember as that of Abraham and Sarah and the writing of their stories into definitive form, the Jewish people went through the rhythm of casting off an older shape of living—one about which archeologists today can only speculate—to build a solid civilization of their own, which we now call Biblical Israel.

Still later, the same community felt its patterns disrupted and its paradigm shattered by the triumphs of Hellenistic-Roman civilization. They paused to absorb and reflect on what they had done. Then they moved to renew their collective identity by shaping what we call Rabbinic Judaism, which flourished for almost another two millennia. Now the Jewish people, amid the shattered fragments of that Rabbinic Judaism, has again paused to absorb and reflect on what we built in those centuries, and to begin the process of renewal and rebirth toward some new form for Jewish peoplehood.

We cannot yet know what that form will be. It may look quite different from the past. Or it may not take on a single shape. It may include both a modified and reinvigorated version of Rabbinic Judaism and a major new paradigm, that of Holistic Judaism, as different from (and as rooted in) both previous Jewish eras as the rabbinic model was different from (and rooted in) the biblical era.

When Jewish life as a whole is transformed, the specifics of the life-cycle change. Since the forms of the individual life-cycle were so different for shepherds, farmers, and orchard-keepers living in a single land from what they were for wanderers in Europe and Africa and Asia, these two eras of the Jewish macro-life-cycle came up with different versions of the Jewish micro-life-cycle. And now, melted down in the intense heat of Modernity into a still newer form, the Jewish people has begun again to reshape the individual life-cycle, and to reshape the ways of celebrating its turning points. We can dimly—only dimly—see the emerging contours of what might be a new approach to the life-cycle as a spiritual path.

In this book we make all three models available, to educate and inspire the Jews of our oncoming future.

Think back to the beginning of the twentieth century—the mid-fifty-seventh century, in Jewish time. What were then the markers of a Jewish life-path?

- Very shortly after birth, the circumcision of a male child. In a few places, in honor of even a girl baby's birth the father might be invited to read Torah; but for most households, no ceremony at all to welcome a daughter. A few weeks later, for a firstborn son, a ceremony of "redemption."

- As puberty approached, most boys would begin preparing for a formal synagogue ceremony of recognition that they had come of age to responsibly observe the traditional precepts—including the one of reading part of the weekly Torah portion. In many communities, a girl who whispered to her mother that she had begun menstruating might get her face slapped as a ritual acknowledgment. In a few communities, when a girl reached twelve her family would note the milestone in a public way—but never would she herself be invited to lead a public reading in the synagogue.

- A few more years into full adulthood, most of the men would take a central role in the ceremony of marrying women, who were mostly passive in the public ritual. Many of the women (but far fewer than would have been the case still one century earlier) would then during their marriages separate from their husbands during their menstrual periods, and end that separation with a ritual immersion in the *mikva*.

- For millions of Jewish men and women, there were separations that lasted not for weeks but years—as millions of men left their towns and villages and wives behind to cross the ocean to America, bringing the wives only later. These separations were marked with tears and foreboding, but never were they made the focus of formal Jewish ritual.

- Some years after marriage, there might for a very few be a divorce—more of these few in the somewhat secularized American setting than in the traditional communities of Eastern Europe, North Africa, the Near and Middle East. For many among these few, the only "ceremony" would take place in the civil law courts. Since men as a body were in total control of all political and almost all economic machinery, individual men were almost always in control of the divorce arrangements. For the tiny number of couples who were divorced in a context traditional enough for the divorce to include an event in Jewish law, the man would play the far more active role.

- An infinitesimal number of non-Jews were joining the Jewish people, and were marking the change with ritual immersion and (for some of the men) with a real or symbolic circumcision.

- And then, for most people between fifty-five and sixty-five or so, death came. Women and men found themselves more or less equally the focus of a set of mourning rituals—though among the mourners, men once again took the preeminent role.

And that was it.

Large parts of the Jewish community were in full flight from many of the markers of Jewish celebration, but birthtime (for boys) and perhaps early puberty (for boys), marriage, and death were still the nexus-points of Jewish ceremonial observance.

Now—just a century later—look at the differences:

- Girl babies are welcomed with more and more richness and intensity of celebration; in some communities, with ceremonies equal to (though different from) the welcoming of boys.

- Many girls welcome their twelfth or thirteenth birthdays with synagogue-based ceremonies identical for entering womanhood to those the boys observe for entering manhood at thirteen.

- A small but growing number of young women are celebrating their first menstrual period in joy, some even publicly.

- Women and men marry much later, and many of their wedding ceremonies treat them as equals who are joining in a partnership and covenant. In more and more communities, two men or two women may also celebrate beneath a *ḥuppa*.

- Probably even fewer women are going to the *mikva* after their menstrual periods, but the ceremony has become a matter of public debate and dialogue. Ritual immersion itself—in a traditional *mikva* or not—is being practiced by men as well as women on occasions like the beginning of Shabbat or of a holyday.

- Many more couples are finding a divorce—and a Jewish divorce—necessary, and if they do, the ceremony is much more likely to treat the separating women and men as equals.

- Great numbers of people who were not born into Jewish households are choosing to become Jews, and are undertaking the traditional ritual forms for doing so.

- Somewhere around age fifty or sixty, many Jews—instead of preparing to die—are looking forward to another thirty years of life, and may be preparing to change careers, partners, relationships with their children, or spiritual paths. Many of them are finding it important to take public note of this major change in their lives. The women, especially, as they reach menopause, may be marking the event with ritual.

- And when, much older than their great-grandparents, they do die, the men and the women among their families and friends will likely find the ceremonies of grief to be equally available to them.

- Perhaps even more startling, people who are facing the myriad vicissitudes of life—abortions and stillbirths, adoptions and serious emotional/sexual relationships other than marriage, major illnesses, leaving the childhood home, finding a job, changing cities of residence—are seeking ways to observe, celebrate, or mourn these events with Jewish metaphors and symbols. Instead of fleeing Jewish symbols to mark their life-changes, many Jews are seeking to create new Jewish ceremonies and revivify the old ones.

Why is all this happening, and what do we make of it?

In the century just past, two aspects of Jewish time drastically changed. For individual Jews, along with their neighbors of many other communities and traditions in a world transformed, the life-cycle itself has been transformed. Most of us live a great deal longer than our forebears of a century ago. And our lives are much more varied (though fewer of us may be undertaking that biggest of all changes, a move across the oceans to a new homeland and a new tongue).

We not only live longer, we change our spouses, our jobs, our vocations, our homes much more often. Whole sections of our lives, like the time between fifty and seventy and the time between seventy and ninety, are filled with new experiences. Maturation is stretched out, so that even life-chunks that most of us lived through a century ago—like the years from thirteen to twenty-three—are much richer in variety and in the modulations of growing up. So the simpler markers of a simpler life no longer satisfy.

And for the Jewish people as a whole, times have changed. The rush of transformation in just one century has both enriched and scarred the Jewish world.

- Women and men within the Jewish world as well as outside it are treating each other far more equally.
- Where many Jews lived for millennia, there are now scarcely any, and the ghosts of mass murder hover in the air.
- Where few Jews had lived for millennia, there are now millions.
- Relationships between the Jewish people and many other peoples have been transformed: (a) Jews who were once powerless now hold not only political and military might in a state of their own but political, economic, and cultural power in a way unheard of in societies where they remain a minority. (b) Religious communities that at one time described Judaism as depraved and Godforsaken now honor it; Jewish teachers and leaders who were once ignorant of or hostile to other religious and spiritual communities now dignify them in respectful dialogue.

- Jews, along with all other peoples, are facing an uncertain and troubling future in the relationship between human beings and the earth.

And, after a period of embarrassed retrenchment and retreat in the face of a triumphant Modernity, Judaism and Jewish culture are experiencing twin renaissances: a surge of "restoration," trying to spit out Modernity and return to a richer Judaism of the past; and a surge of "renewal," trying to digest Modernity and move forward to a richer Judaism of the future.

In short, if an entire people can be said to have a collective life-cycle, the Jewish people has in the past century been living through both a death and a rebirth. In part from the teachings of Rabbi Zalman Schachter-Shalomi, we have learned to think about this crisis as comparable to two previous upheavals in Jewish life: one during that misty era in which Biblical Israel was formed, and the far clearer one in which Biblical Judaism died and Rabbinic Judaism came into being. In our own generation, these simultaneous life-cycle changes in the individual and collective lives of Jews are rooted in the same worldwide change; the great upheaval of Modernity.

Given all this, how do Jewish individuals, households, neighborhoods, congregations, on-line collectivities, give shape to their lives not as a meaningless bunch of unexpected buffetings and benefits but as a coherent whole?

The Fourfold Path

For the Jewish people as for many other peoples, the most basic pattern of the life-cycle was anciently understood at the most nakedly biological level: birth, marriage, the fruitful "harvest" of birthing children from that connection, and ultimately, death.

Long ago, the Jewish people took that fourfold pattern for understanding the individual lifetime and used it as a framework for inscribing the four seasons of the year. Birth became the springtime re-birthing of the earth and the birthing of the Jewish people and its free-dom. Marriage became the encounter and covenant with God at Sinai. Fulfillment through giving fruitful birth to the next generation of chil-dren became the harvest of the earth and the harvesting of all history in the redemption of the world. Death became the wintry time for in-ward retreat to reflect, distill the best wisdom of the last generation, and sow it underground, to be drawn on for the next springtime birthing and sprouting, in the next turn of the spiral.

By seeing the cycle of the year and the cycle of a lifetime through analogous metaphors, Judaism enriched them both. And it gave itself the beginnings of a way to understand the ebb and flow of its own life-history as a people, in which its own life-paths were born, came to fruition, withered, and were seeded into a transformed life-path for a new historical epoch.

In the process, the life-cycle events that every individual lived through were themselves transformed. The celebrations and obser-vances, the very meanings of these events—of birth, marriage, child-rearing, and death—themselves have changed.

We are going through just such a transformation now.

If this were not true—if we were living in one of the long periods of Jewish stability, of "the tradition"—this book could be a simple handbook: Here is how to celebrate a birth, mourn a death. Do it.

But in a period of Jewish upheaval like the present one, our lives are more complex:

- Now that, in the aborning Judaism, women and men are treating each other with ever fuller equality, what does that mean for celebrating birth, adolescence, marriage?
- We live much longer; what does that mean for the period of ma-turity that now may encompass two or three educations, voca-tions, and careers, successive families, different continents?
- Gay men and lesbians have become an important presence in some arenas of Jewish life; what does that mean for their cele-

brations in families where for one generation that would be anathema, for another fully joyful?

So, you might say, fine: Let's just start with where we are, ignore the past. What difference does it make that our ancient Mother Sarah had a weaning party for her son Isaac all those thousands of years ago? What difference does it make that the Rabbis of the Talmud argued over when a girl became a woman, when a boy became a man? If we are dancing in the midst of a Jewish earthquake, why pay attention to the landscape as it was so long ago?

One answer is that there is richness in this past—richness we would be silly to deny ourselves. Who would have imagined that we might find the elements of a midlife transformation ceremony in the life of Abraham, in an eerie mystical experience he had when he was ninety-nine? Yet there it is, and here it is—being used today as people come to new points in their own lives.

Another answer is that the "past" need not be over. Some aspects of Rabbinic Judaism are changing, some are not. Many Jews still— and will—honor it and practice it, as it was and is. Some Jews who are walking the path of a new paradigm in one arena of their lives are also walking the rabbinic paradigm in another. So all of us have a stake in understanding it well.

Jewish thought, Jewish practice, Jewish time itself, always have gone forward by seeming to go backward. By drawing on an ancient teaching, we create something new. We do not live in a circle, or on a straight line—but in spirals, great and small, that always beckon us forward by showing us something old we had all but forgotten.

And so this book is both a spiritual handbook and a spiritual history: a handbook for celebrating the moments of turning in our own life-cycles, and a guide through the spiritual changes in the life of the people as a whole as these have been manifested in the changing life-cycles of those who went before us.

So we look at how Jews have celebrated their individual life-cycles throughout their history—when Biblical Judaism was being born, becoming mature, and withering; when Rabbinic Judaism was being born, maturing, and undergoing its own crisis of the last few centuries; when our own generation has begun to reshape the ceremonies of our lives as our life-cycles themselves have been transformed in the modern world.

As Judaism has drawn on the four major biological events that we have noted, like other cultures it has not left them at this simplistic level. It has woven social, cultural, and spiritual growth in and around these biological markers, and has given meaning to the lives of Jews by giving Jewish meaning—symbols, cross-references—to these universal human passages.

The Spirals of a Life

These great epochal transformations of Jewish rebirth have drawn on the hard-won wisdom of biology: that a burst of creativity must be encoded into a mature calm; that what looks like death may seed new life.

In the process of giving Jewish meaning to the cycles of the earth and of a human life, Jews have sometimes created some unique wisdom, some way of seeing life that another culture has seen in a different way. Indeed, the "spiral" sense of time and thought, especially strong in Judaism, was learned in the yearly cycle of the plants that fed an agrarian people, and in the movement of human life from generation to generation. From the trees and the grain of ancient Israel, Jews learned to see time not as an endless circle going nowhere, or as a straight line of unreflective "progress," but as spirals, always returning in order to go forward.

In daily life, this spiral is created by the restful, reflective rhythm of Shabbat—the Sabbath—in several different forms. The "seventh day" turns the endless cycle of sunset/sunrise into a spiral of reflection and renewal. In the cycle of "moonths," from the new moon through the full moon to its dwindling once again, there is also a Sabbath: The reflective sabbatical month of the High Holy Days (seventh, since we count from the month of spring) gives us the opportunity to turn our lives around. In the cycle of the years in which we spin around the sun, we mark the sabbatical year in which we were taught the land should rest and all debts be forgiven—time out so that our social system could reflect and reconsider our economic and political arrangements. And the cycles whirl their way to the highest pitch in the fiftieth year, the Jubilee, when all land was to be redistributed and no one was to work it. Everyone trusted God to bring forth food for all.

Jewish tradition also makes the spiral into a way to think, a way to renew what the Jewish pathway is. For Jewish thought is grounded in what we call *midrash*: the act of gazing into an old text and seeing something utterly new. Going back to what is ancient in order to go forward into the future. Never ignoring the past, never getting stuck in it. The rabbis of the Talmud proclaimed that whenever they innovated they were actually drawing on the "oral Torah" that had come long before to Moses on Mount Sinai; if Moses returned, they said, he might not recognize the content of the Oral Torah, but he would recognize its process. In this way they were already lifting up this spiral-in-thought to the highest holiness of Jewish tradition.

Indeed, the spirals of the Jewish life-cycle have themselves been recast through such a spiral in thought. For centuries and millennia, the Jewish people, as it sought to wrestle with God, worked out new approaches to the life-cycle itself, by drawing on it and transforming it from generation to generation and era to era of Jewish life.

Why did this spiraling become the basic pattern of Jewish thought, as well as Jewish life-practice? Perhaps it grew originally out of what it meant to be a nomadic/pastoral/hill-farming people who, confronted with the agricultural systems of imperial Babylonia and Egypt, learned these new ways but preserved a memory and a practice of nomadic "gathering" for the sabbatical year of unsowing and unharvesting. Perhaps the spiraling came again out of what it meant to be an agrarian people which then was severed from the soil and turned to words as the way of keeping in touch with God.

A people that lived close to sheep, to fig trees, and to barley might easily learn to see not only a single year of growth but an entire human lifetime as a spiral from seed to fruit and then to seed again—to seed that does not simply repeat the last generation but grows into a new possibility, makes a new turn on the spiral.

And then, when such a people lived through the devastation of its whole identity, it might come to see its own history as such a spiral. When Hellenistic civilization shattered the pattern of life of every traditional Mediterranean culture, including that of Biblical Judaism, the Jews responded with making a *midrash* on themselves, discovering the Oral Torah as a way of renewing Jewish peoplehood without either abandoning the past or staying stuck in it. It was a *midrash* that made the people itself into a fruit tree, moving from seed to fruit, to wintry bareness—while new seed was nurtured underground.

The Fourfold Path in a Single Ritual

Before we consider the life-cycle itself, let us explore some teachings about the general nature of rituals that mark change-points in the life-cycle.

In 1908, the French folklorist/anthropologist Arnold van Gennep wrote a book, published in English as *The Rites of Passage*, that has ever since greatly influenced thought about the structure of such ceremonies. After studying the rites of passage celebrated by many different cultures, he suggested that most of them move through three distinct phases.

The first he called "separation": moving away from the familiar landscape of the social territory and into the unfamiliar. The second he called "the threshold experience": a volcanic, transformative moment when the old identity melts down and a new identity emerges. The third phase he called "incorporation": the movement back into the everyday world.

This threefold pattern to some extent resembles the pattern discerned by the great German Jewish theologian Franz Rosenzweig in the Jewish prayer and festival cycles: creation, revelation, and redemption. Rosenzweig identified the first of these with Pesaḥ, the festival that relives the emergence of the Children of Israel as a newborn people from slavery in the Narrow Place. ("Mitzra-yim," the name of the long narrow Egypt defined by the Nile, means "the Narrow.") "Revelation" he connected with Shavuot, the festival that celebrates the great encounter with God at Sinai; and "redemption" with Sukkot, when we fulfill the promise of that encounter and harvest all history with a Messianic week in leafy huts.

In *Seasons of Our Joy*, Arthur used the language of birth, encounter, and fulfillment for these three festivals. He also pointed out a parallel pattern in the different festivals of the seventh month: Rosh Hashana (birth), Yom Kippur (encounter), and Sukkot (fulfillment).

And Arthur took one more step in *Seasons of Our Joy*: He explored a fourth festival that Rosenzweig never talked about. This was the festival of Sh'mini Atzeret, so shadowy it almost vanishes in the bright glow of Sukkot. Sh'mini Atzeret is the wintry festival of the waning moon, of inwardness, retreat, the nearly invisible seed that drops from the colorful fruit of Sukkot and reenters the earth, quietly bearing the lessons of fulfillment into the next twirl of the spiral, the sprouting of another generation in the spring.

When Rosenzweig analyzed the blessings that surround the *Sh'ma* in daily Jewish prayer, these as well he described as blessings of creation (light and dark), revelation (God's love, through Torah), and redemption (at the Red Sea). Just as he had ignored Sh'mini Atzeret, he ignored the fourth blessing, added only in the evening—*Hashkiveynu*, the blessing of inwardness and sleep.

All this is somewhat similar to what van Gennep did. In our view, he conflated the moment of threshold and meltdown with the moment of full emergence of a new self. At the threshold, the just-aborning new identity meets another: God, or the Holy, or the Ultimate Self, or the volcanic universe. That is why this is a threshold time: at the threshold, two realities meet. And out of this transformative moment comes the full expression of a transformed self. This is not the same thing as the meeting, and it is not the same thing as the reabsorption of the new identity into a changed community.

So we believe that Jewish rituals of life-passage can be better understood in a fourfold way:

The hazy emergence of a new almost-identity from the ground of a previous social role;

the person's earthquake encounter with the Holy, with the Transformative, with God;

the public clarification of a new identity out of this encounter;

the return of the transformed person to the community, in a new role and as a new person.

To look for a moment at one example: In the ceremony that recognizes the growth of a Jewish child into a Bar or Bat Mitzvah, we see the child physically leave the congregation and sit alone in a central place; encounter the Holy Tradition by reading the Torah and prophetic passages; affirm an entry into adulthood by speaking forth his/her own understanding of the Torah and of the event itself; and return to the congregation as an adult, newly empowered.

So we are suggesting a life-pattern in which one might say that the entire life is a "life-cycle ritual," or that each life-cycle ritual is a recapitulation of the whole life-cycle. There is a fractal pattern, in which the macro is replicated in the micro. We have identified at least four arenas in which we dance this pattern: our lives as a whole, the cycle of each year as marked by festivals, the specific markers of the turnings of the life-cycle, and the emergence, encounter, fulfillment, and death-leading-to-rebirth of whole epochs or civilizations of the Jewish people.

At the biological level, for most human beings this pattern is played out in birth, espousal, begetting/bearing children, and death.

But even this pattern is not universal: We are all born and we all die, but not all human beings live through a biological espousal or the pro-creation of children. Since we are not only biological beings, we are delightfully free to draw on this archetype in many ways, dance with it, modify it.

At the emotional/social, intellectual, and spiritual levels, there are many delightful variations on the theme. But the basic theme remains: the birth of a new identity, its encounter with another, the fruitful fulfillment of that encounter, and the "return-forward" of the trans-formed identity into inwardness and death, into a ground that has been forever changed by the emergence of the figure that has now gone in-ward and left seed behind.

Most people are easily drawn to put their energy into relationships with the community around them—which are embodied in the two steps at the beginning and end of the fourfold path.

Yet the first step in the dance, "leaving" the community, is often treated as a perfunctory act. This "leaving" an old role and old rela-tionships is a kind of emotional and spiritual death—and for the sake of the health of the person who is walking the path of spiritual growth, the comforting aspects of the old roles should be celebrated, and their dying should be mourned.

For a baby, at the *b'rit* ceremony the mother might speak of the sense of unity, of Eden in the womb, that may have strengthened both child and mother through the harder times, and yet must now be given up. For a child becoming Bar or Bat Mitzvah, there are some sorrows involved in leaving behind the irresponsibilities of childhood. The night before the ceremony, as evening falls, the child might speak in the midst of family about what it is like to give these up. Two who are wedding are setting aside the actual or potential relationships that might have given them a different-flavored joy. Let them each in the week before the wedding write a letter of goodbye, and then burn the letters with a blessing on both the light and the warmth those relation-ships gave forth. Those who choose to become initiated into the Jew-ish people might, as they met with the *beyt din* (rabbinic court) that would authorize this life-change, name both the joyful and the painful aspects of the spiritual communities in which they were previously members.

And so on through the life-path. For those who do not celebrate and mourn these ghosts are all the more likely to be haunted by them, to carry them along, because they have never truly "left" their previous places in the community.

We hope that those who are planning or taking part in the ceremonies of a life-cycle will pay special attention to the two moments in the middle: the moment of transformative Encounter with the Holy Other, and the moment when the transformed Self shines forth. At Sinai, the Holy One's first word of encounter was *"Anoḥi"*—"I." As we try to grow a *menschlich* Self of our own, we can choose which version of our "I" we will nourish. If we nourish the *Anoḥi* within, our I will resonate with the I of the universe. If we feed only the Ego within, our I may cut itself off from the I of the universe. Deeply living the two central steps in the pathway will help each one of us grow from one age to the next, bringing our *Anoḥi* more and more into tune with the universal Self.

We intend that *A Time for Every Purpose Under Heaven* do four things. These are the ways to read this book that will most help you meet these purposes:

- Help those who are facing a particular life-cycle moment to shape its celebration in a way that both honors Jewish tradition and bespeaks their own values and concerns. For this purpose, check both the specific chapter and the larger section on the life-moment of concern.
- Help those who are about to attend someone else's celebration to understand what is going on, both the visible practices and the reasons behind them. Here, check the specific chapter on the life-moment of concern.

- Give a sense of the history of these ceremonies, how they have changed over the millennia of Jewish history and how they still are changing. In almost every chapter, we first lay out the biblical way of dealing with that life-moment, then the rabbinic way, and then the changes that have been emerging during the past (and perhaps the next) century.
- Show that these are not merely one-shot ceremonial moments—that they fit together, that they help and strengthen people in walking a continuing spiritual path. Together they shape a path to grow and educate a Mensch. For this purpose, read the book with a special eye for moving through a whole life.

May our exploration of these patterns in our individual lives serve the Jewish people in its journey, this generation, from a long-known grounding in old roles, into a new encounter with the Spirit and the clarification of a transformed self that can reenter the communities of earth in a new relationship.

—AOW & POB

Addressing God

THROUGHOUT THIS BOOK, we quote blessings and in other ways refer to God. In doing so, we have drawn on some different practices and traditions about naming and addressing God.

In the classic pattern of Rabbinic Judaism, most written blessings begin: *"Baruḥ ata YHWH eloheynu meleḥ ha-olam"*—where the *YHWH* is a transcription of four Hebrew letters.

At the level of verbal meaning, this "word" is mysterious. Some scholars think the four letters may be a conflation of the letters in the past, present, and future forms of the Hebrew for the verb "to be"—thus, "The One Who Was, Is, Will Be; The Eternal." Others believe they make up the causative form of the verb "to be"—therefore, "The One Who Brings Being into Being."

At the level of sound, each of these letters is a semiconsonant, quite different from a *k*, a *p*, an *r*. They are different also from the Hebrew letter *alef*, which is totally silent. They have no vowels between them. Turning them into the name "Yehovah" or "Yahweh" requires the insertion of vowels that aren't there.

When they are spoken aloud, these four letters are in rabbinic convention replaced by the word *Adonai*, which means "Lord."

As a result, the conventional English translation of this opening to blessing is "Blessed are You, Lord our God, King of the Universe . . ."

Where in this book we talk about the rabbinic tradition, that is the Hebrew and the translation we use.

When we talk about the emerging new life-cycle ceremonies and practices of the last generation, we often use a different formula of blessing. The different formula arises from several strands of thought and feeling that have become especially important in this last generation. The same people who have been creating the new ceremonies have been wrestling with how to understand and "name" God. One of those wrestlings has concerned the image of a masculine and imperious God: King, Lord, Judge. Experiments with "Mother" and "Queen" have mostly felt unsatisfactory, because while they erase God's explicit masculinity they preserve the Up-There God, wholly beyond Her children, Her subjects.

So—why not celebrate an imperious God?

In the last few generations, human powers have expanded to do the things that we had imagined only God could do: destroy all life on earth, create new species, overthrow tyrants, transform psyches. So for many people it seems less true than before that we are simply serfs of a transcendent Power beyond us; many have come to feel that these Godly energies and powers lie within ourselves.

Yet in the past generation, simple atheism has also felt inadequate, as the sense has grown that claiming for human beings full Mastery over life is likely to lead to life's destruction and that we must celebrate what is unmastered as Mystery to be honored, rather than ignorance to be conquered. So for some there has evolved a desire to celebrate God not as Master but as the mysterious interweaving of the threads of life, of all reality.

As efforts have grown to express all this in liturgy, there have emerged new "Names" for God. One such, brought forth by Marcia Falk in *The Book of Blessings*, is *Eyn ha-Ḥayim*—"Wellspring of Life." Another, which the two of us have used more often, consists in the pronunciation—or nonpronunciation—that results when one tries to say *"YHWH"* with no vowels. For many people, this becomes simply a breathing sound. Addressing God as the Breathing Spirit that binds the world together has made sense to many of those who have been renewing Jewish life. For breathing crosses all the boundaries of language; all peoples breathe. It reaches beyond the human species, for all living beings breathe. Indeed, as the trees breathe out what we breathe in, we breathe out what the trees breathe in. Not only does each life-form breathe; our breath binds us together. So some communities have begun to substitute, in the opening phrase of the blessing, *ru-aḥ ha-olam*—"Breathing Spirit of the World"—for *meleḥ*—"king" or "ruler."

Since one of the most ancient biblical names for God is *Yah*, as when the Psalms say *Hallelu-Yah*—"Let us praise God," these communities often use *Yah* instead of *Adonai* as a substitute for *YHWH*, and accentuate the breathing sound of *Yah*. Thus the blessing begins: *"Baruḥ ata Yah eloheynu ru-aḥ ha-olam . . ."*—"Blessed are You, Yahhh, our God, Breathing Spirit of the World . . ."

For some Jews, persevering with old Names and exploring new Names of God are not mutually exclusive. They may experience God sometimes as Ruler, sometimes as Breath. So in cases when most of the ancient phrasing of the blessing continues to be used, we have used brackets to offer alternatives.

Some blessings that we put forward in this book—especially ones connected with new ceremonies—are entirely new. Readers should be aware that in the life-path of traditional Rabbinic Judaism, such new blessings are viewed with disapproval.

For some Jews, the rabbinic teaching to avoid the explicit utterance or writing of the (Hebrew) Names of God has been carried over into the English Names as well. And so some Jews prefer to avoid writing the full word "God," even in English, and generally use

"G-d" instead. But our friend and teacher Reb Zalman Schachter-Shalomi, saying that to him the hyphen seemed very boring, suggested with a twinkle that we might write "G!d" to invoke a sense of radical amazement. For Phyllis this suggestion felt delicious, and she has followed it in her passages in this book. Where the two of us have merged our voices, we say "God."

Encountering Hebrew

WHEN WE PRESENT TRANSLATIONS of Hebrew or Aramaic texts from the Bible, the Talmud, and the prayerbook we have usually done the translation ourselves. We have especially drawn from the approach taken by Everett Fox in his masterly Englishing of *The Five Books of Moses*—an approach he learned from those two great German-Jewish theologians of the first half of the twentieth century, Martin Buber and Franz Rosenzweig. The Buber-Rosenzweig-Fox method is to deliver not an idiomatic and prosaic translation but one that comes as close as possible to the wordplays, breathing patterns, and oral/aural sense of the Hebrew. Text as I-Thou conversation, not chiseled stone.

When we transliterate Hebrew, Aramaic, or Yiddish, we aim not necessarily to replace each letter of the *alef-bet* with an equivalent letter of the Western alphabet but to ease the reader's pronunciation of each word. So we have not distinguished between the letters "khaf" and "chet." (We use a dotted "ḥ" for both.) We have not added an "h" to the ends of words where the "ah" sound is simply delivered by an "a." Where, however, Hebrew words have become well known in English, like "Torah," we have kept the familiar English spelling.

We have used an apostrophe to indicate a silent vowel under a letter—e.g., *Y'rushala-yim*. We have used a hyphen to separate two vowels or two syllables so that they can be pronounced correctly—e.g., *yada-at*; *Y'rushala-yim*.

We have used "a" to make the sound "ah" (papa) as in "Hanukkah"; "e" to make the sound of "eh" (bed) as in "Pesaḥ"; "i" to make the long sound of "ee" (teeth) as in *b'rit* or the short sound "i" (sit) as in *mitzva*; "o" to make the sound of "o" (load) as in *tov*; "u" to make the sound "u" (you) as in "Purim"; "ey" to make the sound "ay" (day) as in *borey*; "ai" to make the sound "ai" (height) as in "Sarai."

PART 1

❧

Sprouting a Self

I

The Fruitful Child

YOU MIGHT IMAGINE that the very first life-cycle ceremony described in Torah is for a newborn baby. It is not. It is indeed about a birth—but one that had not yet happened and perhaps might never happen.

It is an eerie ceremony for a man of advanced middle age who has for decades been looking forward to a child, and is now filled with anxiety because he fears he will never beget one. The ceremony, unlike every other in all of Jewish tradition, happens not in community but for one person who is all alone—except for God.

The anxious Abram—for his name does not yet have the breathing "h" sound in it, the Hebrew letter *hey*—is filled with anxiety that he will have no children. God calls on him to create a dark and awesome space, and, as the space flames up, promises him numberless offspring. (Gen. 15)

We might think that by placing this ceremony of midlife before the one of birthing, the Torah has gotten life out of order. But the sequence reminds us that many of the life-cycle ceremonies that seem to focus on one member of a family may actually be richly involving of others. Think, for instance, how complex are the spiritual journeys of not just the adolescent who stands before the community to chant Torah, or the couple who covenant beneath the wedding canopy, but all those who are connected to them.

Celebrating a birth is even more like this than most of the other life-cycle celebrations. Surely the baby's life has been transformed; an independent identity has come into the world, and most parents will testify that there is much about personality as well as body that is "in there" from the very start. And the child is not merely the synthesis of two parents: something new has been added. As the Talmud teaches, each child has three parents: mother, father, and the God Whose Name is *Eh-yeh Asher Eh-yeh*—"I Will Be Who I Will Be—I Am Becoming Who I Am Becoming." (Exod. 3:14) Birth, like freedom, means the unpredictable has raised its head.

But the eight-day-old child is not yet consciously shaping its own future; the parent is—not only the child's future, but the parent's own. In the great spiral of a life-cycle, birth seems the beginning. From it unfolds the seeking for another identity to encounter—a life-partner, a community, a vision, God. Then from this encounter emerges a fulfillment—perhaps a child, perhaps a vocation, a career, a life-work. For a parent, this moment stands as a time of fruitfulness. So the same moment that in the child's life is a bare beginning, in the parent's life is a fulfillment.

This is one way of understanding why the Torah tells the story of Abraham's and Sarah's midlife transformations "out of order," before the story of their son's birth. As we walk through this book, we will take the Torah's oddity of sequence as a reminder to watch—within each public celebration of a single stage of life—for all its stages, barely hidden. When we look into each spiritual marker, we must remember that what we see is not a snapshot but a multidimensional hologram, in which all the elements of a life can be discerned within each moment.

We will return to this midlife moment of the Torah when we look at the midlife moments in our own society and generation—moments filled with self-questioning, concerned with what we have and have not handed on into the future. (See Chapter 9.) But before we move on, we must note that this double vision of a life-cycle—a midlife transformation embracing a newborn transformation—points to a special quality of the birth-time ceremonies: Though the children are the ceremonial focus, the adults are undertaking, and probably undergoing, much more than the children.

By the time we reach the markers of puberty, this is no longer true—or, at least not as true. A twelve- or thirteen-year-old can reflect on what is happening, may even poke out a hand to change it; the eight-day-old cannot. What the adults do with and for and to the children is more a mirror than a magnifying glass, reflecting their own futures even more than it marks the children's lives.

Let us return to Abram, who has just heard that his life is, in middle age, about to take an unexpected turning: his seed will give rise to many offspring. Let us explore what happens as God's promise to Abram moves toward fruition.

What happens is the gift of a ceremony for celebrating the birth of a child, a ceremony that also represents the birth of a covenant about birth, births so numerous as to give birth to a people. God makes a covenant with the renamed Abraham—for now the *hey*, the Breath of Life, has entered within him—that his seed shall flourish throughout the generations. His wife Sarai, too, experiences a midlife ceremonial transformation. In her actual life, her change may have been as eventful as her husband's multidimensional experience: but the text of Torah presents it as much sketchier. Her name also takes on the breathing *hey*, and she becomes Sarah. Together they learn that Sarah is to bear a child through whom Abraham's desire for blessed offspring will receive a special affirmation—even more special than Abraham's firstborn of his wife Hagar.

This covenant of many generations is to be sealed, appropriately enough, through the generative organ (only Abraham's, not Sarah's): through *B'rit Mila*, the "covenant of cutting"—circumcision, a cutting of the foreskin of the penis. The Voice demands that this ceremony be undertaken for every male of the family eight days after birth, and for every male who is brought into the community. (Gen. 17:3–14)

But none of the first circumcisions is performed on a tiny baby. first Abraham circumcises himself, then his son Ishmael (now thirteen years old), then his male servants. Though Abraham makes himself the model, he knows that he does not stand alone but in community. And the first transfer of covenantal blessing from one generation to the next is not with Isaac, the boy who would come to be seen as the "first Jewish child," but with our cousin Ishmael, who is already at the edge of puberty. Not till a year later, when Isaac is born, does the eighth-day provision go into effect.

Perhaps even at the beginning, it was important that no one enter this generative covenant alone. From the very beginning, it is communal. We share the covenant, the blessing, with others: something every parent knows from the start, something not only Isaac but every child grows up to learn. There have been others before you, whom God and your family have loved; there will be others yet to come.

Especially others yet to come. For circumcision points beyond the birth that has just happened to another birth that will not happen for more than a dozen years: Circumcision focuses on the genitals that will be involved in creating the *child's* children—the generation of the grandchildren.

Abram did not stand alone in his anxiety over procreation. The fear of not having children became the most powerful and perduring of Israelite and Jewish fears, and circumcision became the most powerful and perduring of Israelite and Jewish rituals.

There are echoes of circumcision as an opening for fruitfulness in other aspects of biblical life. As Howard Eilberg-Schwartz has pointed out, removal of the *arela*, or foreskin, is echoed by the practice called *orla* (from the same Hebrew root), in which a fruit tree must be three years old (plus a year of dedication to God) before its fruit can be eaten. Why is this pause called "foreskin"? The time of pausing, waiting, removes a sheath that blocks the tree's fruitfulness. In much the same way, the Torah also speaks about God's removing the "foreskin of the human heart"—that is, cutting away the hard-hearted outer shell in order to soften the heart, make it more fully and spiritually fruitful. Eilberg-Schwartz concludes that circumcision is about fertility—as, indeed, the text of the covenant itself asserts. The point of the covenant is not at this stage an airy spiritual connection or even some ethical instruction, but the down-to-earth promise of overflowing seed and a land broad enough to sow this seed.

This ceremony focuses on men alone. Sarah is informed of her amazing impending pregnancy—How ridiculous, she laughs, seeing that my husband is so old and I don't even menstruate any more!—but when the birth comes, she seems to take no part in celebrating it except to laugh again, this time with joy. Abraham circumcises his son, Abraham names him Isaac—"The Laughing One." And not only does the biblical tradition leave the mother out of the birth-ritual; nowhere does the Bible prescribe a ceremony for the birth of girls.

Nowadays we are used to looking at the Bible with the knowledge that it was written mostly by and for men, that it assumes male dominance of the society as a whole and of the family as well. We may seek the ancient subversive voices (like the Song of Songs) that encourage those of us who are in our own day shaping a Judaism in which women and men are equal. We may learn from the spiritual power and ceremonial eloquence of the biblical men to call forth our own spiritual power and our own eloquent ceremonies.

And at the same time, we can try to learn what lies beneath the surface of male dominance. For instance, the story of the birth of circumcision hints at male anxieties about fruitfulness—as if it is the male, not the female, genitals that are at fault in barrenness and need in some sense to be "opened." Some have suggested that circumcision may betoken a male imitation of menstruation: men learn from women that blood from the genitals is crucial to the cycling of life. But where women do not have to lift a finger to produce this blood, men must lift a knife.

Others have pointed to the later story in which Abraham, preparing to offer Isaac as a sacrifice to God, substitutes instead a ram that is caught in the thicket—and suggest that the foreskin is a kind of "ram," acting as a substitute for what otherwise would be a tragic bind in which the father feels called upon to guarantee his own fruitfulness by sacrificing his firstborn son. And perhaps the Abraham-Isaac story points also to the possibility that some fathers who fear being displaced by their sons may feel the urge to hurt or kill them. From that perspective, circumcision may offer a way both to express and to control that urge, by delicately "opening" the genitals toward future generations instead of cutting them off—or even using the knife to kill.

We might also say that because the cutting of the foreskin necessarily engendered deep anxiety—in fathers even if not in their infant sons—the body-act of circumcision was a way of fully embodying in one stark moment all the different anxieties about sexuality that were felt by the Israelite men who gave shape to the patterns of sexual conduct.

One of the strangest stories in the Torah concerns an act of circumcision. At the Burning Bush, God has just commissioned Moses to become the liberator of the Israelites. Moses asks his Midianite wife Tzipora to join him on the journey back to Egypt. On the road, God speaks out to sum up what will happen: God will honor the people of Israel as God's firstborn. If Pharaoh resists, God will kill Pharaoh's firstborn son.

Suddenly God threatens to kill Moses' own firstborn son—and Moses too. The liberation story seems about to end almost before it has started. And God does not relent till Tzipora circumcises the child. (Exod. 4:18–26)

This story stuns the reader with its abrupt and terrifying interruption of what has so far seemed the orderly saga of the liberator Moses. So we pay attention all the more:

May the crucial ritual of circumcision be intruding on the crucial saga of liberation because it betokens a whole community's rebirth and fruitfulness? Had Moses been blown away by YHWH, the Breath of Life, at the Burning Bush? Has he concluded that since God is making a new covenant, the old rituals of his people are now irrelevant? This possibility gains believability from a later passage of Exodus (12:43–49) which warns that only those men who are circumcised may eat of the Pesaḥ offering. Were some people arguing that liberation from slavery might supersede the old covenant and bring the uncircumcised within the fold?

If that was the issue that arose on the road from Midian to Egypt, what is it about Tzipora that sweeps her into the truth that Moses can't access? Is it because she is a woman, used to sacred blood? Is it because she is a shepherd's daughter, more down-to-earth than Moses, not given to the grandiose visions that excite the Prince of Egypt? In this moment of crisis, we already know that five courageous women— the midwives Shifra and Puah, mother Yocheved, sister Miriam, and Pharaoh's daughter—have made freedom and rebirth possible. Are we now being told that the crucial ritual of circumcision also owes something to a woman's wisdom? Is the Torah remembering that even though in ordinary times men ruled the roost, it was women, when transformation trembled in the wind, who led the struggle? Is this one of the subversive biblical voices that speak to our generation?

And does this story, on top of Abraham's, strengthen the possibility that circumcision is a way of redeeming sons from sacrifice and death and their fathers from profound anxiety?

Notice that all these questions address the parents much more than the child. Where do *they* stand in *their* life-journey? What is being born in them as they celebrate their newborn?

The biblical tradition tells us little more about the circumcision of children. And (except for specifying the eighth day) it tells us almost nothing about how in those days the ceremony was carried out. But it tells us a great deal about the ethnic, ethical, and spiritual meaning of the foreskin and its cutting.

It tells of two mass circumcisions of adults:

- After the leader of the town/clan of Sh'ḥem has raped Dina, the daughter of Jacob and Leah, he says he loves her and wants to marry her. Several of her brothers, Jacob's sons, pretend to agree, on condition that the men of Sh'hem make their way into the clan of Yisrael, through *B'rit Mila*. The Sh'hemites comply with this demand. Then, on the third day, when they are in the most pain, two sons of Jacob slaughter them en masse. Jacob complains that they have made his name stink (and years later, on his deathbed, will curse them as murderers). "Shall our sister be treated as a whore?" they retort. But no one asks Dina's opinion. (Gen. 34:1–30, 49:5–7)

• After the long trek in the Wilderness, as an entirely new generation of Israelites stands at the Jordan, ready to enter the Land and face its many peoples, God tells Joshua to circumcise all the men with flint knives; for none of them were circumcised as they were born. So many men undergo *B'rit Mila* that the place is called Givat Ha-Aralot—Foreskin Hill. (Joshua 5:2–8)

In both of these stories, national pride rather than spiritual growth seems central to the circumcision. But through much of biblical tradition, circumcision intertwines what we might see as the separate arenas of ethical/spiritual devotion and national pride. On the national side, the Philistines and other foreign peoples are referred to with contempt as "uncircumcised." (Judges 14:3, 15:18; Ezek. 32:19, 24–32) On the ethical and spiritual side, the Bible speaks over and over again of uncircumcised lips, hearts, and ears. (Exod. 6:30, Deut. 10:16, Jer. 6:10)

What does this mean? The image seems to be that of a thickened, toughened "foreskin" blocking our ability to hear, to speak, to empathize and love.

The Prophet Jeremiah (9:24–25) pits the national and ethical meanings against each other, with harsh irony the result: "Here!" says YHWH: "The days are coming when I will take note of all with a 'cut foreskin.' For Egypt, Judah; Edom, Ammon, Moab, and all those who [unlike Israel] trim the corners of their beards, dwellers in the Wilderness—they all have foreskins, but the whole House of Israel has fore-skins on its heart!" (See also Jer. 6:10.)

Even when Ezekiel (44:7, 9) denounces Israel for allowing "aliens who are uncircumcised of heart and uncircumcised of flesh" to enter the Holy Temple, it is not clear whether he means ethnic aliens or Is-raelites who, with hearts too blocked and thickened to feel empathy, alienate themselves from the community.

Perhaps the separation in our heads between "national" and "spir-itual/ethical" is itself the problem; it may be hard for us to share the prophets' vision of an entire people committed to an ethical/spiritual vision; their demand for a spirituality so deeply rooted in ethical com-munity that it cannot be lived out by isolated individuals; their insis-tence on a steadfast unity of the flesh with the spirit, ritual with ethics.

From Death to Rebirth: Rabbinic Judaism

The Jewish people as a body has lived through life-cycles on a collec-tive level. Its great flowerings into the community described and cele-brated in the Bible gave way to stagnation and decline as it faced the great material (and even spiritual) successes of Hellenistic-Roman civilization.

So under Roman-Hellenistic pressure, Biblical Judaism died, but not until it had given birth to a new version of itself—indeed, to sev-eral different children. Rabbinic Judaism, Christianity, and (later) Is-lam all drew deeply on the biblical tradition, as well as on various degrees and aspects of Hellenistic culture.

One of the areas in which the new Judaism had to define its own birth-identity was in the arena of birth itself, for circumcision became a serious issue. Several rulers—especially Antiochus Epiphanes of Hellenistic Syria and Emperor Hadrian of Rome—forbade it. Many Jews responded by resisting the decree, and some were executed. On the other hand, some men voluntarily went to the length of undergoing a painful operation to disguise their circumcision, so as to win the approval of Hellenistic officials and to participate in the Greek games. Jews who became Christians argued about whether they should circumcise their children, and whether non-Jews must do so in order to become Christians. Their answer, ultimately, was no.

Perhaps as a result of these doubts and debates, the emerging community of rabbis began to carefully specify the details of *B'rit Mila* as a ceremony. Yehuda HaNasi, the editor of the Mishna, called it more important than all the rest of the precepts of Judaism put together.

The Rabbis ruled that the obligation either to perform *Mila* personally or to find an expert substitute (the *mohel*) rests upon the boy's father; if he fails, upon the rabbinical court; when the child is grown, upon himself. But there is no question that an uncircumcised Jew remains a Jew, no matter how old he is; that is why he is still bound by the obligation. The punishment of *kareyt*—being "cut off" from the people—mentioned by the Torah for failure in this duty was understood by the Rabbis to mean that God would shorten the person's life; no human punishment was assigned.

The Rabbis discussed timing, and decided that the eight-day requirement was more important than even the rules normally governing Shabbat. So they ruled that *Mila* and all necessary preparations must be done even on Shabbat if that was the eighth day (except for unusual situations like a cesarean birth or a birth at dusk when it was unclear whether the eighth day was Shabbat or not).

They made clear that if the child was sick, *Mila* must wait till he was well—indeed, not till seven days after he has recovered, if he has had a general rather than topical illness. And the child was not to be circumcised at all, if in the same family there had previously been deaths that stemmed from *Mila*. (This seems to have been an early recognition of what we now know as the genetic origins of hemophilia, in which any slight cut may start a fatal flow of blood.)

The Rabbis debated whether *Mila* was valid without a procedure called *p'ri-a*—splitting and pulling down the mucosal tissue underneath the foreskin, uncovering the corona of the penis. *P'ri-a* seems to have been done as a way of preventing "reversal" of circumcision—that is, preventing the operation undertaken by some Hellenized Jews to hide the fact that they had been circumcised.

The Rabbis concluded that *p'ri-a* was necessary (Mishna Shabbat 19:6). For Rabbinic *halaḥa*, this settled the matter; but the question has come alive for some Jews today who would like to reduce the pain circumcision sometimes imposes on the child. If Abraham himself did not do *p'ri-a*—as the Talmud acknowledges (TB Yevamot 71b)—then modifications of the surgery seem, to some Jews, more legitimate. (Other modifications have been made in modern times by many traditional *mohalim*: using clamps, local anesthetics, barriers against infection, etc.)

And the Rabbis included in the ceremony some of the blessings that have become honored traditions, inseparable from *B'rit Mila*, to this day. These include the blessing said by the *mohel* on behalf of the father:

> *Baruḥ ata YHWH eloheynu meleḥ [ru-aḥ] ha-olam asher kidshanu b'mitzvotav v'tzivanu al ha-Mila.*
> Blessed are You YHWH our God, Majesty [Breathing Spirit] of the Universe, Who has made us holy through His commandments and commanded us concerning cutting.

The father responds:

> *Baruḥ ata YHWH eloheynu meleḥ [ru-aḥ] ha-olam asher kidshanu b'mitzvotav v'tzivanu l'haḥniso bivrito shel Avraham avinu.*
> Blessed are You YHWH our God, Majesty [Breathing Spirit] of the Universe, Who has made us holy through His commandments and commanded us to bring this one into the covenant of Abraham our father.

And the father continues with the special blessing over a new or a newly reexperienced joy:

Baruḥ ata YHWH eloheynu meleḥ [ru-aḥ] ha-olam sheheḥeyanu v'kiy'manu v'higi-anu laẓman haẓeh!
Blessed are you YHWH our God, Majesty [Breathing Spirit] of the Universe, Who has filled us with life, and lifted us up, and brought us to this moment!

And the community choruses:

K'shem sheniḥnas lab'rit, ken yikanes l'Torah ul'ḥuppa ul'ma-asim tovim.
As he has entered the covenant, so may he also enter into the study of Torah, into the marriage canopy, and into deeds of loving-kindness.

Through this last blessing, the physical focus on the organ for generating the next generation is accompanied by a verbal look ahead to when the child will enter marriage and become a procreator—and this biological vision is surrounded by Torah-study and ethical action, just as the Rabbis created a Judaism of ethics and study to reconfigure a Judaism of the body.

As *B'rit Mila* grew in importance, it became more a communal than a family celebration, and by the ninth century had moved from the home to the synagogue. Along with this shift came a concentration of hopes and fears about protection of the infant from danger, into a focus on the presence of Elijah the Prophet.

According to biblical tradition, Elijah never died but was swept up to Heaven in a fiery chariot. And so, many stories grew up about him as someone who periodically returned to earth to teach wisdom, help the poor, visit Passover Seders, prepare for *Mashi-aḥ* (Messiah)—and protect children. In many Jewish communities it became the custom to set aside a chair for him at every *B'rit Mila*. This *Kisey Eliyahu*, the

Chair (or Throne) of Elijah, might simply be an ordinary chair left empty for him. Or—especially once the *B'rit* became centered in the synagogue—it might be a gorgeously carved and decorated chair, used again and again to welcome the Prophet.

Different ways grew up of explaining Elijah's connection to this role. One is rooted in the Bible's description of Elijah as calling out to God in near-despair that the people had abandoned the covenant. (1 Kings 19:10, 14) For some *midrash*-makers, this was taken to mean specifically the covenant of *Mila*. Since they could see that the people stood firm with the *B'rit*, they imagined God requiring Elijah to show up at every *B'rit*, to witness—in the face of his own assertion—that the covenant still stood. (This teaching may have been a way of reminding skeptics that the *B'rit* had outlasted many critics.)

Another outlook: In the very last verse of the last of the Prophets, Malachi (3:23–24), God says, "Before the coming of the great and awesome day of YHWH, I will send Elijah the Prophet to turn the hearts of fathers to sons [or, parents to children] and the hearts of sons to fathers [or, children to parents], lest I come and smite the earth with utter destruction."

This passage is traditionally read as the *Haftara* (passage from the Prophets) on the Shabbat just before Passover. According to the Torah's story of the Exodus, that was when firstborn children came into jeopardy of death. To invoke Elijah at that moment—especially in his role as peacemaker between the generations—seems to make good sense. By the same token, it would be fitting to welcome him to *B'rit Mila*, at a moment of pain between the generations. And in the very generation when the notion of destroying the earth no longer seems mere fantasy, invoking young and old to join in its protection may take on new weight.

Apparently, however, the unseen Prophet did not suffice as a guide and protector, for the custom arose of inviting an elder of the family or the community to serve as *sandek*, sitting next to Elijah and holding the baby on his knees. Still later, a man and woman who were good friends of the family were added—in Eastern European communities, called the *kvatter* and *kvatterin*—the Yiddish equivalents of the German for "godfather" and "godmother."

In the biblical text, the renaming of Abram and the naming of Isaac are loosely connected with *B'rit Mila*, though not as part of the ceremony. But as rabbinic tradition evolved, the spiritual logic of the ceremony drew the naming and the *Mila* together, for the transformative encounter of the child with God led naturally to his new identity being then publicly named and affirmed. For sure, he was given a Hebrew name by which he could be called up to the Torah when he turned thirteen, and in some communities also a name (in Hebrew, Yiddish, Ladino, or the vernacular of the surrounding society) by which he might be known in other roles.

As a result of the evolution we have sketched, there emerged among the Jews of two millennia and more a ceremony that varied from country to country and home to home but was clearly recognizable everywhere and continues today in much the same form. If we seek in the *B'rit Mila* ceremony the four-step dance that we discussed in our preface, we easily see it emerge:

First the child is brought forward in a special procession from hand to hand.

Then comes the intense, shocking, God-encountering, and transformative moment of *Mila* itself, accompanied by specific blessings.

Then the child's new identity is highlighted, through a kiddush over wine and a traditional blessing that culminates in his being named.

Finally the child reenters the community amid blessings pronounced by family and friends and—as always among Jews ever since the sacred offerings of food at the portable Shrine of Holy Presence in the Wilderness—with a celebratory meal.

The ceremony begins with a blessing by the father. He accepts the responsibility of accomplishing the *B'rit*, and affirms that he has appointed a *mohel* to do so on his behalf (unless, as even now in some families, the father actually does the circumcision himself).

The father often invokes the protection of the Prophet Elijah, and he might begin with a traditional Kabbalistic *kavana*, or statement of intention: *"L'shem yiḥud kudsha briḥu u'sheḥinteh."*—"For the sake of the unification of the Holy Blessed One [Beyond] and the Holy Presence [Within]." *"Hinei, anoḥi ba l'ka-yem mitzvat aseh: u vayom hashmini yimol bisar arlato."*—"Here I am!—I come to fulfill the *mitzva* of action, 'And on the eighth day shall you circumcise the flesh of his foreskin.' " The *mohel* responds with his own affirmation and prayer, as does the *sandek*.

Then the baby is brought into the room—depending on local custom and the desires of the family, perhaps by the mother, the *kvatterin*, and the *kvatter*. The assembled family and friends greet him: *"Baruḥ haba hanimol l'shmona!"*—"Blessed is the one who comes for circumcision on the eighth day!" Various members of the assembly may recite biblical verses that bear on circumcision. (We will deal with these below, in our discussion of *b'rit* ceremonies that have emerged for girls.)

The baby is placed on the *Kisey Eliyahu*, the specially decorated chair symbolically set aside for the Prophet Elijah. The father, the *mohel*, the *sandek*, or one of the family says: *"Zeh hakisey shel Eliyahu zaḥor latov."*—"This is the Seat of Elijah, may he be remembered for good." For some families, this moment has become the time to explain the significance of Elijah's presence.

Then the baby is given to the *sandek*, who sits in another specially bedecked chair and holds the child as he lies upon a table.

Then the central and transformative event unfolds quickly:

- The baby's clothing is rearranged for the ritual.
- The *sandek* holds the baby's legs firmly.
- The father and *mohel* bless the One Who Commands.
- The *mohel* does the actual cutting.

The assembly responds by invoking for the child the blessings of future Torah learning, covenanting with a loving partner, and doing of compassionate deeds (quoted on pages 13–14 above).

Now the child becomes a Self, still separate from the community but fully in its view—and in its hearing. After a traditional blessing over wine, a special kiddush continues:

> *Baruḥ ata YHWH eloheynu meleḥ ha-olam asher kidesh y'did mibeten, v'ḥok bish'ero sam, v'tze-etza-av ḥatam b'ot b'rit kodesh. Al ken bis'ḥar zot, Eyl ḥai ḥelkenu tzurenu, tzavey l'hatzil y'didut sh'erenu mishaḥat l'ma-an b'rito asher sam bivsarenu.*
>
> Blessed are You Who made holy this beloved one from the womb, set a deeply engraved mark in his flesh, and sealed his offspring through this sign of holy covenant. May You therefore, God of Life, our Heritage and our Rock, rescue from devastation what we hold beloved in our bodies, as recompense for our setting this covenant within our bodies.

The blessing then concludes, *"Baruḥ ata YHWH koreyt hab'rit."*—"Blessed are You Who incisively affirms the covenant." And the community drinks from the wine cup.

In many Sephardic communities, the sharing of wine is followed with the sharing of spices or fragrant herbs. First the gathering says the blessing *"Baruḥ ata YHWH eloheyḥu meleḥ ha-olam borey miney atzey isvey b'samim."*—"Blessed are You YHWH, Majesty of the Universe, Who creates species/trees/grasses of spices." Then spices, or branches of herbs, or aromatic oils like rose water are passed from hand to hand, and each participant savors their fragrance.

One powerful explanation for this custom harks back to the Creation story, in which *adam* (the human-earthling) emerges from the *adamah* (earthy-humus). In order to become an independent life-form, the human gives up a *hey*—the breathing sound—from its name. Then God (through the Aspect of YHWH, the Divine Name that sounds like a breath) blows into *adam*'s nostrils the breath of life, so that the human becomes a living breathing being. (Gen. 2:7)

This story sounds a great deal like every birthing. First the child aborning gives up the unconscious "breathing" that comes through the placenta and separates itself from the mother as *adam* separates from *adamah*. Then with a gentle tap, perhaps even a mouth-to-mouth breathing, someone makes sure the new baby is breathing on its own.

So the sharing of spices lets the whole community breathe in and out, breathing this newborn into life and letting this new birth breathe new life into the community—joining with God, the Breath of Life, in this new birthing.

The community then undertakes the naming of the child:

Eloheynu veylohey avoteynu [v'imoteynu] kayem et hayeled hazeh l'aviv ul'imo v'yikarey sh'mo b'yisrael [Ploni ben Almoni v'Alma]. [Ploni] zeh hakaton gadol yi-yeh.
Our God and God of our fathers [and our mothers], lift up this child for his father and his mother, and may his name be called among Israel [insert the child's names, including the names of his parents].

At this point, many families include some biblical passages, especially Ezekiel 16:6. Some may add the passage on Tzipora's circumcision of her and Moses' son. (Exod. 4:24–26)

Then the blessing concludes: "May [repeat his name], this one who is small, grow to be great; as he has entered this covenant, so may he enter Torah, the covenant of *ḥuppa*, and the doing of deeds of loving-kindness."

In this moment, the child who has experienced transformation comes forward as a new Self. Of course, the name is at this stage of life given, not chosen, but nevertheless it carries implications for how the baby as he grows will understand himself and how the community will understand him. Unless the baby needs to nurse or to sleep out of the public eye, this is a good time for the parents to explain the origins of the baby's name—after whom he is being named, what traits of these people they recall for a blessing to this child, what spiritual gifts and meanings they intend to bestow.

Newly named, the new Self is thus returned to the community, itself made new by its receiving this new member.

Others might then follow with specific blessings for the child, and perhaps for the parents.

Finally comes a celebratory meal, preceded by the blessing over bread and followed by a special version of *Birkat haMazon*, the Blessing of the Meal. Within it, several special blessings are added to mark the moment of the *B'rit* by Sephardic Jews.

> *HaRaḥaman, hu y'vareyḥ et ba-al habayit hazeh, avi haben, hu*
> *v'ishto ha-yoledet mey-ata v'ad olam.*
> Compassionate One! Bless the master of this house, father of
> this child, him and his wife who has given birth, from now to
> forever.

> *HaRaḥaman, hu y'vareyḥ et ha-yeled hanolad, uḥ'shem shezikahu*
> *hakadosh baruḥ hu lamila, kaḥ yizakehu likanes la Torah v'la ḥuppa*
> *v'la mitzvot ul'ma-asim tovim v'ḥeyn yehi ratzon—v'nomar ameyn.*
> Compassionate One! Bless the newborn birthling. As You gave
> him the privilege of circumcision, so may You give him the
> privileges of entering into Torah, *ḥuppa*, *mitzvot*, and deeds of
> loving-kindness. May this be your will, and let us say Ameyn!

> *HaRaḥaman, hu y'vareyḥ et ma-alat hasandak v'ha-mohel ush-ar*
> *hamishtadlim bamitzva, heym v'ḥol asher lahem.*
> Compassionate One! Bless the eminent *sandek*, the *mohel*, and all
> others who took part in this *mitzva*, they and all who are
> connected with them.

The B'rit in Kabbala

In the Jewish mystical tradition, Kabbala, *B'rit Mila* took on supernal significance. As the Zohar says,

> It is because of this blood that the world is perfumed with Love
> [*Ḥesed*], and all the worlds survive, as it is written, "If my

covenant be not with day and night, if I have not appointed the ordinances of heaven and earth." [Jeremiah 33:25] . . . There are two crowns united together, and they are the door to all the other crowns: One is Judgment [*Malḥut*] and one is Mercy [*Tiferet/Raḥamim*], and they are perfumed one with the other, male and female. On the male side resides Love, and on the female side Judgment, one white and the other red. And so that they should perfume one another, they are linked to one another. And this covenant [*b'rit*] attaches to them, to "day and night," to Judgment and Love, to Judgment first, and afterward Love rests upon it, and the Whole is perfumed. (Zohar III, 13b–14a, in Isaiah Tishby's *The Wisdom of the Zohar*, III, 1181–82)

This passage is saying that the *B'rit* on the male genitals is what makes sexual intercourse holy, and that if sexual intercourse is done in a holy way, all the worlds (both physical and spiritual) are kept in order. First the male and female sides of God's Own emanations—the *S'firot*—are "perfumed" by this holy intercourse, and then all the other *S'firot* are enlivened as well.

Since neither compassion nor justice, neither unbounded flow nor rigorous boundaries, could survive without each other, nor could the world survive without them both, they must be brought together in sexual union. (The "white" here is identified with male semen, the "red" with female blood.) And it is *B'rit Mila* that keeps this process going.

This theme of sexual intercourse between and within the various aspects of God mirroring (or initiating) sexual intercourse on earth runs through a great deal of Kabbala. It is related to the teaching that Sinai was a supernal Wedding between God and Israel, with the Torah as the wedding contract, and it is related to the teaching that the Song of Songs should be understood as an allegory of the erotic love between God and the People Israel.

Given this focus on sexual union as the energy beneath all Wholeness, the Kabbalists ascribed enormous power to *correct* and *incorrect* sexuality. Joseph, because he used the organ of sexuality correctly (by refusing to use it when Potiphar's wife tried to seduce him), becomes for Kabbala one of the greatest heroes, identified with that *S'fira* that evokes sexual energy at the foundation of the world. Making love in a "correct" way, especially on Friday night (Shabbat) becomes for the Kabbalists a profound spiritual deed that helps to hold all worlds together and to repair the broken places in God's Own Self. On the other hand, those who in Kabbalistic eyes misuse sexuality are believed to bring demonic disaster on the world. The ropes are very taut, the tension very tight.

The focus on *B'rit Mila* as the fulcrum of this worldview raises several problems for Jews of today. First of all, some contemporary Jews are not drawn by a form of mysticism that treats sexuality as the central metaphor for reality, though they may be attracted by other mystical approaches to the world. Secondly, some Jews today are troubled by the notion of laying the orderly process of the universe at the feet—or the genitals—of the unique Jewish covenant with God, rather than in the relationship of all peoples, and each people, to what is Holy and Divine. (The Kabbalists did not explore even the relationship of Ishmael and his biological and spiritual descendants to *B'rit Mila*, though the Torah treats Ishmael's circumcision as a special event.) And finally, the focus on *B'rit Mila* arises from a totally male and totally heterosexual experience of sexuality. There is here no mythic elevation of any covenantal aspect of a woman's or a gay man's sexuality. Indeed, some teachings of Kabbala denigrate many aspects of women's sexuality, treating them as metaphors for spiritual impurity.

Death and Rebirth Again: Modernity

During the past two centuries, Modernity has had something like the same impact on *B'rit Mila* as did the sweep of Hellenistic civilization two thousand years ago. Once again old forms (those of Rabbinic

Judaism) have died; once again old memories have been given new birth into a new gestalt or paradigm.

In the mid-nineteenth century, some Jews proposed to abandon *Mila* as a relic of primitive ritual. But few followed that path. More enticing, however, was a tendency to define circumcision as medically helpful for warding off future disease, and to have the operation done—often with a minimum of ceremony—in the birthing hospital, where a physician rather than a *mohel* performed it.

There is increasing evidence, however, that many Jews are now thirsty for more ritual in their lives—not for ritual by rote, but for ceremonies that will draw on ancient wisdom to speak to their own hearts, minds, and spirits. Some effort has been made to integrate these two somewhat contradictory approaches. Reform Judaism, for example, has begun to train physicians (men and women) as *mohalim* and *mohalot*, to do the surgical circumcision while rabbis preside over the ceremony and seek to fill it with life and spiritual power.

The Covenant with Daughters

So far, the most challenging and enriching effect of Modernity on the Jewish life-path has been the stirring of many Jewish women into asserting their equality in the old forms of Judaism, and creating new forms as well. One result has been the emergence of new rituals for welcoming girl children into the covenant.

It is not likely that as important an event as the birth of a daughter has gone utterly unmarked in Jewish homes for three thousand years. And indeed there are hints of ceremonies, perhaps celebrated by new mothers and their women friends, that were not written down by the men who until our generation shaped the official tradition. In the Bible, for example, mothers are told to stay separate for forty days after a son is born, eighty days after a daughter. So a number of women of childbearing age may have been in a women's community together at any given moment. Did they not celebrate?

In the two thousand years of Rabbinic Judaism, we do know of some traditions that welcomed girls into life and community. Among Sephardim—the Jews who trace their origins to the Spanish and Portuguese communities—girls were named when the mother was ready to rise from childbed, in a joyful home ceremony called *Zeved HaBat*. The baby was carried in on a pillow (as the baby boy was in many communities, to be placed in the *sandek*'s lap). Verses were sung from *Shir HaShirim*, the Song of Songs, that celebrated the beauty of a girl or woman. The community's rabbi recited a blessing for the mother, and then the child's name was announced.

Among Ashkenazim, the Jews of Northern Europe, girls were named in a public ceremony on a Shabbat morning, typically the fourth Shabbat after their birth, when the mother rose from childbed. The father was called up to read from the Torah, the mother stood in the separate women's section, and through the blessing recited after the reading, the baby was given her name.

To the minds of many women and men today, these ceremonies are not enough—for either the daughter or the mother. What many have felt missing is the explicit affirmation that girls are part of the covenant between God and the People Israel.

That gap in the naming ceremonies seemed to match up with the absence of women from the discussions of philosophy and cooking, law and sex, prayer and health, that make up the Talmud; with the absence of women's names from most of the Bible's grand genealogical recitations; with the absence of women's spiritual experience from discussions of the future of Judaism.

In short, the limited celebration of the birth of girls encapsulated the expectation that women would not be part of the "official" great tradition of Torah, but would carry out a quite different religious role, expressing their spiritual lives in totally separate spaces from the men. If adult women and men were both to share in all the sacred moments and spaces, many felt that sharing would have to begin in the mirror-moment of celebrating birth.

So covenant ceremonies for girls (often called by the generic *B'rit Bat*—"covenant of a daughter") emerged in great profusion during the last two decades of the twentieth century.

They have not yet jelled into a single form. Perhaps they never will. Perhaps the new loose networks given us by the photocopier and the Internet will enable small groups of Jews, even single households, to shape their ceremonies with as much independence as the Kurdish Jews, the Indian Jews, the Moroccan Jews, the Roman Jews, used to do. Or perhaps when a profound nerve is struck, lightning-flash communication will in an instant draw millions to a single insight and a single metaphor. Or perhaps both.

What do we have now? Some women have explored the central metaphor of water—the fluid of the womb, the sea, the *mikva* which in the era of Rabbinic Judaism was especially a women's sacred place; the wellsprings connected with Rachel, Rebecca, Tzipora, Miriam.

How then to draw on water for covenanting? Some followed the parallel of *mila*, which represents joining the covenant, for either a newborn boy or an adult male convert to Judaism. Since immersion in the *mikva* is also a step in conversion for adult women (as well as men), it might also provide the pool of meaning through which a baby girl enters the covenant. So some women have used a ceremony in which the central moment is immersion of the baby girl in a bowl of water.

But some women have felt uncomfortable about the echo of *mikva*. For some, *mikva* at the time of menstruation has become a symbol not of women's emancipation but of men's fear of and distaste for women's bodies. For others, the ceremony might seem too similar to Christian infant baptism (even though it is clear that historically, baptism derives from immersion in the *mikva*, not the reverse).

One group of more than a dozen women rabbis have created a ceremony that draws on water in a different way. They call it *Brit Reḥitẓa*, the "Covenant of Washing." Its central metaphor comes from Abraham's washing of the feet of the guests who came to his and

Sarah's tent to announce the impending birth of Isaac. In this cere-mony, the dipping or immersion comes as the central physical event, parallel to the wielding of the *mohel*'s knife. Usually, the water-moment is surrounded with many of the same verses and blessings as those that have resounded for millennia in *B'rit Mila*, with changes like adding Sarah's name along with Abraham's and referring to Miriam's Well, which gave life to the people through their journey in the Wilderness.

In one such ceremony, the moment of the washing is preceded by an explanation, as the *B'rit Mila* is preceded by its biblical origins:

"In our tradition, the *mikva*, or ritual bath, marks the cycles of women's lives. The Talmud tells us that as Abraham entered the covenant through circumcision, Sarah entered the covenant through a *B'rit Reḥitza* ("Covenant of Washing"), a ritual immersion in water. So, today the covenantal ritual act of *B'rit Reḥitza* involves the parents' washing of their daughter's feet. And in the nomadic culture of our ancient forebears, the washing of feet was a sign of ultimate *haḥnasat orḥim*—the welcoming of guests. So what we do today is a way of honoring and welcoming this new family member into the covenant and the tribe."

Mother may say: "As you begin your journey through life, we pray that you will find sustenance in the living waters which Judaism offers to all who draw from the well of our tradition."

Rabbi: *"Baruḥ ata YHWH [Yahh] eloheynu meleḥ [ru-aḥ] ha-olam zoḥer hab'rit birḥitzat ragla-yim."*—"Blessed are You, Adonai [Yahh] our God, Ruler [Breathing Spirit] of the Universe, Who is mindful of the covenant through the washing of feet." Parents (or mother alone) wash the baby's feet.

There follows a new blessing, affirming the God Who calls us to new celebration: *"Baruḥ ata YHWH [Yahh] eloheynu meleḥ [ru-aḥ] ha-olam asher kidshanu b'mitzvotav v'tzivanu l'haḥnisa bivrito shel am Yisra-el."*—"Blessed are You God, Ruler [Breathing Spirit] of the Universe, who has made us holy through the mitzvot, and directed us to bring our daughter into the covenant of Israel."

Taking a different approach, Alana Suskin has focused on the use of salt in Torah as a symbol of everlasting covenant, and developed a ceremony she calls *B'rit Melaḥ* ("Covenant of Salt"):

> [The ceremonial leader says:]
> Salt, meal, and incense are the [means of inducting] priests into service. We thus bring our daughters into a life of service to God.
> [A drop of salt is placed on her tongue.]
> May her tongue always speak Torah.
> [A drop of salt and a few grains of meal are placed on the palms of her hands.]
> May her hands serve God faithfully, and be always engaged in *tikkun olam*, repair of the world.
> [A drop of salt water is placed on her closed eyelids and on her ears.]
> May her eyes see the light of Torah, and may she be blessed to study Torah all her days; may her ears hear the truth of Torah.

Other *B'rit Bat* ceremonies have forgone any "physical," bodily act, and used instead the heartfelt words of Torah about the open heart. Indeed, in one *B'rit Bat* dear to our own hearts—that of our granddaughter Yonit, which came as we were struggling to begin the actual writing/birthing of this book—Arthur's daughter and son-in-law, Shoshana Elkin Waskow and Michael Slater, did precisely this. They quoted one of the Torah's references to circumcision of the heart: "YHWH your God will circumcise your heart and the hearts of your offspring to love YHWH your God with all your heart and every breath, so that you may live." (Deut. 30:6)

In that *b'rit* ceremony, a Chair of Miriam was introduced alongside the Chair of Elijah. During the last generation, Miriam the Prophet has made her appearance alongside Elijah in the Passover Seder, with a cup of clear water that is the *Kos Miriam*, and in the *Havdala* ceremony, with an invocation of her presence to dance and sing for transformation and redemption as she did at the edge of the Sea. Bringing her into the *b'rit* ceremony ensures that a girl child will have as a model a strong woman from the tradition who spoke the word of God with her whole body, and so will strengthen the child to speak and embody Godly words throughout her life.

Reexamining Mila

For some Jews the spread of these ceremonies for welcoming girls into the covenant has crystallized some questions about the nature of the ceremony for boys. If Judaism can be reconfigured in many other ways as we address a new set of life-issues, why not reexamine this tradition as well? Specifically, why use a ritual that causes pain (necessarily without the newborn's consent), if it is possible to enter the covenant through a ritual that does not cause pain? So in our own day, the emergence of new approaches to Judaism has brought forth a new set of reasons for questioning circumcision, on the grounds, not that it differentiates Jews from "the nations," but rather that the compassion taught by Judaism in general should encompass this specific moment as well.

On the other hand, some Jews have insisted that there are good reasons to adhere to the tradition, in addition to the sacred character of the tradition itself:

- Some argue there is no evidence that the pain of circumcision, usually short-lived, has done any serious damage to the psyches of Jewish men. They have suggested that the pain, though real, is fleeting, and may recognize and ritually limit and discharge the pain that often arises between the generations in any case.
- Some have argued that on balance, the evidence is that Jewish men are more compassionate than the men of most other communities, and that perhaps the experience of circumcising sons helps teach compassion.

- Some have suggested that the medical evidence indicates a healthier future for circumcised boys and their sexual partners, though the medical profession is not of one mind about this.
- Some have said that breaking the links of physical similarity between Jewish fathers and sons, as well as the links of tradition between Abraham's generation and our own, would be destructive.

So out of this debate, some Jews—at this point, very few—have drawn on the *B'rit Bat* ceremonies and have for boys as well used rituals other than the act of circumcision. Some have kept the act of *mila* itself as a private event or as a medical procedure and celebrated the covenant and the naming of the child with a joyful gathering. Some have proposed synthesizing the argument for tradition and the argument for change by bringing the *mohel*'s knife to the ceremony and lifting it "in memory of the covenant of cutting between God and Abraham," just as we recite certain prayers in memory of the Temple offerings.

As we have noted, some *b'rit* celebrations for girls have drawn upon the Bible's reference to "circumcisions" of the heart, the lips, and the ears, circumcisions more emotional and spiritual than physical. Perhaps in part because of this initiative, these passages have begun to find their way into the ceremonies for boys as well. For example, the metaphor of "uncircumcised foreskin" as spiritual blockage appears not only in regard to the heart in the Deuteronomic passage quoted above, but also in such verses as:

(Moses speaking to God) Here! The Children of Israel have not hearkened to me; how then will Pharaoh hearken to me, since I am of foreskinned lips? (Exod. 6:12, 30)

(God speaking to the people) Now when you enter the land, and plant any kind of tree for eating, you are to regard its fruit as foreskinned, foreskinned. For three years it is to be considered foreskinned for you, you are not to eat it. (Lev. 19:23)

(God speaking through Jeremiah of the people) To whom shall I speak, give warning that they may hear? Their ears are foreskinned and they cannot listen. (Jer. 6:10)

(And again through Jeremiah) All the nations have foreskins, but the whole House of Israel have foreskins on their hearts. (Jer. 9:26)

(God's accusation through Ezekiel) Aliens foreskinned of heart and foreskinned of flesh [foreigners, or alienated Israelites as well] have been permitted in the Temple. (Ezek. 44:7, 9)

Thus lips, ears, hearts, and very young fruit trees all have some kind of blockage, a thick covering, that needs to be removed.

In the *B'rit Mila* ceremony of our grandson Elior, which took place while we were in the very midst of writing this book, Arthur's son and daughter-in-law, David Waskow and Ketura Persellin, chose to use some of these passages in special prayers and blessings for the child:

HaRaḥaman, Compassionate One, may You open this child's heart. As it is written: So circumcise the foreskin of your heart, and be not stiffnecked. (Deut. 10:16)

HaRaḥaman, may You open this child's ears to the voices of all creation. As it is written: Behold, their ear is uncircumcised, and they cannot hearken. (Jer. 6:10)

HaRaḥaman, may You open this child to loving with all his being. As it is written: YHWH your God will circumcise your heart and the heart of your seed, to love YHWH with all your heart and with all your being, in order that you may live. (Deut 30:6)

Afterwards, as we thought back over the power of these verses, and of the verses on "circumcision of the heart" that had welcomed our other grandchild into the covenant just months before, we could imagine gently touching a knife to the child's lips, ears, and heart, reciting at each touch something like these *HaRaḥaman* prayers. Michael Slater suggests drawing on another metaphor: anointing the child's lips, ears, and heart with oil, for Torah teaches that the whole People Israel is to be a nation of priests (who were anointed). This would also hint that every child carries some of the potentiality of Messianic wholeness, for *Mashi-aḥ* literally means "the anointed one." For some families, such connections of the physical and metaphorical might intensify the "encounter with God" aspect of the ceremony.

And we could also fuse the physical and metaphorical by connecting an ancient Jewish custom of planting trees to celebrate the births of children, with the "foreskin" tradition about fruit trees. Thus at the *b'rit* ceremony, the family could announce the planting of a commemorative fruit tree—whether in Israel, in any tree-deprived community where the child is living, or near the family's home. Years later, the family and friends could celebrate the end of the "foreskin" period of this tree's life.

Naming the Self

In any of these *b'rit* ceremonies, the moment of naming the child should be seen not as anticlimax but as the fulfillment of the covenanting moment. This is when the new Self emerges from the transformative experience. Even though the child has not chosen the name s/he will now bear, almost always the choosing has been done with great care and love.

In most Jewish communities, some member of the family is being remembered and honored in the child's name. In Ashkenazic circles, there is a taboo on naming the child after a living relative. There is no such taboo among Sephardim; to the contrary, there is often a strong desire to honor the living thus. Either way, the choice of whom to honor, whether to transmute Hebrew, Yiddish, Ladino, or English names into some other language, whether to include both father's and mother's names in the classic Jewish *ben/bat* formula, whether to announce a name in English or other local language at the same time, and if so, whether that name should carry a strong Jewish flavor or a mild one or none, be the same as a Hebrew name or not, include both parents' names in the family name or not—all these decisions are expressions of the parents' deeply held value systems, and may have been the subject of complex discussions between the parents themselves.

In many families, other relatives—especially but not only the grandparents—may feel they have a stake in the naming: "What about my sweet sister, who loved you kids so much and looked forward to your child till the day she died?"—"What about hyphenating the last name?"—"What about . . ." These feelings are certainly valid, but they can be addressed in different ways. One is simply silence. Another is pouring out this distress to someone other than the new parents—simply to have a mirror in which to reflect on it. Still another is telling the parents, in the hope they will make the wished-for change. The last might seem the most practical, but—unless the new parents are explicitly asking for advice—it is quite likely to add tension to a ceremony that for millennia has been structured so as to be full of tension. Adding the wrong kind of tension, too. For intervening uninvited contravenes the very flow of the life-cycle that the ceremony is intended to honor. At this moment, the grandparents and others in the family should be handing over with grace and joy the task of parenting to the next generation. That is *their* life-cycle transformation. And the naming of the child is itself one of the first and deepest acts of parenting. So: Hands off.

The Content of Covenant Today

As we see, birthing ceremonies do not address just birth, nor for that matter just "Judaism" in the narrow sense. For at this moment in their own lives, parents are exploring and expressing their own sense of life, family, past, and future:

How broad and how deep is the Jewishness of my own life, and therefore of this child's, to be? Do I expect that from now till twelve or thirteen years from now, Judaism will have little place in my life as I put it on hold till the next ceremony, or do I see this ceremony as a statement that everything in my life, even childbirth and babies and genitals and nursing and childrearing, affect and are affected by my Jewishness?

Am I undertaking this ceremony chiefly because God commanded it, or chiefly out of respect for ancient tradition, or chiefly from pride in sharing Jewish peoplehood today, or chiefly because I look forward to many fruitful generations that may spring from this child, or chiefly because I want to call out to my own generation to help this child grow well in an earth that is healed from its deep wounds and is again filled with life?

What kind of parent do I intend to be? Do I have a partner in my parenting, and if so how do my partner's visions fit with or conflict with mine? How do I feel about the way in which I was parented—and what does the presence (or the absence) of my own parents, the child's grandparents, mean to me? In choosing a name for this child, what qualities and memories and hopes do I intend to affirm?

Who are my community, and how do we fit into each other's lives? What expectations, hopes, and fears do I have about their relationship with this child?

In what ways should we treat women and men as different, in what ways as similar, and how much power do I have to shape the answers to those questions?

Can Jews share the unique wisdoms of Judaism with people who come from other traditions and communities? What if they are part of the family itself? Can we celebrate together? Are there limits?

Especially in our generation, when many families are geographically and emotionally more scattered and more complicated than they used to be, these issues are challenges in the maturation of the parents. The *b'rit* is a conscious event in their life-cycle even more than in the baby's. So in shaping and understanding the ceremonies that welcome an infant, we must be clear what we are saying and hearing about the parents' sense of life and of Judaism.

Indeed, this realization—which we have faced again and again in this one chapter of our book, as we face it in this one chapter of our lives—suggests there might be more conscious attention to the spiritual growth of parents as the birth of a child grows near.

Today, many marriages begin before the wedding day, when the rabbi, cantor, or other Jew who will preside counsels seriously with the couple before they enter on this awesome partnership. S/he often asks them to draw up a "real-life *k'tuba*" of their agreement, often asks them to shape the ceremony itself with a conscious eye to their own intentions—by heart in truth, so not by rote.

In the same vein, should a parent on the verge of a birth realize that the world is about to change again, and come to a conscious understanding of the change? Should a parent take some days, with or without a spiritual counselor, to examine these issues in a serious way? To shape a *k'tuba*, a written agreement, with the child-to-be and with other members of the family? To shape the ceremony with a conscious eye to what it says of the values of body, mind, heart, and spirit?

Finally, what does the covenant of childbirth mean to grandparents? What does it mean to see your children enter the "parenting" passage of the life-cycle that you yourself have lived through? What does it mean to see them take the first steps into the joys and mistakes, the terrors and the puzzles, that defined a large part of your own life for decades past? What does it mean to reassess your own parenting in the light of theirs, and to imagine what wisdom won from your own struggles you will and won't be able to transmit to them? What will it mean to continue parenting them as they embark on parenthood?

And since this *b'rit* ceremony brings to birth some new aspect of the grandparent's own life (even if s/he has already begun the process with another child), what is the covenant the grandparent might make with this new child and with God?

∽ 2 ∽

Firstborns in Community

THE UNCANNY SHADOW-TIME of earliest infancy seems to call forth not just one sacred action but a series of them, to move the newborn and the parents into the fullness of the surrounding community.

Jewish tradition saw the first birthing of any mother as an especially uncanny time: the very birth of birthing. In every nerve and pore of her body, the mother now for the first time experiences the risky, all-consuming, awesome labor of bringing a baby into the world. For both mothers and fathers, the firstborn introduces the unknown territory of parenthood. And as the firstborn child begins to look around the world, later siblings may seem to start out weaker, less coherent, less self-possessed, less self-aware than s/he has already become—and perhaps in the firstborn's eyes, more thoroughly cared-for and protected than s/he remembers being.

So for everyone involved, this first birthing can take on strong spiritual meaning.

In the most ancient Jewish tradition, this first adventure into shaping the next generation was observed with special ceremony—and still is in many Jewish homes today. The ceremony is known as *Pidyon haBen*—"redemption of the son."

Before we examine what this ceremony may mean today, let us try to understand the special role of the firstborn in Biblical Israel, where *Pidyon haBen* first appears.

Many stories in the Book of Genesis show us how special the first-born was—or at least was conventionally expected to be. And yet, strangely enough, in the stories of Cain and Abel, Ishmael and Isaac, Esau and Jacob, Leah and Rachel, Reuben and Joseph, Zeraḥ and Peretz, Manasseh and Efra-yim, God again and again chooses the latter-born for special favor. And each time, what makes this favoring of the younger brother remarkable is that it was not supposed to be this way. Each time, it is seen as a troubling reversal of the "normal" order. For normally, it is the firstborn who is entitled to a special blessing, a special inheritance.

When God favors second-born Abel's offering, Cain is outraged (Gen. 4:1–16) at being overlooked.

Only under God's explicit instructions does Abraham agree to send his elder son Ishmael into the wilderness, shifting his attention to his second son, Isaac. (Gen. 21:9–13)

For Jacob to "buy" the firstborn right from his famished brother, Esau, with a bowl of lentil soup, and then to steal the firstborn blessing with a false-faced goatskin, was a scandal. (Gen. 25:29–34, 27:19–41)

And this same Jacob becomes the fulcrum of a whole series of first-born reversals. When he seeks the second-born Rachel for a wife, La-ban hands him firstborn Leah and scornfully points out that decent folk don't let a younger sister marry early—mocking Jacob's twisting of the firstborn blessing. (Gen. 29:26)

When Jacob comes to bless his grandsons, he crosses his arms to bless not the elder but the younger with the right hand, even though his son Joseph protests. (Gen. 48)

When he is handing out the family blessings to all his sons, he goes out of his way to mention that Reuben is his firstborn, "first-fruit of my vigor"—and then condemns him fiercely. (Gen. 49:3)

Even those untroubled twins, Zeraḥ and Peretz, defy the firstborn norm. One reaches out quickly from the womb, is marked with a crimson thread on the wrist, and then turns shy, returning to the womb while his "second" brother emerges first. (Gen. 38:27–30) This "second" becomes God's favorite, fated to give rise to King David and Messiah. (Ruth 4:18–22)

Even when we leave the family dramas of Genesis behind, the firstborn reversals persist in Exodus. Moses outshines his older brother and older sister, though the three of them are able to work together in a way quite different from the siblings of Genesis. When the two older ones criticize Moses, God comes down, with vigor, on Moses' side.

And the People Israel itself becomes God's "firstborn," even though it is clearly younger, weaker, less cultured, poorer than its elder brother Egypt.

What, then, is that "normal" privilege of the firstborn that God so persistently reverses? The laws of inheritance of the People Israel, as laid out in Deuteronomy (21:15–17), provide that a double portion go to the father's oldest son, even if the mother of that son be "hated." Thus, if there are three sons, the firstborn gets two-fourths of the land, flocks, and other property; if there are twelve sons, the eldest gets two-thirteenths.

The blessings that Abraham, Isaac, and Jacob all bestow on sons other than their firstborns may be in part "spiritual," but they certainly include material benefits—especially access to the land, from which flowed all the blessings of prosperity. Indeed, all the gifts and responsibilities that we call spiritual were connected with the land as well. Whether it was Abraham offering goats and birds to God, or Jacob anointing with oil a stone that he erected to God in the shimmering desert, or Aaron bringing sheep, bulls, barley, bread, to the Shrine of Holy Presence, or Solomon slaughtering whole droves of cattle to hallow the Temple in Jerusalem; whether it was honoring the restfulness of grain and animals on the Shabbat day, or allowing the entire earth to rest for a year of every seven—the wind of God danced always on the earth. If elder sons were privileged to receive more of these earthy benefits, in return they must also give more of their energy to that earthy Breath of Holiness.

The crisis of what it means to be a firstborn shrieks out in sharpest agony in the Exodus. God proclaims Israel God's Own firstborn—and warns that if the Egypt that prides itself on being elder brother of the nations will not allow the blessing to be thus reversed, then it is the firstborn of all Egyptians who must die.

And in the story of the Exodus, they do. Only in the Israelite houses where the doorposts have been smeared with blood from a slaughtered lamb, are the firstborn spared.

If we let our eyes look into these houses, suddenly we may see the one house in which a human being lives whose doorway is always smeared with blood: the womb as every mother gives birth. From those houses where the Israelites can signal that they are ready for their birthing—from those houses, the firstborns and all their new-born families come forth to break the birthing waters of the Sea.

Even amid the intense immediacy of this story of a volcanic up-heaval beyond a revolution, so important is the firstborn theme that the story pauses (Exod. 13:1–2) to institute a practice for the future:

> YHWH worded so to Moses, saying: "Make holy for Me every firstborn that breaks open the womb; among the Children of Israel, whether human or animal, it is Mine."

And the Torah continues (Exod. 13:11–15):

> When YHWH has brought you into the Land of the Canaanites . . . you shall transfer to YHWH all that breaks open the womb: every womb-breaker that is offspring of your animals, the males are for YHWH. Every womb-breaker of a donkey [which was not itself an acceptable animal for ritual offering] you are to re-

deem with a lamb; if you do not redeem it, then you must break
its neck. And every human firstborn among your sons [or "children"] you must redeem.

And the Torah teaches that when a child asks, a parent—probably
the father—must explain:

> Because YHWH killed every firstborn throughout the Tight and
> Narrow Land [*Mitzra-yim*, Egypt], from every human firstborn to
> every animal firstborn, therefore I slaughter for YHWH every
> male womb-breaker [of the flock and herd], and redeem every
> firstborn of my sons."

But another way of understanding "redemption of the son,"
Pidyon haBen, arises from the place in Torah that describes its actual
practice. Here (Num. 3:40–50, 8:14–19, 18:12–18) *Pidyon haBen* is
deeply connected with holy service at the Place of God's Presence, the
portable *Mishkan* in the Wilderness.

The Torah describes the assignment of the tribe of Levi to minis-
ter at the *Mishkan*. First the Levite males who were one month old and
older were counted. Their numbers came to 22,000. Then all the firstborn males of the entire people were counted, and the number came to
22,273. God tells Moses to replace the firstborns with the Levites, and
to redeem the 273 leftover firstborns by paying five shekels each to the
Kohanim, or priests, Aaron and his sons.

What does this mean? It seems likely that until this moment, the
firstborn (son) in every family was in effect a priest, able to channel
the Divine energy through ceremonies that kept the earth and the people in right relationship. Each family could, on its own, stay directly in
touch with God and so receive the blessings of fruitfulness. But this
sacred role was also filled with awe and danger. Any error in its per-
formance could lead to death (as befell Aaron's own two oldest sons).

But now, this function was transferred to the tribe of Levites, to
assist the *Kohanim* by ministering at the *Mishkan* and so to channel

God's blessings for the people as a whole. No longer could a family undertake service to God on its own, no longer could it separate itself from the wider community. Instead, the people was irrevocably united.

This sacred role evidently could be transferred only through a one-to-one exchange. It seems the people as a whole needed a certain number of souls devoted to sacred service, and if that number of firstborns was to be replaced, an equal number of Levites must take up their service.

But there were more firstborns than Levites. So the leftover firstborns had to be replaced in a way different from simple personal substitution. Each had to be "redeemed" from his sacred and dangerous role by paying the *Kohanim* five shekels.

The Torah also looks at this practice from the vantage point of Aaron, the *Kohanim*, and the Levites who served them. (Num. 18:12–16, 8:13–19) Here it becomes clear that not only the firstborn of the flock and herd but also the "first fruits" of olive oil, wine, grain, and other crops are especially dedicated to God and are given to the priests to eat. Even the firstborns of taboo animals are dedicated to God, but since these animals could not be eaten they are redeemed by paying five shekels each to the *Kohanim*, like firstborn human beings.

So we see that the firstborn son may have had a special role, awesome and dangerous, as a channel for God's blessing (or the failure of blessing) for the land's prosperity, as well as carrying the special aura of awe and danger from the risk of death on the night of Exodus. One Torah text (Num. 8:16–17) fuses these two aspects of the firstborn's uniqueness:

> For given-over, given-over are they [the Levites] to Me from the midst of the Children of Israel; in place of the one who breaks open every womb, the firstborn of every one of the Children of Israel, I have taken them for Myself. For Mine is every firstborn among the Children of Israel, of man and of beast; at the time I

struck down every firstborn in the Land of Narrows/Egypt, I took them as holy for Myself.

We may note one more aspect of the sense of awe and danger that surrounds the firstborn. The story of the Binding of Isaac (his mother Sarah's firstborn) perhaps suggests a memory of a time when the ritual slaughter of a firstborn was actually required, before God intervened to stay Abraham's hand. We note in this connection that, at least to Abraham, saving Isaac apparently required the slaughter of a substitute—a ram. (Gen. 22:12–13)

In much the same way, the Torah connects the sparing of the Israelite firstborns from death on the night of the Exodus from Egypt with the slaughter of the Pesaḥ lamb. So the notion of redeeming a firstborn through a substitute may have had deep spiritual significance even before the redemption through shekels for the Levites.

It is the five-shekel redemption ceremony that was reshaped by the proto-Rabbis by the time the Mishna was encoded (ca. 200 CE); that persisted through centuries of Rabbinic Judaism; and that in traditional Jewish families has life still today.

Why did this happen? Of all the biblical life-cycle ceremonies, we might have imagined that this one would most easily drop away when the Temple service came to an end and Rabbinic Judaism, attuned to the far-flung Diaspora, emerged. With no single land from which the foods of Israel might grow, no Temple offerings of the foods gathered from across that land, what was the point of *Kohanim* and Levites? In a Judaism newly built on words of prayer and words of Torah-study as a way of getting in touch with God, a Judaism focused on a group of men chosen for their verbal skills, highly trained in verbal lore and learning, what was the point of a hereditary caste drawn from ancient experts in ritual offerings of plants and animals and in the care of sacred Temple tools and instruments?

Certainly, in the new rabbinic form of Judaism, the ceremony of *Pidyon haBen* changed. Yet it survived, perhaps precisely because it was an anachronism. Living in the midst of so much change, and with so little connection left to any land for which they might still feel responsible, the Jewish people may have felt, under these conditions, precisely an urgent need to preserve whatever link they could to the earthy old Judaism. And here—in the intimate family details of first birthings, in the biology not of a whole people in its land but of a single household—perhaps the archaic biology of tribes and castes could find a place in the new paradigm. Preserving some version of *Pidyon haBen* may even have helped reconcile *Kohanim* and Levites to the loss of most of the special roles that had been theirs so long as the Temple stood.

If the *Pidyon* were to survive in widely dispersed Jewish communities, its rules and procedures needed to be pinned down. The Mishna (in which the early Rabbis harked back to the latter days of the Temple offerings) began by unfolding who is a "womb-opener" for redemption purposes:

- A girl is not, and if she is the firstborn of her mother, then no subsequent child calls forth the *Pidyon*.
- A father's first offspring who is not the mother's firstborn does not bring forth the *Pidyon haBen* ceremony. The womb is what is crucial here.
- Any child of a father who is a *Kohen* or a *Levi* or of a mother whose father was a *Kohen* or *Levi* does not require redemption. (The records of these rankings have been carefully, though not flawlessly, kept by many generations of Jewish families.)
- A fetus miscarried before the fortieth day of pregnancy does not count as a womb-opener (so that the next child still does); but any later miscarriage or stillborn child does count as a womb-opener in the sense that a next-born child will not bring forth the redemption ceremony.
- A child delivered by cesarean section is not considered to have "opened" the womb (and so does not require a redemption cere-

mony), but its birth cancels the obligation in regard to further children.

The rabbinic tradition worked out the ceremony of *Pidyon haBen* that is still in use today.

Since the tradition viewed the completion of thirty days of life (when the moon is at the same place in its phases as when the child was born) as a successful test of the child's viability, the *Pidyon* ceremony takes place on the thirty-first day (unless it is a Shabbat or festival day, in which case the ceremony takes place on the next weekday).

The father presents the child to a *Kohen*, saying *"Zeh b'ni b'hori, hu peter rehem l'imo, v'hakadosh baruh hu tziva lifdoto."*—"This is my son, my firstborn who opened his mother's womb." The father then quotes the biblical passages (Num. 18:16 and Exod. 13:2) that prescribe the redemption. The *Kohen* may then ask the mother to declare: *"Zeh b'ni b'hori lo hipalti."*—"This is my son, my firstborn, and I have not miscarried."

The father hands his son over to the *Kohen*. The *Kohen* explains, quoting from the Torah (Num. 18:16): *"U'fdu-yav miben hodesh tifdeh b'erha kesef hameshet sh'kalim b'shekel hakodesh, esrim geyra."*—"This is a firstborn son, and the Blessed Holy One has commanded to redeem him, saying, 'And its redemption-price—from the age of a month you are to redeem—according to your assessment, silver, five shekels in the Holy-Shrine shekels, that is, twenty grains each.' "

Then he recites a formula asking whether the father wishes to redeem his son: *"Mai ba-it t'fey, liteyn li binha b'horha she-hu peter rehem l'imo, o ba-it lifdoto b'ad hamesh s'la-im k'dimhuyavta midoraita?"*—"Which do you prefer, to give away your firstborn son who opened his mother's womb, or do you prefer to redeem him for five shekels as you are required to do by the Torah?"

The father answers: *"Hafetz ani lifdot et b'ni, v'heylah d'mey pidyono k'dimhayavna midoraita."*—"I wish to redeem my son. I set forth to you the cost of his redemption, as is written in Torah," and hands the equivalent of five silver shekels (today five American silver dollars or similar amounts in other currencies) to the *Kohen*. He also recites a blessing upon the *mitzva* of redemption: *"Baruḥ ata YHWH eloheynu meleḥ [ru-aḥ] ha-olam, asher kidshanu b'mitzvotav v'tzivanu, al Pidyon haBen."*—"Blessed is the Breath of Life, our God, Who makes us holy through commandments [or, connection], and has breathed into us the sacred commandment/connection of redeeming a son."

And then the father says the *Sheheḥeyanu* blessing, praising God for "giving us life, lifting us up, and bringing us to this moment."

The *Kohen* swings the silver coins above the child's head, saying: *"Zeh taḥat zeh, zeh ḥiluf zeh, zeh maḥul al zeh."*—"This in place of that, this in exchange for that, this pardoned because of that," and returns the child to his father. Together the *Kohen* and the parents bless the child: *"V'yikanes zeh haben l'ḥayim l'Torah ul'yirat shama-yim. Y'hi ra-tzon she-k'shem sheniḥnas l'pidyon ken yikanes l'Torah ul'ḥuppa ul'ma-asim tovim."*—"May this child enter into life, Torah, and a sense of awe toward heaven. As this child has entered into redemption, so may he enter into Torah, the wedding canopy, and good deeds."

The *Kohen* places his right hand on the child's head, and pronounces over him two ancient blessings. The first is the blessing Jacob gave to his grandsons Manasseh and Ephraim, crossing his arms so as to intertwine the blessings of the firstborn and the later-born: *"Y'simḥa Elohim k'efra-yim v'ḥim'nasheh."*—"May God make you like Ephraim and Manasseh." This pair, coming at the end of the Book of Genesis, is the first set of biblical siblings who experience both the recognition and the dissolution of tension between older and younger. The blessing affirms the hope that all those who begin with more power and with less, with more wealth and with less, can learn to heal their imbalance and live in peace and equality. It is an especially powerful blessing for firstborns, who may begin with greater power than do those children who follow. It is an even more powerful reminder to the parents, who might plan how to prevent a cycle of siblings' arrogance and fear from curdling the family's sweet life.

Then the *Kohen* continues with the threefold blessing traditionally reserved for priests to recite:

Y'vareḥ'ḥa YHWH v'yishm'reḥa.
Ya-eyr YHWH panav eyleḥa viḥuneka.
Yisa YHWH panav eyleḥa v'yaseym l'ḥa shalom.
May [*Yah*, *Adonai*, Breath of Life, Eternal, God, or Lord]
    bless you and keep you.
May [*Yah* or *Adonai*, etc.] light up God's Face for you and
    pour out love for you.
May God's Face lift up toward you and give you peace.

Then the *Kohen* recites the blessing over wine: *"Baruḥ ata YHWH eloheynu meleḥ [ru-aḥ] ha-olam, borey p'ri hagafen."*—"Blessed is the Breath of Life, our God, Who creates the fruit of the vine." He shares a cup of wine with the child's parents. There follows a joyful meal, as in most Jewish ceremonies. In this case, even more than most, the meal reminds us of how the Temple service of the *Kohanim* and Levites focused on offerings of food to God.

Unless the *Kohen* whom the family has invited is himself very poor, in our day it is likely that the *Kohen* will either return the money to the father or devote the money to *tz'daka* (a socially responsible charity).

In the Jewish community of Rabat, Morocco, the ceremony was customarily interrupted when the *Kohen* would pick up the baby and move to leave the house. High drama would follow, as the mother shrieked at the imminent loss of her baby. Only then would the father redeem him and the *Kohen*, with a show of reluctance, return him.

Many Jewish families today have serious concerns and reservations about *Pidyon haBen*:

- Those who feel strongly about minimizing differences between firstborn and other children are of course concerned.
- So are those who oppose such hereditary distinctions as the ancient rankings of *Kohen*, *Levi*, and *Yisra-el*.

- And increasing numbers of Jews are, in the name of gender equality, concerned about the limitation of the ceremony to boys.

The simplest of these to address would seem to be the gender question. Firstborn girls could simply be redeemed as boys have been. Once this step is taken, it is also easy to include children born of a cesarean section, children whose birth follows a miscarriage, even perhaps an adopted first child.

The other questions are harder to address, but some families have done so. Some have used new forms that focus not on a *Kohen* but on a rabbi or some other respected Jewish teacher. The focus in such ceremonies has shifted from payment for Levitical redemption to giving money for *tz'daka* to a worthy cause—perhaps one that echoes the Exodus by striving to free human beings from slavery and oppression.

Indeed, the Reconstructionist denomination has responded to some of these concerns by developing what it calls a "Welcoming Ceremony for First Children and Their Parents," drawing on the traditional concept of *Pidyon haBen* but quite different in its theology and symbolism.

The Welcoming Ceremony affirms the specialness of a firstborn, but in other ways takes a much more egalitarian stance than the traditional *Pidyon haBen*. Both boys and girls are involved, as are all "parents"—mothers as well as fathers, but also language carefully calibrated to recognize that the parents may be two men or two women.

This Welcoming Ceremony also disconnects the firstborn from priesthood, and quotes the Torah's language of redemption only as a historical reference. Instead, the ceremony focuses on the "five shekels" as a token of *tz'daka* (socially responsible gifts of money to the poor) and invites the parents to pledge themselves to act on behalf of justice and compassion.

In place of acceptance of five shekels by a *Kohen*, the Welcoming Ceremony has five different people who have been appointed as "messengers," each to receive one silver coin. The core of the ceremony has the parents' blessing affirm that what they are doing is a *mitzva*—

". . . *v'tzivanu al kidush hab'θorot [hab'θorim]*"—". . . Who has commanded/connected us to make holy our firstborns."

The parents then ask the messengers collectively, *"Ha-im atem muhanim um'zumanim lih'yot sh'lihim ne'emanim lidvar mitzva?"*— "Are you ready and willing to be faithful messengers for the sake of a *mitzva?*"

When the five messengers accept this mission, the parents hand the child and one silver dollar to each of them in turn and declare to each: "Be our messenger to deliver this money to [name of *tz'daka* organization] in order to build a world of justice for the sake of this child."

Each of the messengers responds: *"Kibalti et hakesef v'eh-yeh shali-ah ne'eman l'ma-anhem ul'ma-an ha-yalda/ha-yeled."*—"I have received the money, and I will be a faithful messenger for you and for the child."

And for the *"Zeh tahat zeh"* passage, the Welcoming Ceremony creatively translates the passage as "Justice instead of greed, caring instead of selfishness, this commitment for the blessing of new life."

The ceremony then ends with blessings for the child and with a celebratory meal.

There is at least one interesting aspect of the biblical version of *Pidyon haBen* that could conceivably give it new energy in the Judaism of today and tomorrow:

It was the only Jewish life-cycle ceremony that human beings shared with the firstborns and first fruits of other species. This was of course a serious fact of biblical life, and in halakhic principle, it is still true today—even though it is rarely practiced, even in traditional Jewish families. In theory, nonetheless, firstborn sheep, cattle, and goats owned by Jews ought still to be redeemed by being turned over to a *Kohen*.

Since there is no Temple, they cannot be used for sacrifice. So in the rare cases when this practice is actually carried out, the *Kohen* keeps the animals until they die (or become accidentally blemished so that they could not be used in a Temple offering anyway—in which case they can be eaten).

In an era of increasing concern for all species and for the wounded earth, could *Pidyon haBen* be given new life as a way of expressing human empathy and solidarity with the dangers that we share with other species?

Indeed, this concern can be easily drawn from the biblical connection of *Pidyon haBen* with God's protection of the Israelite firstborns on the night of Exodus. For the point of the protection given Israelite firstborns was that Egyptian firstborns suffered from Pharaoh's arrogance. Nor did these Egyptian firstborns suffer alone: Their deaths were but the final plague in a series in which the rivers and lakes, the earth and air, the animals and plants, had been befouled, also as a result of Pharaoh's arrogance. Beneath the surface of the biblical *Pidyon*, can we hear the redemption of plants and animals as well as human firstborns as an echo and reversal of the danger that they shared in the Tight and Narrow Space?

Today, how many are the rivers that have (like the Nile in Pharaoh's day) run red with blood from the extinction of the species on their banks? Could the redemption of human firstborns be carried out on the banks of an endangered lake or river, in the midst of a croaking chorus of endangered frogs? Could we bring to a *Kohen* or a rabbi not only a human child but also seedlings, beetles, earthworms for redemption? Or, if not the plants and animals themselves, our awareness that today they also need to be redeemed from the deadly dangers that they face?

In this approach, their redemption would come not through ritual slaughter but through liberation from danger, just as it does for the human firstborn. (This is what "redemption" means in another Jewish context, *Pidyon Shevu-yim*—the redemption of captives.)

Finally, there remains the question of what it means to single out firstborns from their later siblings. Here I myself (Arthur speaking) have learned a great deal by intertwining my own life with the biblical stories of the sibling problems that plague the firstborns of Genesis. As a firstborn, I was brought up short by my younger brother's challenge in the middle of our lives, to rethink our relationship. When for the first time the two of us became aware *with* each other of how our birth order had affected our lives, we were able to become true brothers in a deeper sense.

Obviously, the *Pidyon* ceremony does not make a newborn child aware of what it means to be a firstborn. But perhaps the very act of affirming a first birth as a special one can remind the parents to make sure the specialness does not breed bitterness.

And in our day, when many people become parents ten or twenty years later in their lives than did their own parents or grandparents, *Pidyon haBen* may be an important step in the parents' own life-path. Surely, for many people a sense of awe and danger continues to hover over firstborns—not only for the child but for parents embarking on a new exploration.

So the *Pidyon* can offer parents a time to reflect on what it means to become responsible for guiding a new life. They may well have more responsibility on their own shoulders than most of the generations of Rabbinic Judaism had, since the village it takes to rear a child may not be there organically around them, but may take a conscious effort to create. At best, they will have already begun during this pregnancy to reexamine not the formal *k'tuba*, the written contract of their marriage, but the real ongoing practice of their lives together. At best, they will have taken time to plan the changes they will need to make. They will have made some initial decisions about the early raising of this child. The *Pidyon* may then become a time for them to say in the presence of their family, their "village," and God how they intend to walk the next part of their life-path. Indeed, just as the original Levitical redemption brought previously autonomous families and clans into a much closer relationship with the wider Israelite community, so today the isolated nuclear families forged by Modernity might be able to use *Pidyon* to help shape new communities of childbearing.

We have seen that in the great shift from independent clans to the united twelve-tribe People Israel, *Pidyon haBen* may have played a major role in shaping that united future. And we have also seen that in the great shift from Biblical to Rabbinic Judaism, perhaps the preservation of *Pidyon haBen* served the purpose of preserving an important symbolic connection to the earth-food-and-body Judaism of the past. Today, as we face the analogous transformations of the Modern Age, perhaps *Pidyon* can once again help us look to the future. The Jewish people has become far more conscious of the need to weave a new community with the earth and all its species than Jews have been since biblical days. And Jews have become more conscious than they have ever been of the disintegration of the extended family and the shtetl, and therefore the need for intentionally creating new forms of family. If renewing *Pidyon* can help to shape these new forms of community with the earth and with each other, then it can become redemptive at a deeper level.

Biblical Judaism saw the moment of birth as eerie, uncanny, for the mother as well as the child. The mother entered *tuma*, a state of taboo that could not be mixed with the other awesome status, *k'dusha*. *K'dusha* applied especially where the community as a whole could experience the Presence of God—in the portable Shrine or *Mishkan* in the Wilderness, and ultimately at the Holy Temple in Jerusalem. Someone in a state of *tuma* could not enter there.

Tuma applied whenever life was endangered, newly gained, or lost—for example, in cases of a disease that brought on dead-white skin; after menstruation, a seminal emission, or some other genital discharge; and after touching a dead body. In these situations, most people would probably find themselves intensely inwardly focused, to the exclusion of communal concerns.

So a woman who had given birth entered the inwardly focused, taboo state of *tuma*. This eerie state lasted for forty days if her child was a boy; eighty if it was a girl. (Lev. 12) During this time she could not touch instruments of *k'dusha* or enter the Shrine or the Temple precincts. At the end of this time, she would bring the *Kohen* (priest) an offering (a lamb or a pigeon, depending on what she could afford), which he would "bring near" as an offering to God. Thus she would again become *t'hora*, which is often translated "pure" but may more accurately mean "clear, clarified."

Why the difference in length of *tuma*-time for the birth of a baby girl as against a boy? Most interpreters have assumed the norm was the time that applied to males, and have treated the longer period of eighty days for girls as the aberration. Trying to understand this aberration, some have suggested that the birth of a birth-giver is even more uncanny than the birth of a begetter.

But out of the experience of mothering, I (Phyllis speaking) begin from a different place. In my own experience, eighty days is about right for the length of time needed for a mother to focus on her newborn child, shutting out the distractions of other parts of life—not dealing with other children, her partner, or the community at large. That eighty days of seclusion for mother and child allows the two to bond most effectively.

Why, then, a shorter time for the baby boy? Perhaps the men of ancient Israel were urgent that a baby boy be brought much sooner into the men's community. Perhaps these feelings echo yet today in the sense that for most girls, identification with the mother is likely to be less troublesome; for boys, it is a near-far matter. The closer mother and son cling to each other, the more apparent that they are unlike. The boy's individuation may be more complicated.

Since birth-time *tuma* was focused on not approaching the Shrine or Temple, it vanished as a category once the Temple had been destroyed. (Only the *tuma* associated with menstruation, which is separately referred to in the Torah without a connection to the Temple, survived the Destruction.) So the post-birth withdrawal of mother and child from ordinary social life did not continue in Rabbinic Judaism, nor did the ceremonial reentry of the mother into the *t'hora* state on the fortieth or eightieth day.

Is there any aspect of the biblical teaching of the mother-and-child's withdrawal that might be useful to us today?

It could teach us to take more seriously the need for time away from ordinary work, in favor of intimate time for the family. Modern economics and culture have driven our patterns of the use of time toward ignoring not only Shabbat, the seventh day of Restful-time, but also all the sabbatical moments of Being and Loving that could cradle and transform our times of Making and Doing.

Reserving time for parents to focus on a new human being seems spiritually, psychologically, and medically vital. What would it mean to make this not only possible but almost universal?

First, there would need to be surcease from the struggle to make a living. In most Western countries, there are provisions for paid maternity/paternity leave; but in the United States, no law and no custom requires parents to be paid while they are caring for a newborn. Assuming that paid leave were available for eighty days after a birth (as an obligation of the employer or a benefit from the government), would that be enough to match the depth of *tuma*?

Not unless something more than money were involved.

Tuma was a state so sacred that it canceled out the ordinary obligations to the Temple. A secular society's recompense in the form of money would help to make inward reflection and loving connection possible, but more is needed:

Time to sleep on the baby's schedule. Time for parents to renew their own sexual and emotional relationship with unhurried calm. Time to read each other a short story, a poem, a psalm. Time to meditate, to sing a sacred chant.

Eighty days to walk the next turning in the spiral of their lives.

~ 3 ~

Further into Childhood

WHEN PHYLLIS PUBLISHED in a leading Jewish magazine an article describing her ceremony celebrating menopause (see Chapter 9), there were a slew of letters to the editor in response, most of them negative. One expressed outrage at making such an intimate event as menopause the focus of a semipublic ritual. "Next somebody will propose a weaning ceremony," wrote the angry (male) reader.

We read this openmouthed, uncertain whether to guffaw or weep. The third life-cycle ceremony described in Torah is the great feast that Abraham (so says the text) gave when Isaac was weaned. (Gen. 21:8) (We can't believe that Sarah wasn't at least as much involved, and maybe more.)

And indeed, there is now on record, written in this past generation, a weaning ritual for Jewish mothers and their babies.

The point here seems to be that in many aspects of the bearing and rearing of a child, the involvement of women in shaping Jewish ritual has made an enormous difference.

Perhaps this has been happening all along. Perhaps women have all along been honoring, celebrating, wailing, weeping, at the extraordinary moments of conceiving, bearing, birthing, losing children—weaning them, bewording them, sending them to school, nursing them through illness. Perhaps women have even all along told each other what they were doing to celebrate and honor and deepen these moments. But if so, there has been no written record, and millions of women in our world have never heard the stories. Now they can.

In just a moment we will return to that question of a weaning ceremony. But first, we want to note that in the past two decades, a series of buried agonies of birthing women have erupted into public view. Despite the many biblical stories of parents who have trouble conceiving (and women who bear the burden of that trouble), there have not been "official" Jewish liturgies for infertility, for miscarriages and stillbirths, for choosing to end a pregnancy, for crucial moments of anxiety and hope in the midst of pregnancy, for prayers with friends just before labor and in its painful midst, for a healthy delivery.

Now there are such liturgies and prayers, created and collected by many different hands. Many seem to us both strong and healing. One book about these passages we found extraordinary: Rabbi Nina Beth Cardin's *Tears of Sorrow, Seeds of Hope*. We found there both a sense of the Spirit and practical specifics. Those who hope to be parents and know they are facing these questions, those who expect to be parents and know they might face these questions, and those who take responsibility in the Jewish community to guide the life-passage, would all do well to absorb the lessons of this book.

Cardin's method, as well as her content, is exemplary. She has searched back through Jewish history and spiritual life to pluck the silent strings that are needed for these sad, mysterious melodies:

Rebekah's outcry when she feels torn apart by the struggle of twins in her womb.

Rachel's painful plea to her husband to give her a child.

The naming of Reuben: "See, a son!," a reflection of Leah's fear that without children she could not win her husband's love.

Hannah's lament when she has no children, and her celebration when Samuel is born, and her willingness to offer him to God as a *nazir* and priest and ultimately prophet.

And far more recent outcries of Jewish women—prayers in Yiddish, in Ladino, in English—as they pleaded, grieved, and celebrated.

And the use of ritual objects that were by the official tradition often seen only sideways and askance: red threads from Rachel's Tomb wrapped around the wrists of wistful women; the red stone mentioned in the Talmud as a fertility amulet; the red seeds of fruitful pomegranate.

Cardin points out that the red stone's redness echoes the womb; the root of the word for "human being," *adam*, is close cousin to the word *adom*, meaning "red"; and in the breast-plate of the High Priest, the ruby stone represented the tribe of Reuben/"See, a son!"

"The physicality of the stone," she writes, "allows women to touch what does not yet exist and to cradle in their palms the hope of their dreams." She proposes that a woman should hold the stone in her hands and say:

Dear God, Eyl Shaddai [God of the Nourishing Breast], my mothers took comfort in red stones, these smooth, cool symbols of their deep, dark wombs. My mothers recited Your names and the names of the angels You appointed to look after them. They wrote these names on the walls of their rooms and wore these names upon their breasts.

Although I may not know Your names or the names of your angels, with this stone of my mothers I reach out to You. In taking up this stone I take up their faith. As I place this stone

upon my heart, may You place my prayers upon Your heart, too.
God, you answered the prayers of my mothers. Join my prayers
to theirs and answer me. Let others say of me one day, Look, she
has a child.

In this suggestion we hear not only that women are creating ceremonies for events that women experience more fully than men. We
hear not only that women are bringing these experiences, these responses, fully into the light from the dark underground where the men
who defined Judaism have left them unseen for centuries. We hear
also that forms of religion are being recovered and publicly honored
that some women have cherished quietly and that have been scath-
ingly dismissed by the official (male) rabbis and scholars as mere
"popular religion," somewhere between paganism and superstition.

The question we might ask is whether the earthiness and physicality of this sort of practice is indeed "lower" in value than the word-
focused religion of official Rabbinic Judaism, or, to the contrary,
expresses important connections with the body and the earth that Rabbinic Judaism has scanted.

The separation of the Jewish people from the body and the earth
that accompanied its departure from the Land of Israel was in part
transcended by the new rabbinic religion that used words as a path
to God. But the new path, as it marginalized the body as a channel
to God, may also have concealed a wound—the alienation of the
physical.

The prayer that Cardin proposes to accompany connection with
the red stones does not describe them as imbued with "magical" powers but does honor the associations they evoke. Perhaps the connection of the stones with the prayer points toward a synthesis of word
and body that might heal a long-standing Jewish wound. And perhaps
the action of a woman rabbi in resurfacing the "red stones" is one
step toward bringing the marginalized spiritual experience of Jewish
women into the center of a future Judaism.

The red stone or any of the other emerging ceremonies that bespeak anxiety or grief, sad surrender or unexpected joy, can be configured in the four-step dance we have earlier described—from leaving the common community and meeting the Mysterious God, to the coming forward of a new self—parent or child—and returning to a community transformed by its sharing of the experience.

If despite these pleas there is no birthing, if indeed despite them there is a stillbirth or miscarriage, some parents may find themselves without a clear path of grieving. For in the past, much of the tradition has ruled that for a baby who dies in utero or in childbirth before drawing an independent breath there are only limited rituals of burial, no *tahara* of the body and no sitting *shiva*.

Cardin, however, suggests how to draw on the traditions of mourning in new ways. (See the last chapter of our book for a guide to them.) As warrant to mourn when the conventional tradition has fallen silent or fearful, she quotes a teaching of the most recent major code of Jewish law, the *Shulḥan Aruḥ*: "Anyone who chooses to be stringent on himself to mourn for someone for whom he is not obligated, is not prevented from doing so."

Cardin is not alone. More and more often, rabbis and other knowledgeable Jews are ready to offer communal and spiritual support to grieving parents.

If, on the other hand, from the healing powers of medical science and of prayerful pleading there has emerged not a dead end but the birthing and maturing of a new life, there will come a time to wean the youngster.

The *Second Jewish Catalog* includes a ceremony by Shoshana and Mel Silberman for weaning a child. They suggest it be held in synagogue on the first Shabbat after weaning, or perhaps at home for the weaning itself, as Shabbat ends and the *Havdala* ceremony differentiates between Being-time and Doing-time: a time especially appropriate for moving from Edenic breast-feeding to the harder, more independent work of solid food.

Their ceremony includes recitations by the mother of the passage from Genesis about the weaning of Isaac (others have added the weaning of the Prophet Samuel [1 Sam. 1:23]) of a *midrash* connecting Torah and the flow of milk, and of various blessings that express rejoicing in the ability to nurse. It ends with the parents saying the blessing over wine and letting the child sip a few drops of wine, and then—as in an Eastern European custom—with someone other than the parents leading the blessing over bread and formally offering the child a taste of bread, signifying the child's first step toward independence, away from the nurturing of home into the sharing of a wider community.

We would add some thoughts: One of the major names of God, *Shaddai* or *Eyl Shaddai*, was the name by which God was especially known to the Patriarchs and Matriarchs. *Shadda-yim* is the Hebrew word for "breasts." Especially in the blessing that Jacob gave to his son Joseph, he invoked the God-name *Shaddai* to give Joseph "blessings of the breasts and of the womb." (Gen. 49:25)

> May your father's God on High become your help,
> and may *Shaddai* become your blessing—
> Blessings of the heavens, from above,
> Blessings of the deep, crouching below—
> Blessings of the breasts [*shadda-yim*] and of the womb.

It was *Shaddai* Who foretold the birth of Isaac. (Gen. 17:1) This was the Nurturing, Nourishing God.

Then in the crisis of the Exodus from slavery, God changed the Name by which the Israelites can cry out for liberation. (Exod. 6:2–3) Now they will take to heart the name "YHWH," the Breath of Life Who can be a gentle breeze or the Hurricane that parts the waters. This name is the shortened form of the Name *Eh-yeh Asher Eh-yeh*—"I Will Be Who I Will Be," Who speaks to Moses at the Burning Bush.

This transition is one from simple nurture to—"Get up and go!" Perhaps the weaning ceremony should begin by invoking *Eyl*

Shaddai, the God Who nurtures at the breast, and end with the Name Who calls for independent action.

The next ceremony to honor a new stage of independence is the custom of *apshiren*, Yiddish for "shearing off" or cutting the hair at the age of three. At this point, in strongly traditional families, the small boys begin to wear earlocks—*peyess* or *peyot*—that is, "corners" to their hair, as in the command "You shall not cut the corners of your beards." To make *peyot* appear, the rest of the hair had to be cut.

At the same time, many boys in traditional homes may begin to wear the *arba kanfot*, or "four corners"—an undershirt shaped like a lightweight poncho, with *tzitzit*, specially knotted fringes, tied into the four corners of the garment. (The *tallit*, or prayer shawl, is in theory just a special case of the wearing of *tzitzit*; in ancient lore, such poncho-like four-cornered garments with *tzitzit* were worn all day, not only in the synagogue.)

This ceremony at the age of three may be connected with the sense that by this time the child has learned to control his innards so that he will not be likely to befoul his *tzitzit*.

For most traditional children, the *apshiren* takes place in the scattered Jewish towns and neighborhoods where they live. But during the last generation among some Israelis, the custom has emerged of gathering in the tens of thousands in the northern town of Meron, the burial place of the ancient mystic Rabbi Shimon bar Yoḥai. Rabbi Shimon is traditionally regarded as the author of the great Kabbalistic text the Zohar. He is said to have died on Lag B'Omer, a midspring day of outdoor merriment. So on that day, the crowds gather in Meron to honor him with ecstatic song and dance, and there to cut the hair of their three-year-olds.

Today, even for a child in whose life the *arba kanfot* is no issue, the three-year-old's haircut can become a time for a first conscious introduction into some aspect of a Jewish life—some matter in which s/he can be asked to be responsible. Perhaps learning some melodic, joyful version of *haMotzi*, the blessing over bread. Perhaps learning to set aside pennies for children who are hungry. Perhaps saying the *Sh'ma* together as the child goes to sleep.

With any or all of these, the deepest enrichment might come from using the fourfold pattern we have outlined: first, teaching that an important act of growing up is about to happen; second, actually experiencing the physical intensity of the haircut; third, letting the child actually act on one of the more grown-up responsibilities we have mentioned, perhaps in this moment a blessing over food; fourth, welcoming the child with food and song and laughter back among friends and family.

In many Jewish communities, the next stage of growth was entering school. In some, cookies were baked with the letters of the Hebrew *alef-bet* upon them, or honey was smeared on the letters themselves, and the beginning of school became a ceremony of sweet learning.

Some Jewish families that have adopted children have developed ceremonies for welcoming them into the family. In addition, if the child was not born into a Jewish family, the family of adoption might decide on a conversion. This follows the same practice described for adults in Chapter 11. When the child reaches the age of *mitzvot* (twelve or thirteen), s/he is permitted by Jewish law to choose whether to continue on this Jewish path or to renounce it. (T.B. Ketub 11a)

All these celebrations, those observed for centuries and those developed in the most recent decade, teach a deeper lesson: Freed to imagine and to act, the creative energy of the Jewish people can connect the playful with the serious, tears of anguish with tears of merriment beyond all boundaries. God will appear, people will rejoice, and Judaism will reawaken. As each of the young grows toward being more fully a Self, the Jews as a whole grow toward being more fully a People.

~ 4 ~

Joining in the Mitzvot

WHEN THE TALMUD ASKED THE QUESTION "At what point does a boy become obligated to fulfill the *mitzvot?*" it answered, "When he has two pubic hairs."

At once it added that we do not like to go checking on each boy's growth, and so for communal and legal purposes we redefine this moment as the day after he becomes thirteen years old.

On how many pulpits in American synagogues is this connection between puberty and the age of becoming Bar Mitzvah mentioned—as a proud family and a band of excited friends gather to hear a nervous young man chant a passage from the Prophets?

Very few, if any. And the reason is clear: The embarrassment now extends not only to the individual body-check but even to mentioning puberty in public. Or perhaps the embarrassment arises from mentioning the undoable. That is, there are strong taboos in American society against most forms of sexual expression for thirteen-year-olds. So it may feel less troublesome to repress the knowledge of thirteen-year-olds as sexual beings altogether than to remember it and then teach how to integrate sexuality into a teenager's life.

Yet all the major life-cycle ceremonies of classical Rabbinic Judaism are keyed to bodily change: birth; choosing a sexual partner; death. For the Rabbis, ethical potential and sexual potency were connected. Responsibility for carrying out communal and Divine precepts came due upon reaching sexual adulthood.

Why is this—and why has it become shameful to say so?

First of all, did the Rabbis simply inherit this definition of a crucial life-change from Biblical Judaism? No, they did not. For the Torah, the age when most men entered adulthood was twenty, when they became capable of paying taxes and bearing arms. That is the age defined by the census in the Wilderness. (Exod. 30:11–14; Num. 1:2–3, 26:1–3) For Levite men to do service in the Holy Shrine, they had to be thirty years old. (Num. 4:2–3, 21–23, 29–30) The Torah's only mention of a turning point at age thirteen is its reference to the circumcision of Ishmael, Abraham's first son, at that age.

Why was the onset of sexual energy a less important life-cycle moment for Biblical Israel than it was for the Rabbis? Perhaps for a national entity, adulthood for the sake of war and taxes was more crucial than it was for a dispersed people who had no army and a much more varied economic life. Conversely, for a people whose domestic lives were central to its identity, as in Rabbinic Judaism, sexual adulthood and restrictions on sexual behavior may have been more crucial.

What the two different concepts of adulthood share, in their different contexts, is that the individuals whose fragile, brand-new identities were celebrated around their birth-times have now become powerful enough to make both joy and trouble. To kill or refuse to kill (the Torah exempts from the army those who are too faint-hearted to risk death and those who are too gentle-hearted to risk killing [Deut. 20:8]); to support the communal economy, or not; to create the intense emotions that flow from sex and to beget children, or not—all these posed some danger of disturbance or transcendence.

One might say that while biblical tradition focuses on specific rules of sexual behavior—especially on forbidding men to have sex with another man's wife or with near relatives—the Rabbis treated all sexuality as fraught with danger. They evidently believed that the most difficult task of a grown-up human being (or at least a male) is controlling the sexual urge; so to insist that all the *mitzvot*—commands or precepts—were operative at puberty meant that the community was bracing itself to govern those urges.

There is much in rabbinic lore to support this notion. The Rabbis repeatedly tell tales of the *yetzer hara*—the impulse toward evil—by which they mean primarily the sexual urge. They also recognize how valuable is this urge: Without it, they declare, not an egg would be laid in all the Land of Israel; and so their struggle is to control it, not to do away with it.

Their focus on the danger of no eggs being laid fits into the Rabbis' basic approach to sexuality. For they operated within three basic "rules" about sex:

1. Men are in charge within each household, as they are in the society as a whole.
2. The main point (though not the only purpose) of sex is the procreation of children.
3. Sex is pleasurable, and the pleasure is sacred.

For the Rabbis, then, entering upon the body-time of sexual potential meant that it was possible to have children, and obligatory to do so—and to rear them. Forms of sexuality that could not lead to the procreation and rearing of children the Rabbis either forbade—like same-sex relationships and sexual relations during parts of the menstrual rhythm when women are least likely to conceive—or frowned upon, like masturbation and like uncommitted relationships, which might be less effective in rearing children than long-term marriages.

What about girls and womanhood? The Rabbis said that at twelve, a girl could be promised in marriage. Six months later, a girl who had

not yet been promised was no longer considered to be under her father's authority, and became responsible for herself. Notice that these
ages too, like that of the boys, were closely connected with sexual maturity. By twelve-and-a half if not by twelve, the girl-becoming-woman
became bound by the *mitzvot*. More accurately, she became bound by
some of them, mostly those not focused on a specific time-obligation.

There were three time-bound actions to which women were obligated. All of them focused on the home: lighting Shabbat candles at
the proper time on Friday evening; separating from the dough of new
bread a portion like the sacrificial offering that was brought near to
God by the High Priest at the Temple; following the rules of physical
separation from their husbands, during and after the menstrual period.

Notable among the time-bound *mitzvot* in which women were *not*
obligated to take part was communal prayer at its specified times.
Since they were not obligated, according to rabbinic understanding,
women could not act as delegates-to-God on behalf of men, who *were*
obligated. And so girls who were becoming women could not serve as
congregational prayer leaders, and thus could not honor their change
in status by the public act of leading prayer, as could their brothers.

So the life-cycle moment of entering puberty set the terms of adult
life: Women's roles were focused on the private sphere of home and
domestic activities, men's on public acts of prayer and Torah-study. If
girls had celebrated becoming "Bat Mitzvah," the ritual might have focused on candle-lighting or challah-baking. But mostly, there was no
formal ritual.

To look at what the Bar/Bat Mitzvah ritual has actually become,
we must expand our vision beyond the question of physical growth
into sexual maturity (without altogether losing sight of that powerful
question). Let us begin with boys, since the involvement of girls-
becoming-women comes much later in Jewish history.

In the understanding of the Talmud, a Jewish male became both
obligated and empowered to perform the *mitzvot*—therefore a "Bar
Mitzvah," a "son of the commandments"—simply by reaching the age
of thirteen years and one day. No ceremony was required. At that

point the boy, rather than his father, becomes liable for vows he makes; from then on he can testify before a rabbinical court, can be counted in the *minyan* of Jews necessary for certain parts of communal prayer, and can buy and sell property.

It was only much later in Jewish history that this moment became the focus of ceremony. The simplest and clearest shift in daily public behavior was that at thirteen, boys became obligated to put on *t'fillin*. These are leather straps that Jewish men traditionally bind around the arm and head each morning except for Shabbat and festival days, each strap attached to a tiny leather box containing parchments bearing Torah passages affirming that God is One. So the first occasion of putting on *t'fillin* at a weekday morning service became a time of ceremonial focus, and often the boy-becoming-man would teach a *drasha*—an interpretation of Torah—on that occasion. The process of binding the *t'fillin* each morning follows a careful ceremonial path, and some have suggested that the daily binding symbolizes and acts out a commitment to restrain one's arms and eyes from actions or observations that are unholy. Thus, at just the moment when the young man is taking on new power to act in the world, he affirms that from now on he will need to focus that power in ways that will enhance the Unity of life, not shatter it. And he enters into the lifelong process of reinterpreting Torah so as to find guidance on this path.

But over the centuries, perhaps the *t'fillin* ceremony came to seem too small, too private, even perhaps too easy, to make for a totally fulfilling rite of passage. For whatever reason, another ceremony became more widespread.

In some Jewish communities, boys younger than thirteen had occasionally read from the Torah in public on behalf of the community, even though they did not yet count in *minyan*. But the idea became stronger that someone who was not obligated to perform the *mitzva* of Torah reading could not discharge the obligation on behalf of those to whom it applied, and so could not perform this task on behalf of the community. So in many communities, fulfilling the *mitzva* of reading the Torah was thus restricted to males thirteen or older, and this focused much more attention on formally becoming eligible to do so. What has emerged is a major public event, usually on Shabbat morning, in which the thirteen-year-old reads the last passage, called the *Maftir*, of the week's Torah portion, and then reads the *Haftara*, the selection from the Prophets traditionally assigned for the week. (*Maftir* and *Haftara* both stem from the Hebrew for "completion" or "conclusion.") Most boys also speak about the Torah portion or about some other aspect of their lives.

This is the core of the Bar Mitzvah event, the moment at the heart of the ritual when there is the deepest and closest encounter with God, or with the boy's own wrestling with his life. It crystallizes the life-path that Jewish men have been ideally expected to walk: not only hearing God's Voice through the words of Torah and the Prophets, but also engaging with these words—wrestling with them—so as to bring into the world their own new Torah.

Only in this way could they become full adult members of the people *"Yisra-el."* For the very name of the people echoes the night of terror and transformation in which Jacob turned his lifelong struggle with his brother into a Wrestle with the Nameless One, and was himself renamed *Yisra-el*, "Godwrestler." So the encounter with God is intended to feel like an earthquake, shaking the new thirteen-year-old loose from his old attachments and assumptions. His response, his own *d'var Torah*, is intended to bespeak his adulthood—his ability to do what for centuries Jewish men have done, teach their own Torah.

We must note that the "wrestling" metaphor point us in the direction of something that is missing as well as something that is present. Unlike the adolescent rites of passage of many other cultures, this ceremony focuses on verbal rather than physical skills. It is neither sexual nor athletic nor military nor pastoral nor agricultural. The body skills of Biblical Judaism are nowhere exercised.

This befits the verbal focus of Rabbinic Judaism, but raises the question whether in our generation, verbal and intellectual skills are the only ones that befit a Jewish adult. We will address this question more fully later in this chapter.

We intend to examine more closely the ritual path on the day of the ceremony. But before we talk about what the youngster does who arises to the pulpit, we must take into account one major change that has taken place during the past century—a change in *who* will be standing on the *bima*.

For larger and larger parts of the Jewish people, girls at twelve or thirteen years of age are undertaking exactly the same ceremony as boys. For American Jews, this process famously began in 1922 when Rabbi Mordecai Kaplan, the founder of Reconstructionism, arranged for his daughter Judith to celebrate becoming a Bat Mitzvah at a public synagogue ceremony. But in fact her ceremony did not involve a full *aliya* to the Torah, and was thus a much-diminished version of what boys did. It bore considerable resemblance to a way of celebrating this passage in the synagogue that some girls in Italy and France had begun even earlier, and Rabbi Kaplan may have used for his daughter's rite what he had heard or seen of an Italian ceremony.

Elsewhere, too, in Jewish life, girls entering adulthood had begun to take part in a public ceremony. Late in the nineteenth century, Joseph Ḥayyim Eliyahu ben Moshe of Baghdad, Ben Ish Ḥai, wrote (as translated by Howard Tzvi Adelman):

> And also the daughter on the day that she enters the obligation of the commandments, even though they don't usually make for her a *s'uda* [celebratory meal], nevertheless that day will be one of happiness. She should wear Sabbath clothing and if she is able to do so she should wear new clothing and bless the *Sheheḥeyanu* prayer [for the One "Who gives us life, lifts us up, and carries us to this moment"] and be ready for her entry to the yoke of the commandments. There are those who are accustomed to make her birthday every year into a holiday. It is a good sign, and this we do in our house.

Another Bat Mitzvah ceremony, in the synagogue, was celebrated in Lwow in 1902 by Rabbi Dr. Yehezkel Caro, "rabbi for the enlightened Jews."

What gave long-term importance to Judith Kaplan's moment was that American culture supported transforming this hesitant beginning into wholehearted change. By the end of the twentieth century, in almost all non-Orthodox congregations girls were celebrating their coming-of-age as *b'not mitzva* through much the same ceremonies their brothers experienced.

Indeed, by the end of the century, many Orthodox synagogues were doing the same kind of limited ceremony short of a full *aliya* that Rabbi Kaplan had originally arranged for his daughter. And even among *haredi* ("ultra-Orthodox") communities, some girls' schools were holding a special breakfast for the class of twelve-year-olds, to which mothers were invited. In some American *haredi* communities, each girl signs up for a Sunday near her birthday on which to have a lunch and speak a *d'var Torah*. Some have proposed a party where the Bat Mitzvah might separate challah for the first time, or do another *mitzva* particular to women. Chabad-Lubavitch Hasidic communities celebrate a girl's becoming Bat Mitzvah with the girl choosing a teaching of the seventh Lubavitcher Rebbe to learn and discuss at a gathering of her friends and family.

At the same moment that adolescent girls in large numbers began to join in the traditional male celebration, many of their mothers, and even their grandmothers, decided to affirm and transform their own commitment to Judaism by celebrating as adults the Torah-reading they had not been allowed to do as adolescents. For many, the fusion of joy and awe that came with celebrating what they had been so long denied brought them closer to the "earthquake" moment of transformation in God's presence than the same events were stirring in their daughters or their sons.

The implications of this wave of what came to be called "adult Bat Mitzvah" we will examine later in our journey, among the "midlife transformation" rituals.

So now girls as well as boys will come up to the *bima* and reach out to the Torah scroll. What will the new Bar/Bat Mitzvah do in taking on this ritual of sacred transformation?

To some extent, this will depend on the degree of the youngster's knowledge and skill in dealing with prayer, Torah, and Hebrew. Some will lead the congregation in large or small sections of the Shabbat prayers. Some will read a number of passages from the Torah. But nowadays, most children will come up to read from the Torah scroll one special *aliya* (literally, "ascent"; in practice, one of the sections of Torah marked for reading on that day in the Jewish calendar).

This *aliya* begins like those of the older adults with being called up to the Torah, by Hebrew name—but for the new Bar/Bat Mitzvah, usually with a specially elevated twirl to the melody, letting everyone know: *"This is special!"*

Then, using the same words by which the community had been called into being and into prayer early in the service, the newest of newcomers calls the elders, family, friends, together: *"Barḥu et YHWH ham'vorah!"*—"Let us bless that One Who is worthy to be blessed." And the community, far from ignoring or shrugging off this newly fledged member, responds full-throated, with excitement: *"Baruḥ YHWH ham'vorah l'olam va-ed!"*—"Yes!—That One Who is worthy of blessing is indeed blessed, for ever and beyond!"

At that point, the new Bar/Bat Mitzvah continues in the same way as would any adult, repeating the affirmation and moving into a blessing that affirms God as the giver of Torah. Like many traditional *b'rahot*, it begins with a full statement of blessing—the *P'tiha*, or opening—and then has a brief closing, called the *ḥatima* (seal). In the traditional form it says, *"Baruḥ ata YHWH eloheynu meleḥ ha-olam asher baḥar banu mikol ha-amim v'natan lanu et Torato. Baruḥ ata YHWH noteyn haTorah."*—"Blessed are You, YHWH [pronounced "Adonai"] our God, Ruler of the Universe, Who has chosen us from all the peoples and has given us the Torah. Blessed are You, YHWH, Who has given us the Torah."

In some congregations, other versions of these *b'rahot* have emerged, as a result of wrestling with different ways to imagine God and with the notion (to some, discomfiting) that God has chosen the Jewish people. In some, these blessings become *"Baruḥ ata YHWH eloheynu ru-aḥ ha-olam asher baḥar banu im kol ha-amim v'natan lanu et Torato. B'ruḥa at Yahh notenet haTorah.*"—"Blessed are You, YHWH [pronounced "Yahh"] our God, *Life-Breath* of the Universe, Who has chosen us *along with* all the peoples and has given us the Torah." (Here the *ḥatima* has the pronoun and verb for God in feminine form.) In still others, the blessing affirms *"asher kervanu l'avodato"*—"the One who has brought us near to His service."

Then comes the most intense, and for many youngsters the most difficult, part of the ceremony: They read from the parchment scroll itself a passage of the Torah. The writing in the scroll has no vowels marked, no melodic notes indicated, and no punctuation for the ends of phrases or sentences. So new readers (and many veterans as well) usually must memorize the text and its melody, which heightens the sense of strain, or perhaps of excitement. Moreover, for many readers, new or veteran, the sense of contact with primordial wisdom is strongest here. For some readers, the absence of vowels, melody, and punctuation becomes a hint, a hiddenness, a mystery. The beautifully inscribed letters may come to seem veils, holding within themselves what they do not reveal. Then the *leyning* draws forth not the chill of rote repetition but a passion to unveil the mystery. So for many different reasons and with many different emotions, most youngsters find the Torah reading the volcanically hot heart of the ordeal.

When the Torah passage is complete, there comes another set of blessings: *"Baruḥ ata YHWH eloheynu meleḥ [ru-ah] ha-olam asher natan lanu Torat emet v'ḥayey olam nata b'toḥeynu. Baruḥ ata [B'ruḥa at] YHWH noteyn [notenet] haTorah."*—"Blessed are You, YHWH our God, Ruler of the Universe, Who has given us a Torah of truth and has planted within us life everlasting. Blessed are You, YHWH, Who has given us the Torah."

The congregation catches its breath. There will be a *Mi shebeyraḥ*, "May the One Who blessed our forebears bless those who have come today to honor the Torah, the Shabbat, the place where this is all happening and the Place that holds all places in place." The congregation will say the Kaddish that acts as a sort of punctuation, a pause between the different parts of the service.

Then the youngster turns to the *Haftara*. Again, there are blessings to begin the reading. They celebrate the God Who blows the breath of truth through human throats; the God Who speaks and the world changes; a fitting introduction to the Prophets who spoke with such power that, although in their own generations the world changed little, for millennia their outcry has strengthened those who seek to transform reality toward justice and peace.

Reading the *Haftara*, while still intense, is usually less stressful than the Torah reading, because the Prophetic portion is printed in a booklet, with the vowels and the melody indicated. The melody, or *trop*, written in a minor key, is somewhat more plaintive than the major key of the Torah *trop*, as if to say, on behalf of the Prophets, "Oh, if only you would make all be the way that I call out to you!"

After the *Haftara*, again there are blessings. In the traditional form, they look forward to the coming of Elijah the Prophet, herald of Messiah, and of Messiah himself. In the liturgy of the Reconstructionist community, they gaze toward that world Elijah is supposed to bring about—the world in which the hearts of children and the hearts of parents have been turned toward each other, lest the earth be utterly destroyed.

Usually at this point, when the Bar/Bat Mitzvah has completed the hardest parts of the sacred task, the congregation begins to sing:

> *Siman tov u-mazal tov u-mazal tov u-siman tov (3)*
> *Y'hey lanu*
> *Y'hey lanu, y'hey lanu, u-l'hol Yisra-el (2)*
> (see page 122 for translation)

Then the newcomer speaks his or her own truth, a *d'var Torah* based on wrestling with the texts and with all the unwritten but deeply inscribed processes of the past year, and distilling from them a personal wisdom. This moment can be either the deepest or the most shallow of the whole event. The newly responsible Jew can be encouraged to go deep into the feelings of adulthood and of how they link to a passage of Torah or to the *Haftara*, or else just to say whatever pops into his/her head. The deeper the plunge into the transformative encounter with Torah, the likelier to be transformed is the new self that comes back to the community as an adult.

The parents come up and speak their sense of pride, joy, nostalgic sorrow. They bless the one who was their child—still is, but changed. The traditional blessing is: *"Baruḥ sheptarani mey-onsho shel ẓeh."*— "Blessed is the One Who releases me from the burden of this one." This originally meant the burden of responsibility for whatever sins the child might commit, which until the moment of maturity rested on the parents, or more particularly the father. Today it might well mean: "Blessed is the One Who leaves no longer on my own shoulders the sole responsibility for teaching, guiding this youngster—but now gives me a community to share that task." Some parents nowadays say instead, *"Sheheḥeyanu"*—"Blessed is the One Who has filled us with life, lifted us up, and carried us to this moment." Either explicitly or implicitly, these blessings are a public affirmation that the family, not only the child, has been transformed. It no longer has the old shape.

After these blessings, and perhaps the presentation of some formal ritual gifts from the congregation, the excitement lessens. The Bar/Bat Mitzvah returns from the pulpit to the congregation—not going back, but going forward. For everyone knows the youngster has a new place in the family and the community, and the family has achieved a new relationship to the community as a whole.

In a few observances of this coming of age, we have seen the congregation embody in a powerful new practice an ancient teaching of the relationship between parents and children. The teaching appears in the last passage of the last of the Prophets. God speaks through Malachi to say: "Before the coming of the great and awesome day of YHWH, I will send Elijah the Prophet to turn the hearts of parents to the children and the hearts of children to the parents, lest I come and smite the earth with utter destruction." (This passage is traditionally read as part of the *Haftara* on the Shabbat just before Passover.)

This is how we have seen the ancient prophecy embodied in our day. First the new Bar/Bat Mitzvah speaks briefly about the danger of utter destruction in which the web of earthly life now stands, the danger facing the generations of the future. Then all the generation of children in the congregation—all those too young to be *b'ney mitzva*—come up to the front, to face the congregation. The older generation rises to face them. And each generation says aloud, in turn, the following: "We ourselves will become Elijah the Prophet, coming to turn the hearts of parents to children and the hearts of children to the parents, lest the earth be utterly destroyed."

In our experience, this moment is both challenging and healing.

So far, we have focused on the obvious star performer in this rite of passage: the adolescent boy or girl. But, as with the childhood ceremonies, and probably even more, the public celebration of becoming Bar/Bat Mitzvah both betokens and creates enormous changes in the entire family. Indeed, it would be fruitful to look again at the whole Bar/Bat Mitzvah process and ritual by seeing the whole family as the "hero," the actor who is undertaking a life-cycle transformation.

About a year before the moment of public celebration, the family begins to change. Whether the family becomes conscious of the fact or not, it is facing an enormous new task: both honoring and managing the rambunctious energies of an eleven- or twelve-year-old for a year-long effort to succeed in a difficult task; planning a major event and paying for it; organizing a diverse group of people to come and to establish a new relationship with each other; defining its own relationship to Judaism and its own place in a larger family and a surrounding community. The more conscious and self-aware the family is in carrying out this great task, the more likely it will succeed in accomplishing its own journey to a healthy place in a new stage of maturity.

This self-awareness is what makes the task part of a spiritual journey. All the other parts will happen willy-nilly: The family *will* have to deal with family and community relationships and politics, with an unpredictable youngster, with its own understanding of Judaism, and so on. Whether it realizes that this process is part of its own growth, whether it can reflect on the process as it happens—that will determine whether the family has its own transformative God-experience.

There are two different aspects or versions of God with which the emerging Bar/Bat Mitzvah and the family will be wrestling: One is the official version of God, Who is named in the Torah and the prayerbook. The other is the experience of Wholeness and of the attempt to achieve Wholeness, as it emerges in planning this powerful event. For some people, this Wholeness and the God in the books will be the same; for others, they will be understood as different, and even perhaps contradictory.

So let us look at the ritual from the standpoint that the whole family is the sacred hero on the sacred journey.

The most basic questions (not necessarily the ones that first appear) are: What new responsibilities does the family expect to turn over to the Bar/Bat Mitzvah? Does this event matter? When the youngster has made clear a new Self by speaking publicly about a new understanding of Torah, can s/he carry this new Self into the active world?

What are the possibilities?

- Choosing once a year where a certain proportion of the family money for *tz'daka* will be given, after doing research on the various possibilities;
- Managing the family recycling program: organizing the trash into recyclable categories, mulching organic food leftovers, etc;
- Chanting from the Torah scroll on Shabbat, three times a year;
- Writing three *divrey Torah* a year, to share with the family or the synagogue.

The family should make clear from the beginning that these discussions and possibilities will be on the agenda. (For the sake of everyone's sanity, the discussion may have to wait till after the Great Shabbat itself.) Shortly after the transformative day, close enough to make clear this is still part—perhaps the most crucial part—of the "mitzvah" process, these questions should be put forward for weekly discussion. And then the family should make decisions that get recorded in a family contract—a new sort of *k'tuba*.

Meanwhile, the very first intimations of the wrestle with reality may come long before the crucial birthday, as the family seeks to choose a date for the synagogue ceremonial.

- How does the birthday work with family needs, school schedules, the timing of other Bar/Bat Mitzvah celebrations at the same congregation?
- Does the family already have ties to a congregation that will organically become the venue for the ceremony, or does it need to choose a congregation, or even create an ad hoc one to meet its needs most authentically?

How do Jewish teachings and practices themselves interact with the family's situation?

For example, how does the youngster feel about the content of the various possible Torah portions and *Haftarot*? Would s/he like to choose a date according to the Torah content, rather than accept the content that comes with the date? Does s/he want to read some part of the weekly portion other than the conventional *Maftir* (the last few lines of the portion), because s/he finds the alternative passage more meaningful, more life-connected?

If crucial family members and friends reside elsewhere and live in accordance with the traditional practice of not traveling on Shabbat, might the whole thing be easier if it is set not on Shabbat but on a Monday that is a secular holiday (like Labor Day or Memorial Day), since traditionally the Torah is read on Monday and Thursday mornings as well as Shabbat?

Might the family want to set the Torah reading in the late-afternoon Shabbat service (when traditionally the beginning of the Torah portion for the next Shabbat is read), then celebrate the end of Shabbat with the *Havdala* ceremony, and then move into a Saturday-night party?

What seems the simple matter of setting the date may thus become the family's first revelation of its journey into a new understanding of itself, its community, Judaism and the Jewish people, its relationship to God or some other way of talking about wholeness.

How to define the task that the youngster is facing? Is it defined "by the book," or does it make sense to define it in terms of this specific individual—just far enough beyond the youngster's grasp as to be challenging but not so far that failure is likely? Who decides: a rabbi, the parents, or the parents, child, and rabbi together? What are the roles of older and younger siblings? Even the act of sitting together with a pubescent child to examine these issues may begin the process of the family's changing in its own life cycle.

And slowly, other issues will arise. Who should be invited? What are the boundaries of "the family," which of the youngster's friends, which of adult family friends and relatives? Do certain names make one of the parents or the children quail? If so, how to deal with these people?

Arthur recalls: As my Bar Mitzvah date came closer, I recall my mother in a frenzy, trying to decide which aunt or uncle should get to speak at which moment, be called up for which Torah passage, say which blessing. I asked: "Why are you so upset about all this?" She answered: "Because of the *koved* ["honor"]! Knowing little Yiddish, I thought she had said, "Because of the covet!" Although that made me a little sad, it also seemed realistic that some of these relatives were coveting more glory, and that juggling all this "covet" was hard to do.

Now that I also know the Yiddish word, the joke—the pun—

seems more cosmic than linguistic. The envy is the dark side of the honor. The more *koved*, the more "covet."

Two generations later, with much larger numbers of divorces, remarriages, loving relationships not defined as marriages, blended and unblended families, the task is even harder. Can the divorced mother and father bear to stand together, at this moment when their child comes front and center? And what about new beloveds, spouses, in-laws, grandparents? Yet juggling both the *koved* and the "covet" is what the family must do. If the child's task is to "grow up" by becoming a verbal virtuoso, the family's is to "grow up" by creating a more expansive sense of relationship.

For the family, the ritual process of leaving its previous status may take all year, as these issues arise and are addressed. The most eerie threshold moment of encounter with the sacred and of self-transformation may well be not in the synagogue service, as it is for the youngster, but in the party that comes later in the day—perhaps on Saturday night.

This party is when the most danger looms: What might the scary aunt actually do, will anyone get unbearably drunk, what family secret may be flung into public view as an ugly weapon? And here, too, loom the greatest opportunities for joyful transformation. What reconciliation may happen between weeping cousins, what sudden generosity of spirit may suddenly move an old curmudgeon to raise a toast to the life-work of an unthanked nephew, what tears of love may move the entire assemblage into an awe-filled silence?

"The party" has led a double life in much of American Jewish practice. The family may well have poured a great deal of money, effort, and anxiety into preparing it, and thus has defined it as a very important part of the event. It often follows its own ritualized pattern and ceremonials. But the reigning ritual expert and manager is likely to be not a rabbi but a caterer. And in the "official" view of spokespersons for Judaism—indeed, often in the explicit statements of the rabbis who find themselves shunted to one side as evening comes on and the party unfolds—all this public outpouring of energy makes "the party" spiritually and Jewishly suspect. Not "really" important at all. (This may remind us of the way in which most Jewish families treat Hanukkah as a major festival, while many of the rabbinic guardians of Judaism insist that it is "supposed" to be only a minor one.)

But the party is not as illegitimate an offspring of the Bar/Bat Mitzvah celebration as it is sometimes made out to be. Already in the Talmud, the Rabbis were saying that the achievement of adult responsibilities should be celebrated with a *s'udat mitzva*—that is, a meal affirming the sacred obligation—just as a wedding is. The ancient Jewish tradition that God is served through food and dance and music—a sense that was central in the sacrificial offerings and the Levitical chant and dance at the ancient Holy Temple—is thus renewed in the celebratory *s'uda*.

For the youngsters who come to celebrate with dance and music, the party may be the last survival or the first renewal of the Talmudic teaching about those pubic hairs—the teaching that the Bar/Bat Mitzvah is entering a new, more sexually charged stage of life.

From either of these standpoints, the real question is not whether the party is a distraction from spiritual maturation, but whether it is an avenue of spiritual maturation: whether it is indeed celebrated with a sense of *mitzva*; whether the family sees its whole self—not only the youngster—as newly involved with the web of connection-making and precept-observing that are the *mitzvot*.

What strengthens this aspect of the party? Focusing on connections to the One Who suffuses the entire world with holiness:

- Limiting the expense, and devoting part of the cost to *tz'daka*—socially responsible help for the poor and for social change to end poverty. (Many Bar/Bat Mitzvah celebrants designate some percentage of the cost to Mazon, a Jewish antihunger foundation, or to a similar group.)

- Making arrangements ahead of time to deliver leftover un-opened food or food from unused pots and pans to soup kitchens or centers for the homeless.
- Asking about the labor practices of any hotel or catering hall—or even synagogue!—where the party may be held. Are the workers represented by a union? Are janitors and food workers being paid a living wage, not just the minimum wage? What are their work hours?
- Making sure that the blessing that precedes the eating is said not by rote formula but with a *kavana*, an intentional focusing, on the food as the fruit of the One Who appears in the intertwining of sun and soil, rain and wind, human work and human rest.
- And to make such a blessing real, applying eco-kosher standards to the party: using food with as earth-friendly packaging as pos-sible, recycling table leftovers for composting and mulching, etc.
- Since parties are often where gifts are brought for the new Bar/Bat Mitzvah, explicitly asking guests to channel part of any gift into *tz'daka*.
- Limiting the use of alcohol to what may gently change the state of consciousness but not bring on aggression, nastiness, or stu-por; providing nonalcoholic alternatives (including grape juice for the wine of a ritual *kiddush*); making sure that the younger guests do not violate state laws about access to alcohol.
- Encouraging the next generation to enjoy their own music and dancing, not in a totally separate party but while sharing space and time with the grown-ups. Recognizing that among many (though probably not all) of these younger guests a new alert-ness to sexuality may be arising, while providing boundaries and guidelines for its expression.

At its richest, the evening may include for the newly transformed family some moment in which it can make its new self clear. Perhaps that comes in the ritual of lighting thirteen candles and invoking thir-teen blessings that has become a part of many Bar/Bat Mitzvah celebrations. Perhaps it comes in a declaration by the family as a whole of an action it intends to perform together to serve the needs of the poor, or the sick, or the wounded earth.

Finally, the family—now renewed—rejoins a community of families, no longer the center of attention. This reality might usefully be symbolized at the party by asking someone not in the central celebrating party to lead *Birkat haMazon*, the blessing after the meal. Again, as with the introductory *haMotzi*, whether *Birkat haMazon* is done with the traditional text or with some newer versions that have recently arisen, it would be important to encourage not a rote recitation but a focus on the Unity of life.

These last thoughts move us in the direction of some possible new approaches to the celebration of moving toward adulthood, under the new circumstances of a world and a Judaism that are being transformed. We will now turn to explore these in more depth.

~ 5 ~

Embodying God

A S WE HAVE SEEN, one of the great changes in celebration of
the life-cycle during the past century has been the joining of
girls in full equality in the Torah-oriented observance of becoming *b'not mitzva*, alongside their brothers. This change has emphasized the ways in which girls and boys, women and men, are similar in
intellectual abilities and in their relationship to a community rooted in
words.

At the same time, with much less public fanfare, another change
has been proceeding—also focused on girls, but in this case emphasiz-
ing the bodily dissimilarities between women and men. That has been
the emergence of ceremonies welcoming Jewish girls into womanhood as they experience menarche—the onset of the menstrual cycle.

Ironically, this practice echoes—with a difference—the Talmud's
assertion that the "true" date of becoming bound by the *mitzvot* is
when two pubic hairs appear. First we will look at how this tentative
exploration of ceremonies for menarche is being currently understood
and practiced by girls and women, and then look at its implications for

boys and men, and perhaps in a broader way for all youngsters who are Jewishly entering an adult Jewish community. Most deeply: What may the role of the body be, in an emerging Judaism that learns from but is not bounded by the Judaism of the last two thousand years as the Rabbis defined it?

Phyllis recalls: There we stood, at the banks of the river in the dark of the night under the full moon, an outer circle of women and an inner circle of young girls, celebrating the entrance of my daughter into womanhood. How we got there is a tale, not of geography but of inner space.

Changes in consciousness . . . not a plunge from a precipice but small steps, one at a time, seeds that look as if they've been scattered to the winds but somehow take root.

I first heard the notion of a Jewish menarche ceremony in 1979, from Mary and Everett Gendler, at the first Ḥavurah Conference. The idea excited me but also made me feel vaguely uncomfortable. The unconscious process had begun.

During the years that followed, the dormant seeds received nourishment from the way I was feeling about my own body and celebrating it. About a year before, my women's group, at one of our weekly meetings, talked about the books that had informed us as women and feminists. Another piece.

And then, at the East Coast Jewish Women's Conference in October 1983, I attended a session run by several members of the Philadelphia Jewish Feminist Liturgy Group. They posed a question that stirred my imagination: If we women frequently feel ourselves outside of the tradition, if we often struggle to find meaning in ceremonies that are male-oriented or irrelevant to our modern lives, what moments of life that are significant to us have cried out for community acknowledgment, support, celebration?

My answer was clear. The vague seeds of five years before had, by then, taken firm root. Though many other life-moments came to mind, the one that called loudest, with thoughts of my rapidly maturing twelve-year-old daughter in the background, was the onset of menstruation.

I began to talk about the idea—with her and with friends, both female and male—and though I knew there were already some ceremonies that had been devised and enacted, I didn't want to hear about them. My own images were coming fast—full moon, water, books. Ideas were beginning to flower, but when would this life-changing moment come about? I feared it would happen deep in the winter, or when Morissa was away at camp.

In early May 1984, barely two weeks before Morissa's thirteenth birthday and four weeks before our planned synagogue celebration of her becoming Bat Mitzvah, at the time of Rosh Ḥodesh *Iyyar*, while she and I were working on her Bat Mitzvah *parasha*, the moment of change came. It was a quiet moment between the two of us, not at all embarrassing or shameful (as I remember my own entrance into womanhood). We talked about whom we would tell—which relatives, which friends—and who would tell the men in our lives—her dad, grandpa, brother, my partner.

This was the moment I had been waiting to celebrate with her, but all my creative energies were wrapped up in Morissa's synagogue celebration. Could I stretch myself for this ceremony now, or would it have to wait another month? The answer was clear, even compelling. When, on the new moon, in the very month of calendric adolescence and spiritual adulthood, my daughter also reached biological womanhood, it felt like a blessing from the universe. We all pray to be integrated, whole; here, in her thirteenth year, body, spirit, and age had come together to proclaim "woman." How could we mortals do less than sing praises to the Source of this miracle?

So invitations hastily went out: dear friends, my women's group, Ḥavurat Rey-im of Teaneck, B'nai Or of New York, my educational-professional Counseling-Learning network, and others who had been long and deep parts of our lives. We invited women to bring their young daughters—those who were not yet biologically women—in the hope that this ceremony might make the onset of womanhood easier for them. I asked women to join us at 9:15 p.m. on the night of the full moon on the New Jersey banks of the Hudson River. I asked them each to bring for Morissa some "woman-Torah": a poem or essay or book that had been significant in their learning about themselves as women.

Responses to our invitation were mixed. From some people there were joyous hallelu-yahs: About time for what's significant in a woman's life to be celebrated! From others, more dubious responses: In a book, it sounds exciting, but in real life? What kind of ceremony is this going to be—rooted in Judaism or in witchcraft? Maybe, said some, we should be proud of the first menstruation, but doesn't it really call for a more private and personal celebration? I don't know about your daughter, said some, but I—or my daughter—wouldn't want such a ceremony.

These messages/doubts penetrated me—hints of a discarded voice of fear and convention—and finally I turned in question to Morissa. Your *"aliya"* to the Torah, your period, your thirteenth birthday, I told her, are all merely symbols. They are not what being a woman is about. To me, the bridge from childhood to womanhood is about *decision-making and commitment.*

It's so much easier, when people ask where you stand, to retreat behind ambivalence, uncertainty, to make no decisions or to keep changing your mind. It's so hard—when you know that some people want you to do this or think that—to take an opposing position, and then stick with it when the going gets tough. Many people wear the outer symbols that mark the change of age, but few indeed learn that coming of age is about checking out who you are at a given moment and taking responsibility for that person.

So, I told Morissa, there is no wrong answer to the question I'm about to ask. It requires only that you look into yourself and answer from your own truth: Do you or do you not want a woman-ceremony? Whatever your answer, I assured her, it is making a decision and standing firm with it that is the real celebration of maturity.

Morissa answered firmly that she intended to have the ceremony.

The night arrived—not exactly as imagined, but powerful nonetheless. Rain clouds and thick trees hid the full moon. An early closing of the Palisades Interstate Park forced us to move from the flowing Hudson to a trickling brook. The arrival of police cars—keeping the neighborhood safe—gave this most natural of ceremonies a hint of the forbidden and eerie.

More than a dozen of us, holding candles to share with the moon the task of illuminating the dark, gathered in a circle with Morissa and the other young girls in the center. We sang the song "Love Is the Only Answer" from a David Zeller album, which ends with the words "watch our circle grow."

As I gazed at the faces of loved friends in the circle, I realized that a world of possibilities of living as a woman were represented in that circle: married women with children; unmarried women with children; married women without children; unmarried women with lovers either male or female; unmarried women without lovers. The straight-and-narrow slice of the world which was offered to me as truth-and-all when I began to menstruate, has, like the full moon, swelled with possibilities for Morissa and the young women of her generation. But do we dare show it to our children?

I began the ceremony by supplying some background:

We bring the ordinary into holy consciousness through ceremony/service/celebration. By moving a life-moment from its private enclosure, often clouded with secrecy, fear, shame, and curse, we confront those feelings that have lived for generations within us, and replace them with pride in the miraculous workings of our body.

For many of us who have grown up with ambivalent messages from our mothers and grandmothers, this affirming message does not come so easily to pass on to our daughters. We don't really know where or why we hide this life passage—which many cultures don't hide—but we have internalized the need for secrecy.

We have finally come of age as women to ask: What have we lost in our failure to take pride in our changing bodies? What does that say about our feelings for ourselves, our daughters, our community of sisters? It is time to use ceremony to purge us from feelings of shame, disconnectedness, ordinariness.

This ceremony of menstruation calls for a moonlit night: the moon, like a woman's cycle, waxing and waning; the full moon like an egg bursting forth from the ovary fully ripe. The full moon, coming right in the middle of Morissa's cycle, gives a feeling of congruence, of being on target, of being in touch with the Holy One of Being. How absolutely right it feels tonight, to celebrate Morissa's fullness with that of the moon and our "weave of women" (as Esther Broner's novel has named it)! The very ceremony is a microcosm of what it means to be a woman, to speak a special intuitive language with other women and the universe.

As Jews, we symbolically give our children the Torah as their inheritance/path of life upon their Bat/Bar Mitzvah. So, for menarche, I called upon the women in the circle to hand down to Morissa a teaching that had come from their own or other people's woman-experience.

Some spoke to Morissa from themselves; others read from books or poems or stories. People spoke about friendship; about pregnancy and childbirth; about belonging to community; about learning that women friends were not to be discarded when men came into their lives. I said—with some trepidation—that while she was still too young for my message, I welcomed her to a time when her mind and heart would catch up with her body, and she would be able to experience, as I have, the sheer pleasure of living in a woman's body.

Friends gave Morissa all kinds of books, as widely divergent as the lifestyles of the women present: *A Gift from the Sea* by Anne Morrow Lindbergh; an anthology of women poets; *Dreaming the Dark* by Starhawk; *The Little Prince* by Antoine de Saint-Exupéry; *The Moon Is*

Always Female by Marge Piercy; a book of short stories to remind Morissa that reading makes for companions of infinite imagination; *The Women's Room* by Marilyn French; *Our Bodies, Ourselves* by the Boston Women's Health Collective; some specific poems; *A Child Is Born*, the photographic collection by Linnart Nielson of embryo/fetus developing throughout pregnancy into childbirth; and several blank books waiting to be written by Morissa herself. Though many of the books were beyond Morissa's understanding or interest right then, they stood on her shelves as a legacy to explore when she would be ready, like treasure chests in the attic.

So, too, many of the words said or read to her were more than she could fully take in that night, but Morissa did know that she had received a welcoming full of love and hope.

From our Native American sisters we had learned of a menarche ceremony—including men as well as women—in which the community sits in watch through the night over the rising cornbread. The night before Morissa's ceremony, she and I sat up through most of the night, kneading, talking, and watching the rising challah. It was her first time to take charge (not merely to assist me) in the baking of challah. We brought her baked loaves to her ceremony, inviting women to savor the taste but to save a small piece for the *Tashliḥ* to follow.

Along with the moon as symbol, the ceremony called for water: water reminding us of the birth waters which bring forth new selves; and of Miryam, who sweetened the water in the desert so that it was fit to drink. Had the night been warmer, another month toward summer's heat, I would have chosen a site where we could have used water for a *mikva* (ritual bath)—not from the tradition that calls for cleansing what is impure, but rather from the place of rebirthing our consciousness.

We often take for granted that extraordinary blessing which is our naturally functioning bodies. By immersing ourselves fully into cold water, we are startled to awareness that what is with us all the time is itself a miracle. By purifying our vision, we can see the (w)holiness that is all-present. In lieu of a *mikva* on this cool May night, we used our crumbs of challah for a *Tashliḥ* ceremony.

Tashliḥ (traditionally, the casting of crumbs into a body of running water on Rosh Hashana, as part of the Ten Days of in-looking) does not have to be understood as simply casting off those deadly parts of ourselves we want to be rid of, but rather as a turning around to see a life-giving aspect of those same parts. At this moment marking the transition between childhood and adulthood, I invited everyone in the circle to look into themselves at those aspects that were still childish and immature. Once we were able to identify those parts of ourselves, we might symbolically cast them upon the crumbs of challah into the brook so that the waters might turn them around and allow us to retain our wonder-full childlikeness in a more disciplined, mature fashion.

As we searched within ourselves and lined the banks of the brook, turning the child in ourselves from an out-of-control state into a fine-tuned one, we sang the song "Return Again" (from Shlomo Carlebach via David Zeller's album), which ends with the words "Re-turn to where you are born and reborn again."

We regathered into our inner and outer circles, making a *b'raḥa* over wine. That blessing, like the one for challah, was recited in traditional as well as feminized Hebrew and translated into "midrashic" English.

> *B'ruḥa at Sheḥina, Makor haḤayim, boreyt p'ri hagafen.*
> Blessed are You, Sheḥina, Source/Sorceress of all life, Who has made the fruits of the vine sweet to our taste, in the familiar color of our life-giving blood.

Then, in the fullness of the night, we recited two blessings that are normally part of the morning, not the evening, service:

> *Baruḥ ata YHWH eloheynu ru-aḥ ha-olam she-asani b'tzelem Elohim.*

Blessed are You, Holy One of Being, Mother-and-Father of us all, Who has made me in Your image, like Adam from the Adamah upon creation, with the feminine and masculine sides still intertwined.

B'ruḥa at YHWH eloheynu ru-aḥ ha-olam she-astani isha.
Blessed are You, Holy one of Being, Mother-and-Father of us all, Who has created me predominantly and joyously female.

And then, as we invited Morissa to move from the inner circle where she stood with four other young girls, into our outer circle of women, we sang:

B'ruḥa at YHWH eloheynu ru-aḥ ḥa-olam sheheḥeyatnu v'kiy'matnu v'higi-atnu laẓman haẓeh.
Blessed are You, Holy One of Being, Parent of us all, Who has brought us with great joy to this moment of change in Morissa's life and in the lives of all of us joined in celebration.

In closing we sang again the words to the Zeller song that ends, "watch our circle grow."

As we come to love ourselves, including the wondrous workings of our bodies, the love flows naturally to our daughters and sons, our friends and lovers, our mothers and fathers, our community, and those whom we still consider strangers.

Keyn y'hi ratẓon!—May it be so!

What do we learn from this approach? first, that the entry of women as full equals in Jewish life may mean not that they fit into Torah-as-it-has-been, but that Torah herself changes and grows. Over and over, when we have said this, some people have skeptically asked for specifics. This ceremony, obviously, describes one.

More: the way Phyllis drew on *mikva* and *Tashliḥ* in new ways suggests that hidden at the heart of Torah may be a proto-feminist Sleeping Beauty, waiting for millennia to be wakened by her great-great-granddaughters. Is this the way Rebekah, Rachel, and Miriam, those women of the well, did *mikva* and *Tashliḥ*?

And still more: As the renewal of Judaism has gone forward, women and men have struggled with the tension between the need of women to meet on their own to explore how to create a new Judaism, and the need for a new Judaism to be built by women and men together. Perhaps Morissa's transformation-time suggests a way to resolve that tension. Just as *Kohelet* (Ecclesiastes) teaches us that there is a time for every purpose under Heaven, a time for separating and a time for gathering, perhaps we can honor two different times in the passage of adulthood: the moment at the river when women separate to celebrate menarche, and the moment in the synagogue when women and men gather together to celebrate the Torah-focused ceremony of becoming Bat Mitzvah and Bar Mitzvah.

This emergence of menarche ceremonies raises some interesting questions about new approaches to "body Judaism" in the future life-cycle celebrations of children who are becoming adolescents—boys as well as girls, the body sensual and muscular as well as sexual. Before we look at these implications for the future, let us look back to see how menstruation has been dealt with in the Jewish past, and for some Jewish women in the present.

In the life of Biblical Israel, there was no specific ceremony for menarche. The ceremonial response to menstruation was focused not on its onset but on the continuing rhythm of the menses until menopause.

The rituals surrounding menstruation emerged from Biblical Israel's treatment of menstruation as one special case of a number of bodily flows or boundary-disturbances that brought on a state of being which was called *tuma*. In general, persons who were *tamey* could not enter the Temple precincts until they had waited certain specified periods of time and had taken part in a ritual of clarification.

Tamey has conventionally been translated as "ritually impure," but some recent translations have rendered it as "taboo" or "uncanny"—or even refused to translate it altogether, simply keeping *tamey* in the English text. The category applied also after a male seminal emission, after sexual intercourse, during the course of certain skin disorders, after touching a corpse, to a mother just after childbirth, and to other moments of threshold between life and death. So "taboo" or "uncanny" may be more accurate, though some biblical texts do bespeak a sense of aversion, danger, even unpleasantness in *tuma*.

For us (Phyllis and Arthur) today, "intensely and inwardly focused" seems a useful way of understanding *tamey*. Those who have been in direct physical contact with death, mothers who have just given birth and are caring for very young children, people who are experiencing feelings of exaltation after sexual intercourse—all might be in a state of inward focus that points them away from the communal holiness of the Temple, or from contact with other people.

For a woman in *nida*, the special state of *tuma* surrounding menstruation, the time period of separation from the Temple and its communal life was seven days. And—a unique provision—the specific kind of *tuma* brought on by menstruation made a man with whom she had sex also *tamey* for seven days.

With the destruction of the Temple, however, the practical effect of all these taboo states disappeared, and the rituals for clarifying and ending taboo status disappeared—except for the unique interpersonal effects connected with menstrual *nida*.

In that one case, the taboo status not only did not vanish, it was intensified by the decisions of the Rabbis.

But before we look more deeply into the rabbinic approach to menstruation, let us be as clear as possible about how this worked as ritual for biblical women. If we search for a guide to the actual practice of menstrual *tuma* in biblical times, we may find it useful to look at the contemporary patterns of the Ethiopian Jewish community, since for many centuries it was cut off from rabbinic influence, and has until recently operated more in biblical than in rabbinic patterns.

In Ethiopia, the menstruating women of the community gathered in a special place outside the regular communal boundaries for the seven prescribed days. There they would care only for nursing children, and would cook and clean communally, for and with each other. The men, back home, along with other women would fend for themselves and care for the older children. At any given moment, then, some of the women in the community would be having a sabbatical seven days, a kind of semi-holiday.

For the Ethiopian women, this was a place and time of physical separation but not psychological isolation. In their community, it was considered natural—not secret or taboo—to know where a woman was in her menstrual cycle.

According to the biblical standards, the *tuma* of menstruation was ended, after the seven days, by full bodily immersion in a *mikva*—a gathering of waters either natural, like a river, or an artificial pond that was fed by natural springs or rain. In Ethiopia, a land of many streams, the immersion was usually in a body of natural flowing water; in the Land of Israel, where streams during much of the year are many fewer, an artificial *mikva* was probably more likely. Even an artificial *mikva*, however, would be initiated with a specified amount of rain- or river water—*ma-yim ḥa-yim*, or "living waters." When the Ethiopian women immersed, they also immersed the nursing children who were with them. (Their children often nursed for three or four years.)

After immersing, the woman would return to her household, and in biblical days would again feel free to visit the Temple, bringing an offering.

The operative factor for Biblical Israel was a synthesis of inward focus on the thresholds of life and death, with a special concern for sexuality and procreation, and another special concern with blood.

But then, as biblical Judaism disintegrated under the pressure of Hellenistic-Roman civilization and the Rabbis reshaped Judaism, attitudes toward menstruation changed. The Rabbis seem to have experienced women as profoundly "other," an attitude perhaps learned from Hellenistic culture, even though the Rabbis apparently learned it less strongly than other, more Hellenized Jews. The otherness of women may have seemed at its starkest in the monthly recurrence of menstruation, something altogether alien to men's internal experience, and this must have created a distancing that could easily have become a sense of eeriness, uncanniness. Yet it was men, and only men, who made the rules concerning menstruation.

Without any explicit evidence in their comments, we can imagine that menstruation may have seemed especially eerie to men who spent a great deal of time away from their wives and whose most erotic experience was Torah-study.

Whatever the reasons, as Rabbinic Judaism evolved over the centuries, the regulations governing *nida* tended (at least till the twentieth century) to become more and more strict. A growing fear or disdain of women, especially encouraged by a new wave of infusion of Greek thought into Jewish life through the medieval Jewish philosophers, may have had something to do with this. But even when the greatest of these philosophers, Maimonides (himself generally hostile to women), criticized some new restrictions placed on women in *nida*, the (male) public still tended to adopt them.

In the *Shulḥan Aruḥ*, the most recent major and authoritative code of Jewish law, the following were the regulations governing *nida*:

- Women were obligated to ascertain when their menstrual periods ordinarily began. This could be established by noting three regular recurrences of the flow—that they began on the same day of a (lunar) month; or that they began a regular number of days after the end of the previous menstrual flow; or that they regularly began after some perceptible physical symptoms. Women whose periods came irregularly were obligated to examine themselves and their clothes before joining in sexual intercourse.

- The "beginning" of a flow was defined as the appearance of any spot of blood "as large as a mustard seed" on a woman's body or clothes in a place where it was likely to have come from the genitals. Even if this blood was not in her regular menstrual period and seemed likely to be a non-menstrual discharge (so long as it was not from an actual wound), the entire sequence of the *nida* ritual was followed.

- Beginning at least twelve and preferably twenty-four hours before a woman expected her menstrual period to begin, she and her husband refrained from sex and, indeed, from any physical contact at all. They slept in separate beds, and the husband could not hand her any object, hold her hand, or even do things—like sending her a cup of wine—that would communicate such intimacy and caring that sexual desire might be aroused.

- This separation continued for a minimum of twelve additional days. Beginning with the first spot of blood, the woman counted five full days (including the one on which the blood appeared) as the days of her period. If by that time no more blood was appearing, she put on clean white underclothes, spread clean white sheets on her bed, and began to count seven additional days.

- During these seven days she examined herself twice a day, even inserting a soft white woolen cloth to see whether there was any further discharge of blood. If there was, her menstrual period was not considered ended until this blood no longer appeared, and she began to count the seven days again from this time.

- When seven "white" days were successfully ended, she washed herself thoroughly, cleaned and loosened her hair, pared her nails, cleaned her teeth, and when she was thoroughly clean proceeded (after sundown so as to do so in privacy) to the *mikva*, or ritual bath.

- There she removed anything on her body—clothing, jewelry, nail polish, body paint, caked dough from baking—that might prevent the water from immersing her entirely and throughout.

- She immersed herself entirely (including her hair), letting the water wash over every inch of her body so that all of her was simultaneously immersed, and then recited the blessing, *"Baruḥ ata YHWH eloheynu meleḥ ha-olam asher kidshanu b'mitẓvotav v'tẓivanu al ha-t'vila."*—"Blessed are you, YHWH our God,

Ruler of the Universe, who has made us holy through his commandments and commanded us concerning immersion."

- We should note that the *mikva* (which must begin with *ma-yim ha-yim*—living water like rain, a natural spring or lake, etc.) is a miniature version of the ocean from which all life came and an enlarged version of the womb from which all human life comes. The *mikva* is also used in the ceremony of conversion to Judaism for both women and men—a kind of rebirth—and in some communities as an expression of spiritual rebirth before Shabbat and Yom Kippur. Its use in ending *nida* is especially poignant, since the taboo that springs from the womb within a woman is thus ended by her entering within a larger womb—symbolically, the womb of all life.
- And after *mikva*, the woman returned home to make love with her husband.

In most of Rabbinic Jewish life, women in *nida* usually stayed in their households and continued their usual work, but could not touch or be touched by their husbands, let alone have sexual relations. The immersion occurred at night, almost always in an artificial *mikva*, and there was often a strong atmosphere of secrecy and embarrassment.

This pattern was much more likely than the Biblical/Ethiopian model to encourage a feeling that menstruation is impure. The "slap in the face" that I (Phyllis) and many other women recall as the key ritual for menarche may have fit into that mind-set. As women became more and more emancipated, many reacted to this sense of exclusion and denigration with their own refusal to take part in the ritual. So during the twentieth century, there was a steep decline in the practices of menstrual separation and immersion.

There are now some signs that the emergence of feminist Judaism is leading to an affirmation of women's bodies, including the menstrual cycle. The beginnings of a menstruation-positive ritual for menarche is certainly one such sign. Another may be reports of an increasing observance of the *mikva* ritual in a new key—emphatically not as a purification from the supposed impurity of menstrual blood, but rather as an opportunity for rebirth and renewal. (Let us be clear: So far, it is a minority of Jewish feminists who are affirming this new understanding of the *mikva* process. That any at all are doing so would not have been expected twenty years ago.)

In this atmosphere, it might be useful to refocus attention on the *mikva* itself as a life-cycle ritual. Its pattern reaffirms what we have already seen as a spiral that moves from withdrawal to encounter to transformation to reentry. In either the biblical/Ethiopian or the Rabbinic mode, a woman withdraws from ordinary life—either her regular marriage bed or her entire house and neighborhood, to somewhere outside the walls. Then her separation is intensified: She goes to an even more distinctive place—the *mikva*, built and shaped and watered according to strict rules, suffused with the humidity of a water-world. Usually she enters alone, passing a special guardian—the "*mikva* lady." She makes herself fully vulnerable. Now she encounters God, by immersing entirely in the water. As one line of Torah says, God's Own Self is the *mikva Yisra-el*—the sacred space in which the whole People Israel is gathered together. She emerges a new being: *t'hora*, "pure" or "clear" or perhaps "transparent." A new version of her previous self. And then she returns to "normal" society—to her family and especially to her partner, but as a renewed person.

In what ways is a feminist sensibility transforming the traditional ritual? Some women are going together to the *mikva*, with communal joy rather than secret anxiety. Some are bringing poems, songs, incense. Some are explicitly naming the event one not of washing away the *sh'mutz* (dirt) of blood and ovum "unfulfilled," but one of rebirth from a newer amniotic fluid, a cup-full of the primordial Ocean from which all life was born. Some have radically reduced the time of sexual separation, to the original biblical seven days or even to a single day, signaling that menstruation is remarkable—to be marked and re-marked on—but in no way shameful or disgusting. These experiments in *mikva* all reaffirm the female body in its distinctiveness from that of men.

Some women have celebrated the body-intensity of *mikva* in ways that, rather than distinguishing women from men, emulate and broaden the ways in which men have been using the *mikva*. For centuries, men have plunged into the rebirthing waters before such life-changing events as Shabbat, major festivals, writing a Torah scroll. Women have also begun to use the *mikva* on these occasions, and have added such other life-changing moments as marriage, childbirth, entering on a new career. Some women have affirmed a rhythm of sexual separation followed by immersion in the *mikva* and then a sexual reunion, but have keyed this rhythm to the rhythms of the moon—which men can also dance to—instead of the menstrual period. In this way they avoid any possible denigration of women's bodies as "impure."

For men as well as for women—especially for young women and young men, whose bodies are swiftly changing—all of this is beginning to raise the question: What does it mean to reawaken the Body Jewish?

Is a focus on the words of Torah, important as they are, the only way that boys and girls can share the first steps of an entry into adult Jewish life? Are there ways to hear the echo of the Bible's ancient Body Judaism that do not focus solely on the issues of sexual physiology?

Most obvious, perhaps, as we learn from the menarche ceremony, is that we should be addressing as a Jewish reality the issues of sexual ethics. Where are the rabbis who are prepared to speak honestly to thirteen-year-olds about the fullness of their bodies? (Parents may quail at our naming such an early age, but for many adolescents, sexual explorations begin soon after. Waiting until sixteen may miss the crucial moment.) What rabbis will say in public, honestly, that in this modern world, few are the young women or men who should seek either early marriage or long terms of celibacy? Who will say that it is not wise to marry at sixteen or eighteen, when personalities are still fluid and when commitment to a long-term partnership with another fluid person is likely to breed disaster? And say with equal honesty that waiting to experience sexuality in a serious way until they are married at twenty-five or thirty-five or forty may also be disastrous?

Where are the rabbis who with honesty and joy will teach the Song of Songs to adolescents? Will carry this scarce-read text of biblical tradition out of the back-of-the-Book where some youngsters may discover it with an astonished snicker, and make of it instead a teaching of part of the sacred truth of sacred sexuality? Will bring to light the newer translations like those of Marcia Falk and the Blochs, translations that fully unveil the sensuousness of the Hebrew?

And rediscovering the Body Judaism of the Bible means not only the Judaism of sexuality but also of the earth in which we are immersed. Biblical Judaism focused on herding goats and sheep, planting barley, caring for fruit trees. Few Jews do such work today, but the future of the earth cries out for a new kind of shepherding and tree-keeping. Cries out for us to nurture the planet as a whole, as well as the tiny plots of earth in our own backyards, whether on the eastern shore of the Mediterranean or the western shore of the Pacific, the banks of the Hudson or of the Amazon.

What if boys and girls gathered together under the slender sliver of Rosh Ḥodesh, the New Moon nearest their Bar/Bat Mitzvah Torah-reading—gathered at a brook or river, first to pledge that they would keep its waters sweet, and then to bend their backs and arms to cleansing, sweetening those waters? To pledge that they would act to prevent the scorching of our planet through an overdose of hothouse gases, and then actually plan how to minimize their use of gasoline and learn instead to use their legs and bicycles, rather than becoming addicted to the planet-lethal pleasures of petroleum? What if nature hikes and walks became as necessary an aspect of entering a Jewish teen age as the chanting of Torah in the synagogue? What if the learning and the *doing* of Torah of the earth became a *mitzva* for sons and daughters of the earth and of the Breath of Life?

Imagine that Elijah's Affirmation—"I myself have come to turn the hearts of the parents to the children and the hearts of the children to the parents, lest the earth be utterly destroyed"—were to become not merely powerful words to say aloud as the generations face each other in the synagogue. What if these words were to become a description of reality, a summary of what the children-moving-toward-adulthood had actually done on the nights and days of New Moon just past and would be doing for the New Moons yet to come? What if the ancient celebration of Rosh Ḥodesh were renewed not only as a gathering time for women but also as a time when young women and young men would join each month to renew the healing of the earth?

Imagine a Judaism in which from twelve or thirteen years of age until they left their homes for college, close comradeships of teenage Jews would commit themselves to serve at each New Moon the *Eḥad*—Unity—of earth and rain and wind and sun. Would we need to worry that our next generation might not think that Judaism matters?

Nor is such celebration of the body of the earth the only way in which we could celebrate as sacred the changing bodies of our youngsters:

- Perhaps we learn from the biblical tradition in which the ability to bear arms became a definition of adulthood. Today, needing to seek peace and pursue it, perhaps we ask our children to become not killers but healers—paramedics, learning through even greater intimacy with the body than a soldier's, how to bind up wounds and save a life.

- Perhaps we renew the tradition of the Levites, who brought sacred dance into the Holy Place. Our youngsters who revel in the body-energy of basketball and ballet, the *hora* and karate, could shape the dances that make prayer into the practice where, as the Psalmist says, "All my bones shall praise You."

- And perhaps we honor and renew the ancient priests who carried meat and grain and fruit to feed the poor and landless, calling these offerings sacred as a way of "nearing" God—*korbanot*, from the root *keruv*, meaning "near." Perhaps we ask our children to serve the poor and celebrate God with their own hands, in soup kitchens that bear the stamp of the Holy Altar in our own generation.

In adolescence, we are learning to give fuller shape to the identities that in our births and childhoods first unfolded. We are preparing to meet the Other as more fully ourselves, whether we experience the Other as a God of Unity or as a lover who may call us into encounter.

From tentative experiments in celebrating the bodies of our girls-becoming-women, a Judaism able to come alive in a world of words and sinews could learn how to meet God in new ways. The more deeply we experience God not only as Up There, Out There, but In Here, the more deeply we may feel what it means to meet God in our own bodies. Not wantonly, not carelessly, but in joyful caring.

~ 6 ~

Further into Adulthood

MODERNITY HAS MADE ADULT LIFE SO COMPLEX and the pathway into adulthood so tortuous that many Jewish communities have become dissatisfied with the age of twelve or thirteen as the sole marker of the shift from child to adult.

Almost two hundred years ago, the early Reform Jews of Germany instituted a "confirmation" ceremony to be observed at age sixteen by both young women and young men. The early Reformers intended this to replace the Bar Mitzvah ritual, but the result has been to add a new marker. It has spread to most Reform, Conservative, and Reconstructionist congregations.

Originally, the Reform community in Germany may have modeled "confirmation" on the practice of some Christian churches of "confirming" young adults in their acceptance of Christianity, perhaps originally expressed in infant baptism. Since there is no theological basis in Judaism for one Jew to be more fully a Jew than another (though perhaps more vigorous in observing one or another of the *mitzvot*), this language sat badly on some Jewish shoulders. So some communities have called the event "affirmation," with the emphasis on young people's affirmation of the importance of Judaism in their lives, rather than on the community's acceptance of them as members.

Even though some Jewish communities have rejected this ritual in-novation as "un-Jewish," it is an attempt to digest Modernity into Judaism rather than let Modernity swallow Judaism. It essentially ac-cepts that Modernity has wrought irreversible changes in the life-cycle of Jews, and instead of turning over this new turf entirely to secular modes and practices, it has attempted to "Judaize" the process of fur-ther growing toward adulthood.

There was no biblical or rabbinic model on which to base a confirmation/affirmation ceremony. So new tradition has been free to emerge over the last two centuries.

It is general practice that a whole group or class of sixteen-year-olds go through confirmation together, rather than individually as in the Bar/Bat Mitzvah passage. They study together through a school year (essentially synchronous with the Jewish year that begins on Rosh Hashana) and, typically, celebrate in the midst of their congre-gation on or about Shavuot—the early summer festival that celebrates the giving of the Torah. Thus each group of sixteen-year-olds comes to stand together at the foot of Sinai.

For many confirmation classes, it has become a central part of the ritual to take part in, even to help create, a cantata about some major event in Jewish history or tradition. Sharing the work of this produc-tion helps make the class not merely a formal group but an intertwined community.

The class is also likely to work together or individually on acts of *gemilut ḥasadim*—kindness toward the poor or the disabled through direct service, or perhaps acts of protection and healing for the earth. Working with a soup kitchen to feed the hungry, cleaning up debris at a local stream, leading a Shabbat celebration at a nursing home, are examples of such actions. Many sixteen-year-olds not only are capable of doing these *mitzvot* but find the doing full of joy.

One aspect of Modernity that has rarely been incorporated into this Jewish approach to adolescence has been the advent of the teenage driver. In most places at age sixteen, teenagers are given access to a one-ton machine that can kill, transport its occupants within one hour to a place where no one at all knows them, serve as a bedroom for sexual expression or a temporary hut for living, eating, sleeping, drinking. Any one of these attributes might have in the distant past called forth a response of awe and instruction from any religious or spiritual community. But today the only preparation is training in the bare technology and in the legal regulations that govern operation of the machine.

- No ethical training.
- No instilling of a sense of awe for the car's ability to maim or kill, in a moment of lost focus or anger or exhaustion. Or even in the lost focus of an unknown other, sharing only the same strip of concrete.
- No preparation to use a sacred bedroom wisely.
- No blessing to affirm that the One Who breathes the universe is woven into all the aspects of this auto, and that even its fuel might affect the breathing of the planet.

Yet all these elements of this major step into adulthood could be addressed through wrestling with God and Torah. Not by finding rigid answers, but by seeking higher consciousness.

So—could Jewish parents insist that their sixteen-year-olds receive their permission to drive only after they complete the training for a "Jewish driver's license," alongside the one permitted by the state? Could synagogues that now bemoan how few of their youngsters stay around after Bar/Bat Mitzvah time find serious connection with an entire generation, if they said that receiving a driver's license was a moment in the Jewish life-cycle? Could the confirmation/affirmation ceremony include the presentation of a driver's permit signed by the rabbi and the parents of each sixteen-year-old who has accepted the challenge?

Aside from entering the world of drivers, the next important steps in the maturation of an adult are likely to be the first ongoing sexual relationship, probably before commitment to marriage and family; the first "grown-up" job; the first independent household—usually in that order. For the third of these, the tradition has evolved a ritual practice; for the others, it might enrich the Judaism of the next generation to draw on traditional sources to work out Jewish paths of sacred entry.

To create a new Jewish household, Jews affix a *mezuza* to the doorpost—if possible, within thirty days of moving in. A container made of almost anything—cloth, ceramic, metal, wood—encloses a tiny scroll that has been hand-scribed to say that God is One, and that the daily, earthy aspects of our eyes and hands, our doors and gates, our rising-up and lying-down, our gazing at the mountains and the redwoods, at the beetles and the mosses, all remind us: God *is* One.

On the side that is visible to those who cross the threshold, the container traditionally carries the Hebrew letter *shin*. That letter begins the word *Shaddai*, a name of God that is connected with the word for "breast" and therefore also evokes "mountain," as in the range we call the Grand Tetons. So it has been understood to mean both All-Powerful and All-Nourishing.

The new householder recites two blessings:

Baruh ata YHWH [Yahh] eloheynu meleh [ru-ah] ha-olam asher kidshanu b'mitzvotav v'tzivanu likbo-a mezuza.
Blessed is YHWH our God, Ruler/Breath of the Universe, Who has commanded us [or connected us] in order that we become holy, and taught us the commandment/connection of affixing the *mezuza.*

Baruh ata YHWH eloheynu meleh [ru-ah] ha-olam sheheheyanu v'kiy'manu v'higi-anu lazman hazeh.
Blessed is the One Who has filled us with life, lifted us up, and brought us to this moment.

That person then places the *mezuza* on the doorpost, about one-third of the way from the top, leaning with its head slightly inward, and hammers in the nails that hold it to the doorpost.

Aside from this, the ceremony is open and fluid, welcoming the creativity of new householders. To draw on the wisdom of the now-familiar fourfold pattern, the ceremony . . .

- could begin with welcoming a swirl of people, the community of friends, perhaps some family;
- continue with the person who is setting up a first independent household (or a couple that has decided to live together) coming forward to affix the *mezuza*—making that a transformational moment of standing on the "threshold" of change in the literal as well as the figurative sense;
- set forth the new Self that has emerged in this moment as the new householder speaks about what this moment of new responsibility calls forth: excitements, hopes, fears, sorrows;
- and finally, open up to blessings from the surrounding friends, becoming again part of the community but in a new relationship.

Now let us turn to two important steps into adulthood for which Jewish tradition has not specified a ceremonial depth. First, let us explore how someone might celebrate the beginning of a first ongoing sexual relationship:

The Song of Songs, little known to many Jews who think of the tradition as prudish and puritanical, is one of the great erotic love poems in all world literature.

Most English translations have averted their eyes from its erotic pleasure, but in the last generation two new translations—one by Marcia Falk, the other by Chana and Ariel Bloch—have made that joyful pleasure visible.

In the text of the Song, God is never named; indeed, this is one of only two biblical books in which that is true. Rather than accept the song as a hymn to sensuous joy, the rabbinic tradition reinterpreted the text so as to understand the Song allegorically, as a poem about love between God and the People Israel.

But many of today's communities of Jewish renewal have understood the Song in a new way. To them, and clearly to Falk and the Blochs, it is understood as a profoundly spiritual poem not only because it is so drenched in sensuous love of musky fruit and breasts and bellies, the pleasures of the Garden of Eden for grown-ups, but because the fluidity and flow of the poetry evokes a kind of fluid spiritual path that is very different from the "official" path of Rabbinic Judaism. Whereas the Talmud begins, "From what time can we recite the evening *Sh'ma*?" the Song dances with a recurrent refrain: "Never waken love till it is ripe!"

The pleasure of the Song is not an empty physical completion, but a dance infused with love. Yet the Song is not focused on the structures and strictures of marriage. It emerges from a sense that one might call, "There is a time for fluid love, and a time for focused marriage." So the Song—any passage of it that new lovers might choose, in the Hebrew original or either of these newer English translations—could act as the central element of a ceremony to mark the beginning of a first sexual relationship, a first step on the path to sexual adulthood.

And now let us turn to the beginning of a first "grown-up" job, perhaps one that hints at the possibility of an ongoing calling or career.

There are several passages of Torah that might be brought into such a ceremony. For example, how does Moses welcome the tribe of Levi (the "connectors" or "escorters") into their task of sacred service to the Shrine of God's Presence?

YHWH spoke to Moses, saying: Take the Levites from among the Israelites and clarify who they are. . . . Sprinkle on them water of clarification, and let them go over their whole body with a razor, and wash their clothes. . . . Let them take a bull of the herd,

and with it a meal offering of choice flour with oil mixed in. . . .
Bring the Levites forward before the Tent of Meeting. Assemble
the whole Israelite community and bring the Levites forward
before YHWH. Let the Israelites lean their hands upon the Levites, and let Aaron designate the Levites before YHWH as an
elevation-offering from the Israelites, that they may do the work
of YHWH. (Num. 8:5–11)

Today we can choose to understand that any task that we perform
as sacred, with reverence for the Breath of Life that shapes all work
and restfulness, is a way of serving YHWH in the Tent of the Presence. To begin any work with this intention is a potentially sacred act.
So we can gather friends and family around the one who is taking this
step. They can lean their hands upon his head and give offerings of
tz'daka (money or actions of social responsibility) to those who need
it, and thus make clear the sacred potential of work.

And then, after the new worker has said how s/he sees the task as
sacred, the community can join first in the teachings and then in the
blessings of the Torah, about work:

You shall not abuse a hired hand, one who is afflicted or needy,
whether from among your kinfolk or from your stranger who is
within your land, within your gates. On his payday you must give
him his wage, do not let the sun set on him unpaid, for he is
needy, for it lifts his life-breath, that he not cry out against you
to YHWH, and there be sin upon you! (Deut. 24:14)

When you cut down your harvest in your field, and you forget a
sheaf in the field, you are not to return to get it; for the stranger,
for the orphan, and for the widow shall it be! (Deut. 24:19)

You are to bear in mind that a serf were you in the Land of Narrows, and YHWH your God redeemed you from there. . . .
Therefore I command you to act upon this word! (Deut. 24:18,
24:22)

Six days you may serve and do all your work, but the seventh day is Restful-Shabbat for YHWH your God. Do no work, not you, not your son, not your daughter, not your servant, not your maid, not your ox, not your donkey, not any of your animals, not the stranger who is in your gates—so that your servant and your maid may rest as one-like-yourself. Bear in mind that a serf were you in the Land of Narrows, but YHWH took you out of there with a strong hand and an arm outstretched to sow seed; therefore YHWH commands you to keep the day of Restful-Shabbat. (Deut. 5:13–15)

Blessed shall you be in the city, and blessed shall you be in the field.
Blessed shall be the fruit of your womb, the fruit of your soil, and the fruit of your cattle; the calving of your herd, and the lambing of your flock.
Blessed shall be your basket and your kneading bowl.
Blessed shall you be in your comings and blessed shall you be in your goings. (Deut. 28:3–6)

Then the gathering might add its own blessings, specific to the person and the work s/he is beginning.

In all these ways, the long-extended entry into adulthood that is characteristic in our society can be filled with a sense of sacred possibility, and at each step the emerging Self can be renewed and deepened.

PART 2

Meeting an Other

∾ 7 ∾

The Covenant of *Ḥuppa*

THE HEART OF THE JOURNEY of each life-cycle ceremony is the transformative encounter with God.

The heart of the journey of the Jewish people is its ever-renewing covenant encounter with God at Sinai.

And the heart of the "model" individual Jewish life-journey is the deep encounter with another human being, the creation of a covenant between them. Through almost the entire Jewish past, the primary form of this encounter in the cycle of a life has been a marriage. And to mark the moment, a wedding.

In the Jewish past, marriage has not been the only form such deep interpersonal encounters have taken. Deep and intimate friendships have also fulfilled this need. In our own generation, the creation of "intentional families" and the search for intimate friendships among a wider swath of people have perhaps drawn our attention to the possibility in a deeper way. In the next chapter, we will examine what this means.

For now, we will address the way in which, over centuries and millennia, the Jewish people has explored and deepened the sense of encounter in marriage.

For most of Jewish history, marriage has been the meeting of un-equals (just as the People Israel felt its original meeting with God at Sinai was between unequals). Men took women in marriage. Men were in charge, and the wedding ceremony reflected that. Two men could not make a loving covenant, for each would have to be in charge—and the perceived impossibility blew out the power generator. Two women could not make a loving covenant, for neither would be able to take charge—and the perceived incapability left the motor too cool to turn on.

One man was to be in charge of each family. And God was in charge of all.

If, however, we begin to imagine God not as the King Above but as the Breath Between, the Wellspring Within, the possibility emerges that women and men, women and women, men and men, can make a covenant of equals. And the other way round: Begin to treat women and men as equals, and God's Own Self comes more into the world, ready to stand *with* rather than *above* the human race and the People Israel.

This is not simply an idea of postmoderns. More than three thou-sand years ago, the Prophet Hosea, drawing on the pain of having ex-perienced the faithlessness of his own marriage-partner, hears God's shriek of pain over a faithless partner—Israel. But then Hosea goes beyond the assumptions of a bossy marriage, even one that is formally monogamous, and glimpses for the future a different model altogether (Hosea 2:19, 21):

> And on that day, says YHWH, you shall call me "My man," and shall no longer call me "My boss." . . .
> For I shall betroth you to Me in uprightness and in transforma-tive justice, and in loyal love, and in compassion.

Hosea's vision still assumes a superior partner who "betroths" the other. But we also have the even more subversive model of the Song of Songs. In the Song, neither partner is superior in any way, and marriage itself seems to fade in and out, into a loving erotic delight that suffuses all of life.

The history of Jewish marriage is the history of a long journey from a marriage-pattern where one man might reign over several women, through a marriage-pattern in which one woman served one man and in return he cared for her, toward a pattern of marriage in which a man and woman can covenant together while both stand upright and between them is loyal love and the kind of justice that transforms relationships. In some communities, this evolution has continued into the celebration of marriages between two men or two women.

Biblical Weddings

But let us begin at the beginning. In biblical days, there was a ceremony of marriage, but we have only the barest hints of what it was like. Indeed, most biblical stories of important marriages have no ceremonial tale attached to them: Of Abraham it is written, "Avram and [his brother] Naḥor took [*va-yikaḥ*] wives for themselves; the name of Avram's wife was Sarai." (Gen. 11:29) Of the marriage of Amram (Moses' father) to Yocheved, it is simply noted, "And there went a man of the house of Levi and took [*va-yikaḥ*] a daughter of Levi." Of Moses it is written: "And [Jethro] gave Moses Tzipora his daughter; and she bore him a son."

The marriage of Isaac and Rebekah starts in a more complex fashion, but whether or not with ritual is open to question. When Abraham's servant asks Rebekah's family to send her with him to marry Isaac, the family asks her, *"Hatelḥi im ha-ish hazeh?"*—"Will you go with this man?" and she responds, *"Eyleyḥ"*—"I will go." Then they bless her for fruitful motherhood, and she leaves.

This sounds as if it may have been a ritual formula; if so, it betokened a form of marriage where go-betweens were more crucial than direct communication between the couple. The nearest Rebekah has to a direct ceremonial connection with Isaac is that she veils herself when she sees him for the first time, and he brings her into the tent that had been his mother's. Here again, the formula for celebration and consummation of the marriage—they may have been one and the same—is that "Isaac took [*va-yikah*] Rebekah, and she was for him for a wife." (Gen. 24:55–67)

On the other hand, Jacob's wedding to Leah is celebrated with a drinking-feast, and he has to fulfill a *sh'vua* ("seven"; that is, a week) before he can finally marry Rachel. (Gen. 29) Samson's wedding to a Philistine woman includes the seven days of a drinking-feast with the young men of the community. (Judges 14:12) And one of the Psalms mentions wedding-songs. (Ps. 78:63)

Two biblical passages refer to a man's spreading his robes above a woman as a symbolic act of espousal. (Ezekiel 16:8 and Ruth 3:9)

The clearest, fullest description of a wedding celebration from the biblical period comes from a non-biblical text, I Maccabees 9:39, about a non-Jewish but neighboring people: "There they saw the bridegroom, in the middle of a bustling crowd and a train of baggage, coming to meet the bridal party, escorted by his friends and kinsmen fully armed [this was in the midst of the Maccabean wars] to the sound of drums and instruments of music."

Rabbinic Weddings

By the time the Talmud debates and describes Jewish practice, the Rabbis have defined weddings in much more expansive and specific ways. Legally, they explained, a marriage can begin in any one of three ways:

sh'tar (written deed): through a written version (handed by the man to the woman, who indicates agreement by accepting it) of the oral formula that sets apart and sanctifies this particular woman for this particular man;

kesef (money): through a public act of acquisition (*kinyan*) in which the man transfers a piece of property (usually a ring) to acquire not the whole person of his wife but exclusive authority in regard to a sexual relationship with her;

or *biya* (coming): through actual sexual intercourse, accompanied by a public statement that the two intend marriage.

But while the Rabbis acknowledge that they will regard as a marriage a relationship that has already been begun by any one of these acts, they are averse to beginning with just one of them, and they shape a ceremony that includes the first and second in public reality, and the third as a brief seclusion of the couple that is usually only symbolic.

By the time they had done this shaping, the ceremony had begun to look in its basic rhythms much more like the other life-cycle rituals we have seen—though much more imbued with legal forms and concerns than the B'rit Mila or Bar Mitzvah rituals. The basic pattern continues to be observed in traditional communities today, and some parts of it are drawn on for the sake of their symbolic richness in nontraditional communities.

We have seen that the typical first stage of each life-transformation is the separation of the celebrant from the "ordinary" community. In this case, the separation takes a legal form, in three stages.

First of all, a couple (or their families, if the male was younger than thirteen or the female younger than twelve and a half) agree to what we might call an engagement—*shiduḥin*. (The word *shadḥan* or *shadḥanit*—matchmaker—comes from this word.) This does not change the legal or sexual status of the parties, but it involves promises about when a marriage will take place and especially about the financial arrangements. These clauses are called *t'na-im*, or "conditions," and often the whole process is known as *t'na-im*. Since no marriage can occur without the consent of both parties, the *shiduḥin* can be broken if either party refuses to go through with the wedding. In that case, financial penalties stipulated in the *t'na-im* go into effect.

Often, this agreement becomes the focus of a celebration. A plate is broken as a symbol of contract (and perhaps as a foretaste of the broken glass at the wedding).

The second and much sharper stage of separation was, until the early twelfth century, accomplished a year before the full-fledged wedding. In a ceremony called *Erusin* (betrothal) or *kiddushin* (separation/sanctification), the bride and groom agreed not to have sexual relationships with anyone else, and not (yet) with each other. Since the twelfth century, this ceremony has taken place under the *ḥuppa*, just a few minutes before the wedding ceremony itself.

Though the legal aspects of *Erusin* are preeminent, like most events in Jewish life it is given a celebratory aspect by a preceding blessing—indeed, two. The first is chanted over a cup of wine, and it is followed by one that blesses the God who commands *Erusin*. This blessing traditionally goes as follows: *"Baruḥ ata YHWH eloheynu meleḥ [ru-aḥ] ha-olam asher kidshanu b'mitzvotav v'tzivanu al ha-arayot, v'asar lanu et ha-arusot, v'hitir lanu et han'su-ot lanu al y'dey ḥuppa v'kiddushin. Baruḥ ata YHWH m'kadesh amo yisra-el al y'dey ḥuppa v'kiddushin."*

Literally, this means: "Blessed is YHWH our God, Who made us holy through commandments [or, connections] and commanded/connected us through sexuality, prohibiting it in betrothal and permitting it for us upon *nisu-in*, through the power of *ḥuppa* and separation/sanctification. Blessed are You, YHWH our God, Who makes the People Israel holy through the power of *ḥuppa* and *kiddushin* [the marriage canopy and separation/sanctification]."

The cup of wine is then shared by the couple.

The ceremony continues with a legal act of acquisition, *kinyan*: The groom gives the bride any object worth more than a *p'ruta* (a small coin, so as to make marriage possible for the poor), in order to acquire a preemptive relationship with her—though one not yet to be sexually consummated.

Usually, the groom does this by placing a ring on the bride's right forefinger, reciting: *"Harey at m'kudeshet li, b'taba-at zo, k'dat Moshe v'Yisra-el.*"—"Here! You are separated/sanctified to me, through this ring, according to the practice of Moses and Israel." The legal element of purchase requires that the ring be truly his property. The bride's willingness to let the ring be placed on her finger constitutes acceptance and agreement.

The reference to *dat Moshe v'Yisra-el* means that both primary Torah law (from God through Moses on Mount Sinai) and the decisions of every later generation of judges (*Yisra-el*) are part of the "practice" being observed. Two competent witnesses whose word can later be taken in court have to be present, and a *minyan* of ten is also customary.

To dissolve this betrothal requires a *get* (a formal Jewish divorce), but the betrothal itself does not complete marriage. No sexual relationship or obligation (except abstinence) is created by *Erusin*. Nor is any financial obligation, except that after twelve months, the groom becomes liable for his betrothed's maintenance if they have not completed the marriage in the meantime—assuming the bride makes clear she is ready and willing to marry him.

When the final stage of marriage, called *nisu-in*, is affirmed, there are two crucial changes in the relationship. A *k'tuba* (written contract) defines the financial obligations of the groom if he were to die or divorce his wife; and the couple then begin a sexual relationship.

Legally, the process of *nisu-in* requires first the writing (usually in private, often long in advance of the wedding ceremony) of the *k'tuba*, with its "prenuptial" commitments, then—just before the ceremony—its being formally acknowledged by the groom as embodying his obligation, being witnessed, and finally being read in public and delivered to the bride at the ceremony. Indeed, the *k'tuba* has to be delivered before *nisu-in* can proceed.

The writing follows a basic formula. It begins by specifying the date—the day of the week in relation to the approaching Shabbat, defined according to the name of the Torah portion to be then read, and the day, lunar month, and year since the creation of the world in the Jewish lunar calendar; and the town (often connected with a river) where the wedding is taking place, with the full names of the couple.

Then it specifies their financial arrangements. There are five basic components: (1) the minimum amount defined by Jewish law that the husband must pay the wife in case of divorce or death; (2) *tosefet k'tuba*, a possible additional amount to be paid above the legal minimum; (3) *nedunya*—the dowry, or agreed amount that the wife is considered to be bringing into the marriage (whether she actually does or not)—which the husband can use for investment or expenses, but must return if the marriage ends; (4) *tosefet nedunya*, an increment on the dowry (usually half its amount) to compensate the wife for use of the dowry in investment and trade; (5) additional conditions, especially the amounts due the wife during the marriage for her clothing and other maintenance. The first two of these amounts were determined in large part by the local custom of the place where the couple lived. The first four were sometimes subsumed into a single total amount in the written *k'tuba*.

Over the centuries, the custom arose that for those who could afford it, the *k'tuba* was often illuminated and illustrated with great beauty, to be shown to the world.

Shortly before proceeding to the *ḥuppa*, the groom meets with his chosen witnesses and the *m'sader kiddushin* (literally, "coordinator"—that is, the officiating rabbi or other learned Jew). The groom accepts the obligations of the *k'tuba*. This he does by a traditional symbolic act of acquisition: Before two witnesses, he takes a handkerchief from the hands of the *m'sader*. He lifts the handkerchief and returns it.

Two witnesses then sign the *k'tuba*. They are required to be competent and religiously observant men who would be capable of testifying if need be in a rabbinical court. Neither can be a close relative of the marrying couple, for fear of introducing a conflict of interest into the testimony over how much money has been set aside for the bride.

The *k'tuba* is then handed to the wife, who keeps it as a contractual definition of her rights. (If the *k'tuba* is later lost, even for an hour, the husband cannot touch his wife until it has been found or rewritten.)

In most communities, the *k'tuba* is read aloud under the *ḥuppa* just before *nisu-in*—the ceremony completing marriage—begins. Ceremonially, *nisu-in* then requires the chanting of seven blessings in the presence of a *minyan* of ten males. These blessings continue to be chanted today—with changes introduced by some couples, and in most communities with a *minyan* that counts both women and men:

Baruḥ ata YHWH elohyenu meleḥ [ru-ah] ha-olam, borey p'ri hagafen.

Baruḥ ata YHWH eloheynu meleḥ [ru-ah] ha-olam, shehakol bara liḥvodo.

Baruḥ ata YHWH eloheynu meleḥ [ru-ah] ha-olam, yotzer ha-adam.

Baruḥ ata YHWH eloheynu meleḥ [ru-ah] ha-olam, asher yatzar et ha-adam b'tzalmo, b'tzelem d'mut tavnito, v'hitkin lo mimeno binyan adey-ad. Baruḥ ata YHWH, yotzer ha-adam.

Sos tasis v'tagel ha-akara b'kibutz baneha l'toḥa b'simḥal. Baruḥ ata YHWH m'samey-aḥ tzi-on b'vaneha.

Samey-aḥ t'samaḥ rey-im ha-ahuvim, k'sameyḥeḥa y'tzirḥa b'gan eyden mikedem.

Baruḥ ata YHWH m'samey-aḥ ḥatan v'kala.

Baruḥ ata YHWH eloheynu meleḥ [ru-ah] ha-olam, asher bara sason v'simḥa, ḥatan v'kala, gila, rina, ditza, v'ḥedva, ahava, v'aḥva, v'shalom, v'rey-ut. M'heyra YHWH eloheynu yishama b'arey Yehuda uv'ḥutzot Y'rushala-yim kol sason v'kol simḥa, kol ḥatan v'kol kala, kol mitzhalot ḥatanim mey-ḥupatam un'arim mimishtey n'ginatam. Baruḥ ata YHWH, m'samey-aḥ ḥatan im hakala.

Blessed is the One Who creates the fruit of the vine.

Who created all for Your radiant glory;

Who shapes humankind;

Who shaped humanity in Your image and likeness [usually understood to be echoing the text of Genesis 1, male and female], and made for humans an internal process through which they became self-perpetuating forever [usually understood to mean, sexuality for procreation];

Who makes Zion joyful through her children, though she had
   been a hardened root [a barren mother];
Who makes bride and groom rejoice as did the beloved
   companions in the Garden of Eden;
Who has created joy and gladness, groom and bride, mirth and
   delight, love and fellowship—may You bring again into the
   cities of Judah and the streets of Jerusalem songs, weddings,
   and gladness!—and
Who makes the groom rejoice with the bride.

These *Sheva B'rahot*, or Seven Blessings, are followed by the couple's sharing of another cup of wine.

Then they retreat to a secluded place, perhaps with two witnesses
to guard the door, for still another symbolic enactment of their sexual relationship, now fully lawful. And while they do, their friends
and family begin an "obligatory celebration": sharing the food, in
yet another shadowy reenactment of the offerings at the Altar in
Jerusalem.

Ever since Talmudic times, some rabbis have been distressed at
what seemed to them excessive merriment at the feast that followed
the wedding. At two such feasts that the Talmud records, one rabbi interrupted the laughter by smashing an expensive wine-cup.

Over the years, as the story was retold, the community connected
this intervention with the need for a sense of mourning even at the
time of greatest joy—mourning over the Temple destroyed, and later
a broader sense of mourning for all the imperfections, the cruelties, the
injustices, that remain unhealed in the world.

As the message went forth of punctuating mirth with a dash of
mourning, smashing the glass became a practically universal custom.
Indeed, over the centuries it became hard to find a Jew, or anyone
else, who believed a Jewish wedding could be complete without it—
though it has no standing in the formal code of law.

Beginning in the twelfth century, the separation of a year's time
between the legal statuses and ceremonies of *Erusin* and *nisu-in* dis-

solved. The betrothal was moved under the *ḥuppa*, to be effected just minutes before the full marriage ceremony. (The custom also arose that upon entering the *ḥuppa*, the groom would don a *kittel*—a simple white robe, to be worn also every Yom Kippur and at every Pesaḥ *seder* and then in the coffin after death.)

One might ask: Why keep *Erusin* at all, if its function as a yearlong covenant of "suspended marriage" was being abandoned?

Some might answer that having first established the importance of *Erusin*, the legal mind within the rabbinate felt uncomfortable about abandoning it entirely. But we could also note that the resulting double ceremony had one very important psychological and spiritual impact: It taught that covenanting is a continuing process, that we do not just arrive at a deep relationship and that's it! By showing that even a covenanting partnership can move from level to level, the double ceremony under the *ḥuppa* may have served to remind the couple and the community that their new partnership would have to keep changing and deepening.

From the twelfth century to the twenty-first, the wedding ceremony has stayed essentially the same. It's not difficult to discern in the ritual the familiar fourfold pattern: The couple leave the ordinary community to enter the sacred space of the *ḥuppa*. There the two join in an intense encounter with each other and with God, an encounter that melts them into a new persona. The two of them fulfill and enact this newness by going off together into a secluded space, and only after that do they rejoin the community.

In many communities, there are more elaborations of the ceremony. The community is readied for the forthcoming marriage on the Shabbat just before, when the groom (or the couple) may have an *oyfrufns* (Yiddish for "calling up") to the Torah for one *aliya*. As the blessings after reading Torah are completed, the community throws candy or flowers, singing,

> *Siman tov u-maẓal tov u-maẓal tov u-siman tov (3)*
> *Y'hey lanu*
> *Y'hey lanu, y'hey lanu, u-l'ḥol Yisra-el (2)*

A good star and a good constellation
May there be for us and for all Israel.

Among Ashkenazim, the custom arose that on the wedding day, just before or after the acquisition of the *k'tuba*, the groom would lead a men's group in Torah-study—the *hossen's tisch*, or table. Often this becomes a comedy of Purimtorah, as the groom's friends interrupt him, suggest false inferences from the Talmud, quote nonexistent verses from the Torah—all to suggest that on the day of his marriage his head could not possibly be on serious Torah.

Then the groom is accompanied to visit the bride, who is being adorned among the women. He first looks into her face. At least folk-lorically, this careful gaze prevents any errors along the lines of the substitution of Leah for Rachel in the marriage of Jacob. Nowadays, some couples turn this gaze into a time when their friends can help them see deeply the "seventy" different faces each may wear—angry, curious, joyful, grieving, lustful, bored. This version of *kabbalat panim* (receiving faces) may help strengthen a marriage that must survive and grow through the emergence of all these faces, not just the "nice" ones.

After the older version of this gazing, the groom does what in Yiddish is called *bedeken di kala*—draws a veil over the bride's face, while he, the officiating rabbi, and perhaps the women, chant the blessing that Rebekah's family sang to her just before she left to marry Isaac: *"Ahoteynu! At ha-vi l'alfey r'veva!"*—"Sister! May you grow into thousands of myriads!" (Gen. 24:60) For some couples today, each may come to honor and to "bedeck" the other. Then he (the *hatan*), followed by the bride, walks to the *huppa* (in many communities, set up outside, or under an open skylight that mimics the outdoors). The *m'sader kiddushin* chants: *"Mi adir al hakol, mi baruh al hakol, mi gadol al hakol, hu y'vareyh et hahatan v'hakala."*—"May that One Who is supremely mighty, supremely praised, and supremely great, bless this bridegroom and bride." The bride may walk in seven circles around her husband, suggesting fulfillment of the Messianic prophecy, "In that day a woman shall surround a man," and also invoking what the mystical Kabbalistic tradition calls the seven *s'firot*, or emanations of God: Overflowing loving-kindness, rigorous boundary-making, focused compassion, the rhythmic beat of eternity, the melodic flow of grace, connectivity, collectivity.

Then follow the *Erusin* and *nisu-in* ceremonies, interspersed with the public reading of the *k'tuba* and some Torah commentary and personal comments or wisdom from the *m'sader kiddushin*. If any of the couple's parents has died and so can not stand beneath the *ḥuppa*, there may be a chanting of *Eyl maleh raḥamim*, invoking their memory and picturing them at peace in God's Garden of Delight. Finally: the breaking of the glass, and the retirement of the new couple for *yiḥud*—"unity"—in a private room.

After joyful dancing (which the Talmud treats as an intrinsic part of the sacred ceremony) comes a meal together—again, a sacred celebration. The meal ends not only with the traditional *Birkat haMazon*, the Blessing of Sustenance, but with the addition of the *Sheva Braḥot*—this time with a little twirl in their order. The blessing over wine, which was recited first under the *ḥuppa*, is said last after dinner—as if to hint that the blessings have become a spiral.

For the next week, the *Sheva Braḥot* may be said again after any meal where some "new face" who had not been at the original wedding is present and wishes to rejoice in the marriage. (In our own day, when it is not uncommon for friends of the couple to live far away, some have stretched this time to a year.)

Recent Transformations

Modernity poses challenges to the character of many traditional Jewish ceremonies and life-paths—but perhaps most directly to that of marriages and wedding ceremonies. In this part of the life-cycle, we face changes in gender roles and sexual ethics, changes in the relationship of the Jewish people to other peoples, and changes in the relationship of the Jewish people to God.

Let us then look at how these three areas of change are affecting the nature of Jewish marriage, and therefore the Jewish wedding ceremony.

First: The Jewish community is more and more reorienting its value system toward treating women and men as equal and toward welcoming gay and lesbian Jews into full participation in the community. That is bound to challenge both the legal structure and the symbolism of the traditional wedding ceremonies.

The law and the ceremonies have for centuries been rooted in the model of an active man's acquiring access to an accepting (not quite passive) woman as sexual and emotional partner, in exchange for his financial protection and support of her. Facing the distance between that model and the one of a covenant between equals, Jews have done a considerable amount of experimentation in liturgy and with the *k'tuba* which has so long embodied the legal assumptions of traditional marriage.

Let us look at the *k'tuba* first. It was originally intended as a protection for women, who were economically and socially disempowered in traditional societies. In most recent Jewish contexts, the *k'tuba* text has become petrified, as a formula or mere decoration. For some, the traditional form has ceased to be meaningful at all, and in many Reform congregations the couple receive a marriage certificate from the rabbi that has no special connection to Jewish law. For some, the traditional *k'tuba* has become important in only one way: as a proof of Jewish identity for possible use as a "passport" in Israeli society, where the state, influenced by the Orthodox rabbinate, might demand such proof.

In this atmosphere, many Jewish couples who want to make financial agreements do so in civil law, with Western lawyers, not in a *k'tuba*. For some the *k'tuba* has been revived as a statement of love and devotion, in the couples' own words. Some couples have had it calligraphed, witnessed, and publicly displayed. Others have purchased a well-done poster equivalent with loving sentiments and lovely illustrations.

Some, however, have decided to go back to the roots of the *k'tuba* and to write a serious agreement between them about the issues of real concern—perhaps to be made public at the wedding, perhaps not. Such a "real-life *k'tuba*" might deal with questions of where the couple intend to live. And how they will care for ailing parents. And what they see as their civic and political responsibilities. And what they intend to be their relationships, emotional and financial, with stepchildren. And whether they intend to merge what they own and what they owe, or keep their money separate. And what they intend their sexual relationship to be like. And how they will deal with any intense disagreements that arise between them. And what arrangements they would make if, God forbid, they found it necessary to end their marriage. And whether they see these decisions as immutable, or open to change—by agreement? by the decision of either party? after a specified stretch of time?

Indeed, one way to write such a "real-life *k'tuba*" would be for the couple to make a list of the difficult issues between them—not the ones that have been easy to agree on—and then to work out together their answers to those questions. If they do this, the rabbi or other person they have asked to be their *m'sader*—or perhaps someone else entirely, a couples' counselor—might need to keep insisting that they face these issues, since blurring them might feel more comfortable in the short run.

There is one area of a "real-life *k'tuba*" that may need special attention in our generation because of the changing relationship of *adam* to *adamah*—of the human race to the earth of which we are one species, but the most powerful one. How will the new household relate to issues of consumption of resources in the present planetary crisis? Throughout Jewish history, this has been either an assumption or a question in the form of *kashrut*, the code of proper, kosher eating: For centuries, *kashrut* was assumed and the only question was: "How?" More recently, the question has become explicit: "Will our new household keep kosher, and if so according to what standards?"

And now a couple might ask, "Will our house be *eco*-kosher?"

What fuels will we use for heat, what vehicles for transport, what packaging? What do we think of genetically modified foods, of vegetables grown with pesticides? How much do we need to buy, how much can we reuse, how much can we recycle? Perhaps a real-life *k'tuba* can only begin to explore basic attitudes toward these questions, rather than working out every detail. But the conversation seems crucial. And it can influence decisions about the wedding celebration itself.

In another arena where a new world asks new questions, issues of women-men equality have called into question one major aspect of traditional Jewish divorce. We will deal with this in more detail in the chapter on divorce, but attempts to address it have had an effect on some contemporary *k'tubot*.

The problem is that traditionally, only a Jewish man has had the power to initiate a Jewish divorce, and that without a divorce or a certifiable death, a traditional woman cannot remarry. The result is that in traditional communities, the disappearance of a husband without credible information of his death, or a husband's refusal to initiate a Jewish divorce even if he has received a civil divorce, can prevent the wife's remarriage in a traditional context—forever.

To prevent this, Rabbi Saul Lieberman, a noted Conservative scholar, provided in 1954 for a conditional clause to be added to the *k'tuba* (*t'nai b'kiddushin*) that would permit the Conservative rabbinate's Rabbinical Court to impose damages for failure to obey its requirements in this area. The intention was to make this a civil contract enforceable in civil courts.

The Orthodox community has mostly refused to recognize the Lieberman *t'nai b'kiddushin*. Other attempts have been made to write such *t'na-im*, especially an effort by Rabbi Zalman Schachter-Shalomi aimed at a retroactive annulment of the marriage if either party refuses to initiate or accept a traditional divorce after a civil divorce is decreed, or if the husband disappears for a certain number of years. With the marriage annulled, the parties could remarry. In 1998, the Conservative rabbinate approved a partial version of this *t'nai b'kiddushin*.

In Jewish law, these issues arising from inequality in marriage and divorce are rather stark. But there are more subtle issues that may permeate a marriage but not quite surface in either "law" or "ritual." The long-established patterns of male dominance, in Jewish life and in society at large, can leave—even in couples who wish to be egalitarian—a deposit of automatic deference and dominance. For some couples, it may be important to flag these questions, even to look for them with heightened awareness, as more pervasive and more important than many others are likely to be. Even same-sex couples may find themselves falling into patterns that ape the old ones, with one of the pair dominant.

This is not to say that power is not a necessary part of all human interactions, including marriage. But power can be a dance—a circle dance, in which each dancer gets to step into the other's place—or it can be a frozen, rigid structure. The first is modeled on the God Whose name is "I Will Be Who I Will Be." The second is modeled on the frozen idols carved out from the Flow of life and told to stay put: eyes that cannot see, a nose that cannot breathe.

So we suggest that couples look deeply into the patterns they bring with them as they step toward the *huppa*, to see how to loosen and make fluid the dominance and deference they may have frozen into rigid place.

Now let us turn to recent changes in the liturgy of the wedding ceremony. The first major departure arising from the movement toward treating women and men as equal was the use of "double-ring" ceremonies in many Reform, Conservative, and Reconstructionist weddings. In many such ceremonies, the woman addressed the man with a reverse-gender version of the *Harey at* words of commitment: *"Harey ata m'kudash li b'taba-at zo, k'dat Moshe v'Yisra-el."* As each gave the other a ring and pronounced this formula, the atmosphere of *kinyan*, of acquisition and inequality, was, in many eyes, eliminated.

Indeed, most Orthodox authorities have agreed, and for that very reason have refused to permit the exchange of rings. For, they argue, in such an exchange 1−1 = o, that is, one *p'ruta* (the minimum value of the ring) minus one *p'ruta* equals zero. Since *kinyan* is considered one of the indispensable elements of a halakhic marriage, the man is required to purchase something of value by handing over a commodity of value. Exchanging rings means that nothing of value has been handed over, and therefore nothing has been acquired. No marriage.

To circumvent this problem, some halakhically committed Conservative rabbis who also support the equality of women and men have had brides give a ring to their grooms without voicing the *Harey ata* formula, so this second ring becomes simply a gift, one accompanied by an emotionally strong but halakhically irrelevant passage that the bride chooses from the Song of Songs, or perhaps by the same prophetic passage from Hosea that accompanies the wearing of *t'fillin*:

> *V'eyrastih li l'olam,*
> *V'eyrastih li b'tzedek uv'mishpat,*
> *uv'hesed, uv'rahamim.*
> *V'eyrastih li be-emuna,*
> *v'yada-at et YHWH.*
> For I shall betroth you to Me forever;
> I shall betroth you to Me in uprightness and in
>   transformative justice,
> And in loyal love, and in compassion.
> I shall betroth you to Me in faithfulness,
> And you shall intimately experience the Breath of Life.

Some couples, finding these approaches still too redolent of the acquisitive model, have treated the *Harey at* formula as a quotation inside another declaration. For example, *"Va-ani hin'eni mey-kim et brit huppa itah: Harey at . . ."* That is, "Here! I lift up a covenant of *huppa* with you, 'Here—you are made holy . . .' " This attempt to turn the marriage into an egalitarian *b'rit* draws upon the language of God's covenant with Noah, with the whole human race, and with all living, breathing life.

The feminist theologian and liturgist Rachel Adler, however, argues that the acquisitive mode is still visible and palpable at the root of all these versions. Even the most egalitarian of double-ring ceremonies, she suggests, means that in some sense each person is "acquiring" a property right in the availability of the other. So she has suggested looking elsewhere for a metaphor of marriage. In ancient days, she points out, it was possible to make a business contract between equals. Since no one was being acquired, *kinyan* was not a proper symbol. To seal such a contract, the two partners would each put something precious—coins, a ring—in a small bag. The mixture of property in the bag recognized the joining of two partners, and the bag itself symbolized the relationship. So she urges that today, two partners who intend to be equal in their marriage use this ritual. Along with the changed symbol may come a different affirmation to begin the relationship. When Rabbi Sue Levi Elwell and Nurit Shein used the Adler symbols, they affirmed to each other: *"Harey at m'kudeshet li, bifney k'hilat kodesh ɀu."*—"Here! You are set apart for me, in the eyes of this holy community." And others might use other language focused on *b'rit*, covenant.

In the last years of the twentieth century, reassessment of the nature of marriage was not restricted to questioning the old assumption of inequality between women and men. Three other assumptions were also questioned: the assumptions that sexual relationships other than marriage are forbidden or unholy; the assumption that a Jewish marriage cannot be created between two men or two women; and the assumption that there is no Jewish way to affirm or celebrate a marriage between a Jew and someone of another religious or ethnic community.

First, the issue of nonmarital sexual relationships. This is having an effect on wedding ceremonies directly, because the blessing for *Erusin* is so strongly focused on the prohibition of sexuality without the *huppa*. Most Jews in the world today have had sexual relationships before marriage and do not feel guilty about them; most have probably had an ongoing sexual relationship with the person they are marrying. When most American Jews could not understand the Hebrew, and most translations bowdlerized it, this was usually ignored. Now that more Jews do understand what they (or the *m'sader*) are reciting, some have decided to change the wording. One simple response has been to leave out the passage about prohibited sexuality, and use just the conclusion of the blessing: *"Baruḥ ata YHWH m'kadesh amo Yis-rael al y'dey ḥuppa v'kiddushin"*—"Blessed are You, YHWH our God, Who makes the People Israel holy through the power of *ḥuppa* and *kiddushin* [the marriage canopy and separation/sanctification]."

More deeply, some Jews have begun to explore the possibility of renewing an ancient tradition of *pilegesh* relationship—a sexual rela-tionship other than marriage that does not require the elaborate arrangements of either secular or Jewish divorce, but can be ended by the decision of either party. When women were socially and econom-ically disempowered, the rabbis were generally hostile to this practice because women in a *pilegesh* relationship were not protected. But in an era when women are economically and socially equal to men, the *pilegesh* form makes them (and men) more independent.

There is no traditional ceremony for entering *pilagshut*, and the whole point may be to keep the relationship relatively fluid, not sub-ject to communal formality. But a statement between the couple about what they do expect from each other, made perhaps in the presence of close friends, might make sense. And if they have chosen to live to-gether, they might together affix a *mezuza* to the doorpost of their newly shared home. Such a gentle announcement of a further step in the relationship might be a life-affirming way to draw on Jewish tradi-tion in a new context.

The emergence of Jewishly celebrated gay and lesbian relation-ships opens profound questions for the underlying assumptions about Jewish families, marriages, and *halaḥa*. Same-sex marriage raises some extraordinary questions about the nature of a *k'tuba*. It might not, however, lead to radical changes in the ceremonies of committed life-partners.

Concerning what we have called a "real-life *k'tuba*," a gay or les-bian couple faces special issues because very few jurisdictions have the elaborate legal and institutional fabric concerning child custody, finances, inheritance, health care, divorce, etc., for committed same-sex relationships that they do for heterosexual marriages. What would be an effective "real-life *k'tuba*" for heterosexual couples can assume the existence of these legal arrangements; a "real-life *k'tuba*" for same-sex couples would have to include such arrangements in the *k'tuba* it-self, give them the force of civil contract, and put the practical and emotional and spiritual weight of the Jewish community behind them. At a minimum, pre-marriage Jewish counseling for same-sex couples will have to address issues it probably would not address for hetero-sexual couples.

In an unexpected way, the decision by some Jewish communities to validate same-sex Jewish marriages would place those communities in a relationship to society in general that has some odd parallels to the Jewish situation during the Middle Ages. In those days, the non-Jewish state allowed Jewish communities to create their own civil as well as religious law. In this contemporary situation, and in this one area, Jewish communities might have to create ongoing Jewish case law to address many of the practical issues that are likely to arise.

In regard to wedding ritual, on the other hand, the challenge may not be so deep. Since a spectrum of ways to shape the wedding cere-mony already exist among heterosexual couples, ranging from tradi-tional to radical, many same-sex couples may simply be able to choose some point along the spectrum. It is also true that some gay couples have worked out their own new "commitment" or "covenant" cere-monies, drawing on passages from the religious tradition and from secular Jewish poetry and from their own thoughts and writings to shape the liturgy of such ceremonies. For example, many lesbian wed-dings have used the "Whither thou goest, I will go" passage from the Book of Ruth. Now that rabbis and congregations have emerged that are ready to affirm same-sex relationships as Jewish marriages, more same-sex couples have chosen to use some version of the Jewish wed-ding ceremony—*huppa*, *Sheva B'rahot*, and all—to establish their new marriages.

The most obviously necessary change is in the text of several of the *Sheva B'raḥot*. Where the traditional form specifies bride and groom, this text and its translation (by the two of us, Arthur and Phyllis) do not. Other than this, a gay or lesbian couple might use any of the range of versions of the marriage service, from traditional to Rachel Adler's, that we have described. And a heterosexual couple might decide to use this broader, more inclusive version of the blessings. (The "gender" of God alternates here between masculine and feminine.)

B'ruḥa at YHWH, eloheynu ru-aḥ ha-olam, boreyt p'ri hagafen.
Blessed are You, Yahh our God, Breathing Spirit of the Universe, Who creates the fruit of the vine.

Baruḥ ata YHWH, eloheynu ru-aḥ ha-olam, shehakol bara liḥvodo.
Blessed are You, Yahh our God, Breathing Spirit of the World, Who infuses Radiance into all being.

B'ruḥa at YHWH, eloheynu ru-aḥ ha-olam, yotẓeret ha-adam.
Blessed are You, Yahh our God, Breathing Spirit of the Universe, Who shapes in earthiness the human spirit.

Baruḥ ata YHWH, eloheynu ru-aḥ ha-olam, asher yatẓar et ha-adam b'tẓalmo, b'tẓelem d'mut tavnito, v'hitkin lo mimeno binyan adey ad. B'ruḥa at YHWH, yotẓeret ha-alam.
Blessed are You, Yahh our God, Breathing Spirit of the Universe, who shapes humanity in Your image and likeness and enables us to renew creation by nurturing generations to come. Blessed are You, Yahh, Who shapes in earthiness the human spirit.

Sos tasis v'tagel ha-akara b'kibutẓ baneha l'toḥa b'simḥa. B'ruḥa at YHWH, m'samaḥat tẓi-on b'vaneha.
May all who are deeply rooted rejoice, for those they nourish will spring up to flower and be fruitful. Blessed are You, Yahh, Who gladdens Tzi-on with her offspring.

Samey-aḥ t'samaḥ rey-im ha-ahuvim [rey-ot ha-ahuvot],
k'sameyḥeḥa y'tzirḥa b'gan eyden mikedem. B'ruḥa at YHWH,
m'samaḥat dodim b'ahavatam [dodot b'ahavatan].

May these loving companions rejoice as did God's first creations
in the Garden of Delight. Blessed are You, Yahh Breathing Spirit
of the World, Creator of joy and gladness, Who enables lovers to
rejoice in their love.

Baruḥ ata YHWH eloheynu ru-aḥ ha-olam, asher bara sason v'simḥa,
ahuv v'ahuva, gila, rina, ditza, v'ḥedva, ahava, v'aḥva, v'shalom,
v'rey-ut. M'heyra YHWH eloheynu yishama b'arey Yehuda uv'ḥutzot
Y'rushala-yim kol sason v'kol simḥa, kol ohev v'kolahuv [ohevet
v'kolahuva], kol mitzhalot ahuvim [ahuvot] mey-ḥuppatam
[mey-ḥuppatan] v'shirey shalom mimishtey n'ginatam [n'ginatan].
B'ruḥa at YHWH, m'samaḥat dodim b'ahavatam [dodot b'ahavatan].

Blessed are You, Yahh our God, Breathing Spirit of the World,
Who creates the joy and gladness of soulmate and beloved—
merriment and song, dance and delight, love and harmony, peace
and fellowship. May all soon hear in the cities of Yehuda and the
courtyards of Y'rushala-yim the voice of joy and the voice of
gladness, the voice of lovers' jubilation from their *ḥuppa* and the
celebratory songs of peace. Blessed are You, Yahh, Who fills with
joy the cherishing of lovers.

When one of us—Phyllis—was *m'saderet kiddushin* for the
Elwell-Shein wedding, there was one powerful liturgical innovation
that we might want to explore for other uses. At the moment when the
m'sader kiddushin usually speaks "by the authority of the State and the
Jewish people," one of the rabbis present asked all the others to stand
with him to affirm the wedding—still then, and even today, a new departure. What they said was:

Harey aten m'kadashot aḥat lashniya v'eyney Yisra-el.
Here!—You have set each other apart from all others in the eyes
of the people of Israel.

L'shem she'nihnasten l'huppa ul'vrit ahuvot, keyn tizku lil'mod
ul'lamed Torah, ul'kayeym mitzvat tikkun olam.
As you have come under the *huppa* and signed this lovers'
covenant, may you continue to teach and to learn Torah and to
fulfill the *mitzva* of repairing the world.

Surely one reason for this collective affirmation was that the very
newness of the step called out for more than one authoritative person
to join in the path. But perhaps there was another, less explicit, less de-
liberate reason: Perhaps this was a step toward the whole community's
taking public responsibility for making a halakhic change that for
centuries only rabbis would have felt empowered to make. And indeed, in other contexts we have seen the *m'sader* ask the whole witnessing community to stand and to affirm in their common voice that
"By our authority" the couple is now wedded. What this step does is
to change, ever so gently, the locus of sacred authority to make
change happen. In itself that represents one transformative aspect of
the shift from Rabbinic Judaism toward some new form of Judaism.

Another of the great changes that Modernity has brought our generation is that the boundaries between the Jewish community and
other ethnic or religious communities—formerly very sharp—have
become much more permeable. Ghetto walls have dissolved into
something much more like the fringes on the corners of a prayer
shawl. Can these fringes be made into, not helter-skelter fuzziness, but
a new form of sacred connection?

There are two challenging aspects of these new fringes: When a
non-Jew converts to Judaism and marries a Jew, how does a Jewish
wedding ceremony relate to the convert's non-Jewish family? When a
non-Jew marries a Jew without converting, how does the Jewish community relate to the couple?

Out of past trauma and fear, the classic rabbinic attitude toward
the non-Jewish family of a convert to Judaism has been discomfort
and distance. But huge numbers of conversions to Judaism are being
experienced in this generation, along with a decreased sense of hostil-

ity and fear between the Jewish community and others. So, different attitudes have emerged, and with them at least one proposal for a change in liturgy at the wedding and afterward.

The rabbinic tradition has been to name a convert the child of Abraham and Sarah—as if his or her biological parents had vanished. In the wedding ceremony, calling out that person's name as *ben* or *bat Avraham v'Sarah* (as is traditional) could easily cause great pain to those parents and to their child who is about to be married. (We know of cases where one member of a couple has decided not to convert to Judaism before a wedding for that reason alone.) In fact, of course, the family of origin cannot (and, we would say, should not) be banished from one's life and background. One possible way of averting such pain and saying the real truth is adding to the name, after *ben* or *bat Avraham v'Sarah*, *"mimishpaḥat Jones"*—that is, naming the convert's family of origin.

As to an intermarriage between a Jew and someone who was born into another community and has chosen not to convert, there have been four major reactions in the Jewish world to this situation:

- Some, especially in Orthodox and Conservative circles but also among some Reform and Reconstructionist congregations, have said this is not an option, and that Jewish law and wisdom totally forbid participation in creating such a marriage.
- Some, especially in Reform, Reconstructionist, and Jewish-renewal circles, have responded to couples who commit themselves to shaping a Jewish home and children by using some version of the traditional Jewish wedding ceremony. Among changes that are sometimes made in such ceremonies is the omission of *"k'dat Moshe v'Yisra-el"*—"according to the practice of Moses and Israel" from the marriage affirmation, in order to signal that this marriage departs from Jewish practice.
- Some rabbis have been willing to be present at secular wedding ceremonies, to make a connection between the new couple and the Jewish community without treating this as a Jewish marriage.

- And some rabbis have conducted a wedding ceremony that is totally different from the traditional Jewish ritual but draws on one strand of Torah that addresses the connection of all human beings and all life to covenant with God: the tradition of Noah and his family. Not only Biblical but Rabbinic Judaism saw this tradition as embodying *sheva mitzvot b'ney No-ah*—seven specific obligations that human beings from other than Jewish communities owe to each other and to God.

From this seedling, one of us (Arthur), working with two other rabbis, created a ceremony that uses only the Noah/flood/Rainbow story and symbols. Through sharing earth (olives), ocean (a cup of water), air (a breath, a kiss), and fire (a candle) under the sacred space of a Rainbow Arc, two who come from different families of the children of Noah can choose a new way to encounter God directly while also encountering a covenanting partner. No one could mistake this ceremony for the traditional Jewish wedding. No one could mistake it for the legal formula of a secular state, devoid of Spirit.

Still another change wrought partly by Modernity is the increased likelihood of crisis and transformation in a marriage. As we explained in the Preface in talking about our own marriage and the writing of this book, marriages themselves may go through upheavals and rebirths, midlife transformations. As new possibilities unfold and new identities emerge in one or both of the partners, the original covenant between them may no longer accurately describe their relationship. In traditional societies, most people did not transform themselves during one lifetime. During the Modern age, greater social complexity and more focus on individualism have encouraged such changes of identity. Moreover, so long as marriages still focused on a man, even his self-transformation might not require a transformation in the relationship. His wife might simply follow his lead. But when two different people, with approximately equal social power, live their lives in a context of invitation to self-transformation, upheavals in a marriage become much more likely.

Sometimes these upheavals end the marriage. Since each marriage is an important public and communal fact, the dissolution of any marriage requires a public and communal acknowledgment. And so for divorce, there has long been a ritual for a legal and, if it is well done, a spiritual dissolution of the marriage. In the next section of this book, we describe how the Jews of dim and recent pasts and of the present have dealt, are dealing, with this separation and this ceremony.

But sometimes the marriage may survive through change, and the covenant be renewed. For living through an earthquake in a marriage, for surviving the quake through renewal of the covenant and the transformation of the marriage, there has been no ceremony. Perhaps most people who have lived through such a process have felt too fragile. If the public did not need to know, as it did in the case of a divorce, couples' desire for privacy has meant that public rituals were unlikely.

As we said in our Preface, for us this book itself—our writing of it—became a kind of transformational ritual. Yet clearly not everyone will be in a position to do it this way. Are there other ways?

Retreats and workshops for marriage renewal have begun to appear. They are much more micro-communal than the outpouring of people at a wedding, and perhaps less likely to invoke the Spirit. In a sense they may accomplish what we have called the writing of a "real-life *k'tuba*," a rethinking and revised agreement on the pattern of a life together. The most obvious ritual for the renewal of a marriage would seem to be the renewal of the *huppa* ceremony, new real-life *k'tuba* and all. In some congregations it has become the practice for a number of couples to "renew their vows" simultaneously. But such events are usually scheduled according to the calendar—in the seventh year of marriage, say—rather than according to the internal rhythms of the couples concerned. Perhaps if a couple wishes to celebrate its ability to dance through an earthquake and come out on new solid ground, the couple should invite their closest friends to witness the ceremonial renewal of their relationship.

And finally, how are changes in the Jewish encounter with God affecting marriage, an encounter with another human being? It is no accident that Jewish tradition has described Sinai as the moment when Israel stood beneath the *ḥuppa* of Cloud and Fire, to accept the Torah as its *k'tuba* from the Holy One. If Sinai was the Great Wedding, then each wedding is a small Sinai; and if the Jewish people begins to think of Sinai in new ways, then it must also think of weddings and marriages in new ways.

For many Jews, both formal theology and the popular understanding of God seem to be shifting in the direction of experiencing God as more immanent, more Within and Between, less Beyond. Many of us sense ourselves as "overlapping" with God or being included within God, rather than meeting a God who is outside us.

We cannot yet be sure where these experiences are taking us in shaping the liturgies and forms of marriage. They seem already to have seeded such metaphors for God as *ru-aḥ ha-olam*, "Breath of the World," and *Eyn ha'Ḥa-yim*, "Wellspring of Life." They have awakened us to the Song of Songs as more than a mere allegory of love between God and the People Israel, more than a mere wedding song for two human beings, but as, more deeply, a hymn to joyful, loving pleasure, an invitation to the presence of holiness in all the relationships of human beings with each other and the earth. These experiences may already be encouraging such ceremonial changes as the *kabbalat panim* that unveils the many faces of ourselves to our partners, rather than revealing and seeing only one "correct" face. Or the ceremonial change in which the authority to affirm a wedding as valid and complete is diffused into an entire witnessing community, not just a single rabbi.

They may be encouraging us to see "former" in-laws and "ex"-grandparents (and even in some cases ex-spouses) as still parts of the family, when the family gathers for a wedding. Or they may be giving heart to some tiny experiments in cluster relationships where friendship and family overlap.

As the great life-cycle of the Jewish people moves through turnings measured in millennia, the markers of each Jew's individual life-cycle, measured in decades, also change their form.

~ 8 ~

Binding Souls Together

I N   T H E   E N T I R E   B I B L E, there is one story of an extraordinary
friendship that comes together not because of family but despite it,
not even by reason of a shared future but in the teeth of destiny. It
is the story of Jonathan and David.

So extraordinary is this story that in our own generation people have wondered whether their relationship was also sexual, especially since David wails when he hears of Jonathan's death,
"Your love was wonderful to me, more than the love of women."
(II Sam. 1:26)

The text of the story, in First and Second Samuel, leaves this mysterious. It certainly never spells out a sexual relationship; but it never
says there wasn't one. What it does say is, "Now Jonathan's own self
[*nefesh*: life-essence, life-breath, soul] had become bound up with
David's self, so that Jonathan had grown to love David like his own
self." (I Sam. 18:1) Perhaps the ambiguity about a sexual relationship
is itself a teaching to us, as if the tale is telling us:

Their souls connected; that is what you need to know. Sometimes
souls connect between two men, sometimes between two
women, sometimes between a woman and a man.
Sometimes souls connect in a sexual relationship; sometimes not.
Sometimes souls connect in a nonsexual friendship; sometimes
not. Perhaps they connect in a marriage, perhaps not.
But at a deeper level, all these "sometimes" and "perhapses"
simply do not matter. When souls connect, take time to honor
the connection.

The Talmud (Pirkei Avot 5:19) commented on this friendship,
"Whenever love depends upon a material cause, when the material
cause vanishes, the love vanishes. But if it does not depend upon some
material cause, the love will not vanish, but remain forever. What love
depended on a material cause? The love of Amnon for Tamar. [Which
depended on sexual lust—one of King David's sons raped one of his
daughters.] And what love depended on no such cause? The love of
David and Jonathan." Today we might call this an I-Thou relationship, as distinct from one rooted in I-It: A relationship fully open to
the presence of and the Presence in each other, rather than one in
which the parties are using each other as tools for satisfaction or advancement.

This assessment by *Avot* is particularly striking in that both
Jonathan and David were central players in the great struggle for
power in the early Israelite monarchy. If ever there might have been a
"friendship" in which each might have been using the other as a tool, or
even less crassly keeping the troublesome other at arm's length,
this could have been so. Instead, in the world of material actuality,
Jonathan offers up his hopes of succeeding to the throne, affirming
David's kingship; and the two "cut a covenant in the presence of
YHWH." (I Sam. 23:16–18) Thus they reaffirmed the commitment
each had made to stay loyal to the other not only during their own lives
but into the futures of their families: "May YHWH be between me and
you, between my seed and your seed, for the ages!" (20:15–17, 42)

And there are other mentions in the Talmud of how life-giving is the love of a friend. In Baba Kama 92a, the sages teach: "One who entreats God's mercy for his fellow while he himself is in need of the same thing will be answered first, for it is said, 'YHWH changed the fortune of Job when he prayed for his friend.' " (Job 42:10)

Rabbi Joshua ben Levi said, Whoever sees a friend after a lapse of thirty days should say *"Sheheḥeyanu"* ("Blessed is the One Who has kept us alive till this moment"); after a lapse of twelve months *"meḥayeh hameytim"* ("Blessed is the One Who gives life to the dead"). This second blessing bears a little thought. At first, one might think that the dead person who has been revived is one's friend. But the blessing might mean, "I myself have been feeling deadened by your absence—parched for your presence. Blessed be the One Who has let me drink from the wellspring of your love again, Who has brought me back to life."

In our own generation, we may explore even more deeply the possibility that friends can become a central element in our lives—for some people, perhaps even filling the space that once a spouse or a sibling may, or may not, have filled. There are three reasons that more Jews may in our generation be drawn in this direction.

One is that for some people, the overwhelming focus of Jewish tradition on marriage may not accord with their deepest selves. Unlike some other religious traditions, Judaism has long defined marriage, rather than celibacy, as the most sacred life-path. Even the one respected scholar of the Talmud who was himself not married, Shimon ben Azzai, said that to abstain from begetting children was like shedding blood. (T.B. Sota 9:15) In our generation, in Modernity's individualist atmosphere, more people seem to tune in to their own individual wavelengths, even when these run counter to communal norms. So some people who might never have thought to question their own desires on this matter now may, and some who come to feel marriage is not their own soul's life-path are more likely to pursue another.

Secondly, in the bustle of Modernity many of us find ourselves so mobile that our sisters, our brothers, may or may not turn out to be our intimates. Many Jews in the past generation have created *ḥavurot* (informal fellowships for prayer and study) to be for them "intentional neighborhoods" that come together in time rather than space. In much the same way—but with more intensity—some have sought to create "intentional families," have sought to choose new brothers and new sisters.

Thirdly, even those who do feel deeply drawn toward marriage may also connect with a special friend who is not their spouse. David, after all, was himself engaged in several different passionately committed marriages, yet still felt deeply drawn to Jonathan. So an intimate friendship may not replace a marriage, but stand alongside it, and a beloved may not replace a spouse.

All these explorations have been happening around us, but often awkwardly. Here and there two friends have seen that they were more than friendly, were beloveds yet not romantic lovers, and have not known what to do about it. There has been no form, and certainly no ceremony, to affirm their understanding.

Yet surprisingly enough, the story of Jonathan and David offers us such a possibility. (For the story as a whole, read I Sam 18:1–6, 19:1–7, 20:1–21:1, 23:14–18; II Sam. 1:1–27.)

At the very beginning of their relationship—

And Jonathan and David cut a covenant, because of his love for him, like his own self. Jonathan stripped off the cloak that was upon him, and gave it to David, together with his uniform, his sword, his bow, and his belt. (I Sam. 18:1–4)

So we could create a ceremony, to be held with witnesses, in which the two beloveds could exchange some articles of clothing, and then follow up the hint of Baba Kama about Job: bless each other out of the deep knowledge each one has of what the other needs.

Such a decision could also include what Jonathan and David gave each other in the world of material actuality, as we have seen: a kind of *k'tuba* of inheritance and sharing. So even in this area, two intimate friends could draw on Jewish tradition in paralleling the commitments that are otherwise made in entering marriage.

We have suggested that the heart of the Jewish life-path is the encounter with an Other, an I-Thou meeting that dissolves the previous Self so as to grow a more mature Self, just as a micro-version of such an encounter is at the heart of each life-marker along the path. If we encounter another human being in this way, says Buber, we are in that same moment encountering God.

So let us welcome the possibility that alongside marriage there may emerge another way in which this covenant may flower. Perhaps, drawing on the story of Jonathan and David, we should call it *B'rit haNefesh* (the covenant of soul, of life-breath) or *B'rit ha-M'il* (the covenant of the cloak).

As we danced with the story of these beloved friends, we found ourselves wondering about another biblical pair: Ruth and Naomi. To us this seemed another kind of intimate connection, based not upon a rough equality but on a different mode—Naomi so clearly a nurturing teacher, a mothering guide, to her daughter-in-law. So this story too can become a model for an I-Thouing encounter with an Other.

The question is, to what kind of I-Thouing does the story beckon us? Certainly it was inevitable that in our own generation we would notice. Whereas in the Bible overall, women rarely come into their own; here not merely one but two women are clearly limned and honored. Some, indeed, have seen in this story a warrant for a kind of marriage that most of Jewish tradition has disdained until our day. So it is that the promise Ruth makes to Naomi—"Whither you go, I will go; where you sleep, I will sleep; your people will be my people and your God my God; where you die, there shall I be buried"—has been used in wedding ceremonies between two women.

Beyond this, we ourselves see in this story an archetype of loving relationship across the generations, more clearly loving than any of the Bible's fraught parent-child relationships. We suggest their story be seen as a model for the kind of teacher-learner relationship in which both the elder and the younger partner love and grow. As Naomi guides Ruth, so Ruth fulfills Naomi.

Though the Talmud describes many teacher-student pairs, few are shown with such loving care for each other. The rabbinic pair of Jonathan the Fair and Resh Lakish, for instance, explodes into competitive jealousy and lethal depression, leaving both dead and their heroic friendship thwarted.

What makes the Ruth-Naomi relationship so extraordinary? Perhaps the fact that it fuses fate and choice. They are family—but they could choose to step out of the family tie, as Orpa does in the story. Instead, they choose to make it much stronger. From the place of choosing, they invest their relationship with the sense of destiny. From the place of family, they invest their relationship with the sense of commitment.

So we encourage teachers who meet the student of their dreams, learners who meet the teacher of their lives, to suffuse their search for knowledge with the familial milk of loving-kindness. And we also encourage those family members who miraculously "click"—parents-in-law with children-in-law, grandchildren with grandparents, aunts and uncles with nephews and nieces—to suffuse their relationship with self-awareness and reflection.

And we encourage both those who enter from the place of learning and those who enter from the place of family to draw on the story of Ruth and Naomi as a source of sustenance and celebration. Perhaps reciting its words of commitment can help them water their relationship; perhaps relearning the story together, year by year, can help them think through its implications.

Still more deeply, we encourage all of us to open ourselves to the possibility of this kind of relationship as another pathway of encounter with the Other. Alongside marriage, alongside the intimate friendship of equals, may we place this tale of mentoring in all its depth, human and divine.

PART 3

∿

Harvesting a Life

~ 9 ~

Fulfillment in Midlife

I N OUR LIFE-JOURNEY, beginning a marriage and binding souls together in intimate friendship can be moments of intense encounter, of Meeting, when our previous Self melts into a new shape.

Then we get to walk in those new shoes, and to explore our new Selves. We get to do on a larger life-map what a baby does as its new name is called aloud; what the Bar/Bat Mitzvah does by speaking a new *d'var Torah* for all the world to hear; what the married couple does by entering a room alone; what the Jewish people does each year at Sukkot.

We get to affirm on the life-map of an entire lifetime this harvest, this fulfillment, and to give it a higher clarity. Perhaps we even get to do it in a special ceremony, marking the maturity of the middle of our lives.

For some of us, that new sense of maturity may mean new work, a new career, leaving behind the skills we have accumulated to test out others that we don't yet know. For others, it may mean a new place, even moving across a continent or an ocean, leaving communities not only of birth-family but of work and friendship and celebration, communities we may have spent decades forming.

And for any of us, the maturity could be embodied not in a new choice, but in a new uncertainty. The maturity of openness and pausing. For after all, it may be that deciding to continue in the same place, in the same work, but with a new sense of devotion and intention, will turn out to be our true midlife transformation. When new possibilities open before us, are they really what we mean to explore? And how can we find out?

As we said at the beginning of this book, in our chapter on the *b'rit* of babyhood, there was one Jewish event in the ancient past that could be understood as having played the same role in the course of a lengthy life-span as the moment of naming the baby plays in the briefer time of a *b'rit* ceremony, the same role as Sukkot plays in the course of the year. That event was Abraham's "covenant between the parts," which came in midlife, when he was still Abram, and which predated even *B'rit Mila* as a ceremony in a Jewish life.

But until recently, no one had used the *B'rit Beyn haB'tarim* in this way, and there was no Jewish time set aside specifically for a midlife celebration. Indeed, it was only in our own generation, responding to lengthened life-spans and to the anxieties of Jewish women who felt both tugged and frightened by the possibilities of choosing new life-paths and careers in middle age, that Irene Fine suggested drawing in some limited ways on Abraham's experience to shape a Jewish midlife ceremony.

Why did *B'rit Beyn haB'tarim* slumber in disuse for all this time, and why had no one since Abraham felt the need for a midlife ceremony till now?

The connection between the two *b'rit* ceremonies may suggest the answer. Abraham's *B'rit Beyn haB'tarim* came as the most intense moment in a cascade of covenants, culminating in the announcement of *B'rit Mila*. It came to announce Abraham's entrance into a time of generativity, when he himself would beget a child and many, many offspring.

Why was this *b'rit* needed? (Most children of the time were evidently born without requiring a mystical announcement or a covenant.) Because this period of Abraham's life had been so long delayed. He had lived so long that he now had a "midlife."

For most people of his era, having children was itself their midlife fulfillment. At the biological level, it was the third step in the four-step dance of life: (1) A newborn grows to the point of (2) sexual relationship; (3) from this relationship a new child is born; (4) the parent dies. For Abraham, this biological fulfillment was so long delayed that it became doubtful. And in the process, Abraham's life became much more complex than sheer biology.

Let us look more closely at what happened. The turning point of Abram's life had come much earlier, when he and Sarai responded to God's call (*"Leḥ l'ḥa"*—"Walk forth into your self!") and left behind their country and their kinfolk to journey into "a land that I will show you": a question mark. This deep encounter with each other and with God, however, had so far produced but little fruit. A strange adventure in Egypt which nearly lost the two of them their marriage; a troubled but enduring relationship with Abram's cousin Lot; a local war with petty kings; a blessing from a priest of ancient lineage. And a challenge to God: "Do Your promises of offspring and prosperity have any meaning?"

From this challenge unwound one of the most uncanny tales of Torah. (Gen. 15)

God said to Abram, "Take for Me a three-year-old heifer, a three-year-old nanny-goat, and a three-year-old ram, plus a turtle-dove and pigeon." Abram split the cow, the goat, and the ram in two. He laid each one's half all but touching to its neighbor: a narrow passageway between the walls of flesh. The birds he did not split. Perhaps he did not even kill them. A vulture swooped down upon the carcasses. Abram drove it away.

As the sun began to set, Abram fell into a deep trance. Deep horror, fear, great darkness fell upon him. God told him a dark prophecy shot through with glimmers of bright possibility: For his offspring, four centuries of exile and slavery, and only then redemption. For himself, a life fulfilled so that he would go to his forebears in peace, and be buried in a good ripe age.

And the sun set. Night-blackness fell. A smoking oven, a fiery torch, crossed over between these parted chunks of flesh.

That very day God promised Abram that his offspring would inherit the land between the rivers: the River Nile of the Land of Tight and Narrow Places, *Mitzra-yim*, Egypt, and the Great River of Practical Precision—the Euphrates.

Only after the *B'rit Beyn haB'tarim* did there come the announcement of the first of those offspring, Ishmael, "God Hearkens." It took years more for the announcement of a second, Isaac, "Laughing One." And for new names to be given "Sarah" and "Abraham." Yet somehow it all unfolded from the covenant between the parts.

What happened in that uncanny moment?

We, Phyllis and Arthur, try to see the scene more clearly, more darkly. Two great hills of flesh, ram and goat and cow, male and female. Raw, bloody. Two small and uncut birds, a dove and pigeon. Abram. Dazed. In trance.

Where?

Maybe between the two hills of flesh. Dying in the darkness. Yet moving slowly through the birth canal whose walls enclose him. Moving upward, a sperm aiming toward the hidden fertile center? Moving downward, a new birth aiming toward the airy breathing open? Giving new life, new breath, new birth, to his own self? Looking up as smoke rose like a pillar from the bleeding meat, looking up again as a flash of fire engulfed it? Darkness, blood, death, smoke, fire, rebirth. Echoes of Exodus, Going-forth from Narrows.

Or was he watching from outside, watching as the dove and pigeon, those two small beings, heaved between the two great carcass-sections? A sign of births to come? Of Ishmael and of Isaac?

A new self, born from the self that had been unable to beget. Born *because* he had been unable to beget.

Abram had been a shepherd, a cowherd, a goatherd, wandering amid the meadows and oases. The very products and companions of his labor, he had split. Destroyed them, left them open to the searching eye. They had been no more fulfilling than his body's workings in the tent of Sarai. He had to go beyond them to fulfill them, to bring new meaning and fulfillment to his life.

Only after the "covenant between the parts" do we meet the Abraham we know. The one who struggles with Hagar and Sarah, meets God's messengers with bread and butter, pancakes and veal; once more risks his wife into a royal harem, argues with God lest the righteous die in Sodom, swears oaths of peace that bring a well into the family, endangers the life of one child and then another, bargains to buy a grave to bury Sarah.

In the covenant between the parts, he has become himself. Identified, fulfilled. Able to live because he knows how to die. Able to die because he knows how to live.

What does this mean for us today?

Before we pursue this, let us pause for another question—one that probably occurred to few wrestlers-with-Torah before our own generation. What was going on for Sarai?

We can actually hazard some answers to this question. By the time God's messengers are prophesying Isaac's birth, Sarai is beyond menopause. (Gen. 18:11) But just when did her menstrual periods come to an end? We cannot tell for sure; but let us remember that this process begins in Gen. 15:2–3, when Abram challenges God's assurances. Abram says that so far as he can see, his heir will not come from his body, as God promised, but only from the domestic arrangements he has made—and only a foreigner, Damascus-born, at that. Not only are Abram's thoughts rebellious; his words themselves are bitterly ironic. It is reasonable to guess that he is moved to irony because he *knows* the promise of an heir has turned sour; he knows that Sarai has reached menopause. Before now it was reasonable to hope; from now on, it will take a miracle. So we may easily imagine that for Sarai, the moment of midlife transformation came when she reached menopause, and it was her turning point that gave Abram his turning point.

But how might she have taken this moment as a time of celebration and of maturation? To this we shall indeed return, but with a special note that we do not intend to suggest what might have been assumed by ancient Torah, that women should pursue the biologic transformation of menopause and men the social-psychological-spiritual transformation of a *B'rit Beyn haB'tarim*.

Now let us go back to exploring what the "covenant between the parts" might mean to us.

From darkness and silence, trance and fire, the shattering of his own work and the suffering of his soul, Abram has been reborn into his fullest self. What could we imagine for someone facing, seeking, such a moment? We who have turned a knife into *B'rit Mila*, a brook into a *mikva*, a shattered wineglass into the emblem of a union—what might we do to shape a ceremony with these symbols?

Somewhere between the ages of forty-five and fifty-five, imagine the moment of a soul alone. All Jewish ceremony takes place in community, we say, but just this once perhaps we stand alone, as Abram did.

In the dark, beclouded in fire and in smoke.

What may be our ram, our goat, our cow? The solid ruminative works we have already taken pride in? Will we slay the work we have done in order to explore the possibility of a new shape to our lives?

Our dove and pigeon? Perhaps the tiny fluttering uncertainties we can feel in the trembling of our bellies?

What might be our trance? A meditative silence? Outside? All night? Beneath a sky so filled with mystery it may bear vultures? So many stars—the numbers of the possibilities that are aborning? Or the distance between us and the denouements we wish for?

Can we find a guide who will take us into these uncertainties, will warn us that there is suffering and exile yet to come, but that we can take comfort in good lives and see broader boundaries outstretched before us?

Living through a night of darkness, perhaps a week of silence crowned by one dark silent wakeful night . . .

At the darkest moments just before the dawning, can our guide or we ourselves set on either side of us two rows of roaring torches, rows of *Havdala* candles to mark a separation between the pregnant person we have been becoming all our lives and the newborn person we have snatched from the dying of old selves?

We can begin to shape the grammar of such a midlife ceremony of new selfhood.

The seeker asks a ritual question, and receives a ritual answer:

"Adonai YHWH, ma titen li?"

"My Lord, Breath of Life, what will you give me?"

"Al tira. Anohi mageyn lah."

"Fear not. *I* will be a shield to you."

Then the seeker piles up two large and bulky rows of symbols of the past: "habits," in the form of clothing; jewelry; books, recordings, photographs; some tools of work: enough to make the heart pound and the stomach flutter.

The seeker sits down between these rows of life solidified.

Darkness. Night. Silence.

And a flare of fire just before the dawning. In the unknown, in the mystery, is new light.

The message that arises in the smoke and flame. A warning, a promise. Only the seeker can hear the meaning, record it, choose to tell or not to tell the story.

For Abram and Sarai, the turning points came from a dance of midlife change. Her menopause. His bafflement. What might Sarai have done to give meaning to her menopause while Abram was falling into trance and reverie? In our own generation, women struggling to make midlife changes open up the landscape for men to change as well. What are the women doing as they reach menopause?

Phyllis recalls: As the moon hovered on the edge of Hanukkah, thirty-six—a magical number—of my women friends assembled to celebrate not only the Festival of Light, not only my fiftieth birthday, but also my menopause. Thirty-six women joined together to end an age-old silence. We had gathered not only to speak about menopause but also to celebrate it. Just as my journey beyond menstruation was still unknown to me, so this ceremony I had just created was a journey still unknown to them.

Why did I think it was so important to end the silence about menopause? Three months before my thirteenth birthday, I "got the curse" and "became a woman," to use two common euphemisms about menstruation. My mother whispered the news to her friend Selma and to Mrs. Goldstein who lived next door, and it was thus that I learned about "women's things"—and about whispering. In my seventh-grade classrooms, other girls/women were, like me, embarrassed to talk about the changes that had, or had not yet, happened to them. Nothing could have been more on our minds and less on our lips.

Silence is profound. When we cannot speak about what is happening in our bodies, in our hearts, and in our souls, we draw some reasonable but damaging conclusions. We learn that what is public is limited to the world of our minds and, more likely, to the most superficial layers of our minds. We then begin making the distinction between the inner, consuming conversations we have alone or with an intimate few, and the outer disconnected ones we have with others. The disconnections are not only from others but also from ourselves: We lose the at-one-ment we could feel when we perceive ourselves whole and holy in relation to others.

For much of my adult life, I have wanted to speak about the unspeakable. I have longed to move the body and the emotions and the spirit out of the shadows, where they appear hidden, trivial, shameful, even dirty, into the sunlight, where they are real, important, central, and acceptable. For me, the process of making an inner experience public helps me to see my experience as normal, to speak my experience with passion and sureness, and to feel myself integrated within and without.

In my forty-ninth year, as I began to experience the ending of my menstruations, I decided to break through the silence hovering over this passage, with two circles of friends: women, ranging in age from twenty-one to fifty-eight, gathered from all over the country and from various parts of my life, and the women and men of the P'nai Or Ḥavura and other members of the extraordinary Jewish Renewal neighborhood of Mount Airy in Philadelphia.

For the Mount Airy crowd, we held a Shabbat morning service and a Saturday night Hanukkah-and-birthday party. But in the late afternoon of Shabbat, which was on the winter solstice weekend and just before Hanukkah began, I gathered with my women friends to celebrate my menopause.

To these women I had proposed that we celebrate a *"seder* of womanhood"—the order of the stages of womanhood as I had experienced them in my life. As with the traditional Passover *seder* and the increasingly familiar Tu B'Shvat *seder*, we drank four cups of beverage as we told our individual stories. We are taught in *Pirkei Avot* that fifty is the age of advice-giving; but in keeping with modern feminist practice, rather than giving advice, we shared lessons we had learned from each stage of our woman-life.

For the first cup, I served a bright red sangria. (Cherry-apple cider was served to non–alcohol drinkers.) Sangria, the "drink" of my adolescence, represented my first stage of womanhood, menstruation. The group shared stories, some funny and some sad, about first periods and the silence around them; about later periods and their weightiness in our lives—hoping for them when we feared we might be pregnant, fearing them when we prayed we might be pregnant. We recognized ourselves again and again in each other's stories. Then we drank the first cup.

As we moved on, I suggested a guideline for the remaining three cups: Since everyone in the room had already reached the stage of menstruation, we had all been able to speak from our own experiences. For each of the following cups, women could speak only if they had already reached the stage of life represented by that cup.

The second cup, a sparkling champagne (sparkling apple cider for non–alcohol drinkers), was for my second stage of woman-life—the bubbly, heady introduction to sex and love. Again, we spoke about the silences that had heralded this stage of life: how little we had known about our own bodies, about our own pleasures, about the wide range of potential loving partners (women as well as men). This was not the bawdy, bragging talk of the locker room but rather the sad, sweet talk, long overdue, of innocence and ignorance, of surprise and delight.

The third cup, milk (soymilk for non–dairy drinkers), marked my third stage: pregnancy, childbirth, nursing, child-raising. Not surprisingly, we again spoke of silences—the silence of abortion, of adoption, of not having children, of the sensuality of nursing, of the passionate protection of and connection to our children.

The fourth cup, water (mineral water for purists), represented the totally open possibilities of the fourth stage of woman-life: menopause. Only about eight in the group had reached menopause, and there was a significant difference in our sharing. What I had imagined would be the most silent of the life-stages, and potentially the most depressing, now appeared quite the opposite.

The silence of menopause had already been broken publicly. In spite of our youth-centered culture, several books about menopause had appeared, as well as a *Newsweek* cover story focused on turning fifty. Many of us now felt about reaching fifty what Gloria Steinem felt at forty. "You don't look forty," someone remarked to her. She quipped, "This is what forty looks like!" Rather than experiencing an empty nest at the end of our biologically reproductive lives, many of us at my ceremony felt giddy with freedom, with the chance to forge a new path of our choosing, without obligations. We were asking ourselves, some for the first time, "What do we want to do with this new opportunity?"

While the menopause ceremony suffered some of the awkwardness and embarrassment that accompanies a lifetime of silence, it was also filled with laughter, sorrow, relief, and understanding. I hope the silence that has enveloped so many other important life-turnings will, by the strength of our ceremonies and rituals, our books and our conversations, be similarly broken. Ceremonies and rituals today, like those of old, make each life-stage a time for self-revelation, first to ourselves, then to one another, and then to the larger human community—for breaking out of the tyranny and alienation of silence.

At the end of the ceremony, I read a Marge Piercy poem. When at last that lifelong leak of blood comes to an end, she says, "I will secretly dance and pour out a cup of wine on the earth." Now the dance need no longer be secret. Now menopause may become what the title of her poem calls it: "Something to Look Forward To."

The two life-markers we have just described open up into fullness; they mark a harvest, and a new beginning. Some discussions of midlife passages address the opening to inward contraction, the stage beyond harvest that might be called "going to seed" or "becoming seed." We will explore this stage of life in Part IV. The differences are not absolute: Midlife is woven of too many threads for those of expansion and contraction to be easily disentangled from each other. But there is difference enough for us to pursue in the rest of this chapter some other efforts to celebrate the onset of a new spiral of creative possibility.

In our chapter on Bar and Bat Mitzvah, we mentioned the practice of "adult Bat Mitzvah." It has been undertaken by a growing number of women who grew up in a Jewish world where women did not publicly mark their entrance into the *mitzvot* of reading and learning Torah. Having watched over the years as their daughters, and women who might have been their daughters, were honored and celebrated by their congregations at this passage, many of this older generation have found joy in their own undertaking to learn and in celebrating the advent of a fuller equality for women in Jewish life.

Sometimes older men as well have chosen to take this step. It has drawn especially those men for whom their thirteen-year-old Bar Mitzvah moment was built of boilerplate, a mere recitation from rote memory of a passage from the Torah and of the *Haftara*, bereft of understanding or exploring. No wrestle and no dance. An empowerment that had no power in it.

So in many congregations of many sorts, men and women well versed in many pathways of the world but not in Jewish wisdom have decided to learn, and to share what they have learned. Increasingly, the practice is called becoming a *Bat Torah* or *Bar Torah*, leaving the phrase "Bar/Bat Mitzvah" for the moment of puberty when the Talmud says girls and boys become obligated to fulfill the *mitzvot*.

The *Bar/Bat Torah* practice is straightforward but, at its fullest, not easy. In its fullest version, it could mean learning to make sense of a passage from the Torah and/or one from the Prophets—at least enough biblical Hebrew to understand those specific passages; learning to chant them according to the two distinct traditional trops; learning to shape one's own responses to these passages into a coherent *d'var Torah*; and coming forward on a Shabbat or another day of Torah-reading to do the reading and to lead the congregation toward a deeper understanding of the passages.

But that is the most expansive possibility, and also in one sense the most limited. Since this is a midlife passage for a conscious and self-aware adult, it makes sense for the adult who is thereby shaping a future relationship to Judaism to shape what the event itself is like. In some cases, for example, groups of adults have studied together and shared responsibility for an entire service, thus lessening the burden on any one person and allowing each to choose a responsibility that seems especially fitting.

The *Bat/Bar Torah* experience could also be used not only to mark a transformed relationship to Judaism, but also to mark some other transformation in one's life. (Bat/Bar Mitzvah, analogously, marks a new relationship to the Jewish people—and also a new relationship to one's own body.) So this taking up of Torah could be connected with a change in career, arrival in a new community, a changed relationship with friends and family, and so on.

Since for any adult Jew the most notable occasion of being "Named" is being called up to the Torah, the *Bar/Bat Torah* process offers an additional midlife possibility: changing one's name. The Talmud teaches that just as *t'shuva*, *t'fila*, and *tz'daka*—turning one's life away from misdeeds, prayer, and assisting the poor—so also might changing one's name avert the dangers of severe divine judgment that loom so large at Rosh Hashana. In some traditional synagogues, a sick person might do this so as to avert death.

But it does not take mortal illness to teach us that changing our name can change our identity, our destiny. The David Gruen who became David Ben-Gurion, the Cassius Clay who became Muhammad Ali, the millions of women who have changed names when they married, teach us that. Often the hardest part of a name change (as Muhammad Ali discovered) is getting other people to accept your new identity.

So a *Bat Torah* or *Bar Torah* might take this midlife moment to rethink the name s/he was given soon after birth, and to explore new possibilities. Could my name express more fully who it is I hope to be, or who I am already? Is it my Hebrew name, or my English name, that jangles—or . . . ?

Standing before the congregation; being called to the Torah by a new name; and (after reading from the scroll) explaining the new name might be followed by asking the congregation to repeat the name aloud three times. In Jewish folklore, three times is a *ḥazaka*—a strong and potent assertion of a custom or a truth. So this threefold repetition can make the name change real.

In some midlives, we discover that we can change not by changing our names or our personas but by uncovering the persons who we have always been. We can enter a new life-stage by becoming in public the person we already are in private. Unmasking then becomes a ritual of growth.

During the past generation, this process became particularly well known in reference to gay men, lesbians, and others whose sexual lives did not fit into the census check-off boxes of M and F. The ceremony even took on a label: "coming out of the closet."

In one community we know, this became a Jewish event. In 1985, during a weeklong summer gathering of several hundred members of the movement for Jewish renewal, gay and lesbian participants slowly became convinced that the gathering was "safe space." By Shabbat, they had decided that those who were still closeted could trust the wider community to welcome them as who they really were, and at the same time preserve their confidentiality in other circles where jobs, friendships, families might be at stake.

So they chose to "come out" through a group *aliya*, a rising to the level of Torah-reading. They chose the passage "You shall love your neighbor as yourself," as the one they would arise to. One by one they came up, said their names aloud, and recited the blessings for the Torah-reading—mostly with tremors and with trepidation.

After the Torah passage had been read, each explained what aspect of themselves they had been hiding. Others in the community affirmed their action and the fullness of their membership in the Jewish community, by pinning lavender triangles on themselves. (These triangles were at that point for many gay people a symbol of victimization, resistance, and especially a comradeship with Jews, since the Nazis had compelled gay people to wear them as they compelled Jews to wear the Star of David.)

As the newly uncloseted participants explained their selfhood, others in the gathering were moved to unveil themselves as well.

The chanting of the blessings that came after the reading of the Torah was far different: As the whole community felt itself more whole and holy, the blessings became joyful and triumphant.

Phyllis recalls: Several years before, I had discovered that unmasking an aspect of myself that was not sexual—at least not explicitly sexual—was an astonishingly liberating act.

For me, the transformation came not in one ceremony but in two: one so public that I was practically anonymous; one—even scarier—among my closest friends.

I needed to unmask, because twenty years before, when I was twenty, I had put on a mask. Almost literally: I had put on a wig.

The summer I was twenty years old, my hair fell out in clumps.

Only a week after my senior year began, I was totally bald. Year by year from then on, I hid beneath a wig. Year by year, handmade wig by handmade wig. The wigs hid my baldness from others; they hid my self from myself.

The rest of my hair went too—I have no memory of exactly when. For I felt that if my body was going to treat me so shabbily, I was going to divorce myself from it. Forget it.

Having lost my hair, I believed I had lost my worth.

Slowly, subtly, my life began to contract as I learned how to hide from others. I stole in and out of dorm showers at odd hours when no one else was around to see me take off my wig, wrap it in a towel, and stealthily wash my head. Although the wig was often uncomfortably tight and warm, I kept it on even in the privacy of my room.

I began to fear being discovered, uncovered. Most of all, I was afraid that my stock on the social market had crashed and that I would never marry.

At a party, I was dancing joyously with a young man I was interested in. The speed of the dancing increased until, dizzy, I fell to the ground, and my wig bounced off. I wasn't physically hurt, but I was paralyzed with shame.

But I found a man I wanted to marry—and did—and within the

next few years gave birth to two beautiful, and perfectly hairy, children.

Though this marriage lasted twelve years, it seems to me now that it was doomed from the start to fail. How can one person, not thinking herself worth much, find love and respect to give to another person? Yet the marriage did give me strength. In the privacy of the relationship, I could take off my wig and still feel loved. But even my children learned that although my uncovered head was okay in the privacy of the family, it had to be covered up when anyone else was around.

After my first marriage ended, my ex-husband went to "est," an intensive encounter training. The experience was so transforming for him that he wanted our children to take part as well. But since they lived with me, "est" wouldn't take them unless I attended the training first. I was willing. The training became my first ceremony of unmasking, and turned my life around.

In the very first session, we were told to close our eyes and focus our attention on our bodies—our toes, ankles, knees. . . .

I couldn't do it. Not only did I have no connection to my body parts, I felt dizzy and nauseous as I struggled for awareness and sensation.

The insight came to me at once: For eighteen years I had blocked awareness of my body to avoid dealing with my feelings about losing my hair. At first, that evening, I felt furious at being trapped by the insight. In this intense pressure-cooker training, I wouldn't be able to hide my secret.

That night my inner voices went to war. I swore that I would drop out of the training to avoid revealing myself. I raged at the leaders who were pushing me up against the wall. And, in a whisper, I wondered about the possibility of "dropping the mask" that had separated me for some years from myself and from others.

That night I made up my mind: I couldn't *not* reveal myself any longer.

The next morning, I stood up in what I now see as a life-transforming ceremony in the "est" spiritual tradition: I talked about my secret in front of 275 people.

"This is the most terrifying thing I've ever done," I told them, "but I'm sure that nothing in my life will be right till I stop hiding." The trainer, who had been sarcastic with most other people when they got up to speak, was gentle with me. I think he knew that I had gotten the message I had come for and that I was speaking, with integrity, from the core of my being.

How freeing that moment felt! Once you have told people your "secret," the secret has no more power over you. The amazing thing was that people didn't seem put off by what I had shared. Instead, they began to tell me *their* stories.

I met a woman who had worn a wig for about twenty-five years but then had stopped, and had begun to accent her baldness with striking clothes, makeup, and jewelry. She helped me see a possible pathway.

For two more years, I experimented in going without my wig in public—so long as the place was far from home. I began to realize that there was much more dignity in *choosing* to tell or show what is true about myself than in being exposed. But even so, I experimented as well with medical efforts to get my hair back. Jumping back and forth on a very narrow tightrope.

(Just one of a series of encounters that became my "classics" over the next few years: A woman came up to me, touching my bald head, and said, "How do you get it so smooth?" "What do you mean?" I asked, puzzled. "When I shaved my head last year," she said, "I couldn't get it so smooth." "Why in the world did you shave your head last year?" I asked, totally perplexed. "For the same reason you do it!" she announced, exasperated, as she walked off, certain we had had a clear and intimate conversation.)

And then as I turned forty, I created the second ceremony—this time with my friends. Far scarier.

My fortieth birthday fell at Hanukkah time, a time for moving from the darkness of the first night's candle to the brightness of the eighth night. I invited about two dozen of my friends to my "unmasking" ceremony. I asked them to help me ready myself to bring my bald self more fully into the larger world.

Fear. These are not anonymous "est"ers, or casual passersby on streets far from home. Even dressing to greet them—finding the clothes and earrings that would work attractively with baldness—was a new and scary challenge.

But I also felt a lightness of being, of having nothing to hide, that made it easy to be with myself and with those I loved. I invited my friends that night to "unmask" along with me. I knew that most of them didn't have wigs or physical masks that were as "easy" to take off as mine; I knew too that many of them, like me, were in hiding. And I knew that some of the deepest of friendships grow from trusting to tell and knowing how to hear about those closets we hide ourselves in. So I invited them to join me that night in coming out of their closets, in whatever form that meant.

Often, at parties, people are awkward; we don't know how to connect ourselves in meaningful ways, even to other people whom we'd really like to feel connected to. But this fortieth birthday party was unlike most social gatherings. The conversations all around the room, even among people who hadn't known each other before or in intimate ways, went way beneath the surface that we usually stop at when we are wary or ashamed or guarded. One person's "coming out" becomes an invitation for all of us to come out. We set for one another a deeper level of being seen and seeing one another as we really are.

My birthday merged with Hanukkah. We lit the lights that united them, and I watched the darkness, hiddenness, be filled with light. The secret gone, and loving recognition possible. A new kind of mystery, glowing: the mystery of love. Of the Hanukkah miracle.

So I kept going:

Consciously holding eye contact with strangers. Learning that people most often reflect back what you put out in the world. If I was comfortable with myself, it was this serenity, not the baldness, that was most visible.

Unteaching my children the secrecy I had taught them.

Encouraging—not with words, just with openness—people to ask what they need to know. (No, I don't have cancer; no, I'm not a Buddhist or a nun or an Orthodox Jew. Or a skinhead.)

Feeling grateful that my strangeness helps strangers bridge the distance between us. Many tell me their most intimate secrets, apparently because they see that I have already shared my intimate secret.

Learning to ask people with alopecia first to share one of the most painful experiences that has come from their hair loss, and then what good has come out of it. For most, the second question was much harder to answer than the first. Quiet, quiet—and then someone would speak about having reached a deeper level of love and understanding for people who look "different."

I believe that my baldness has done just that—cut through the mask of pretense and allowed me to be simply me to myself and others. My experience has taught me that "looking different" opens us up to a whole new perspective on the world. It encourages us to be who we are and not who we think we are supposed to be. And that, I believe, is what each of us wants most: to be seen and known on the outside as we know ourselves to be on the inside.

The challenge for each of us is to stop masking our uniqueness and to bless the opportunities—like my loss of hair—that allow us to be ourselves. In "midlife," our creation of ceremonies to welcome these new identities goes a long way in our coming wholly into ourselves with community to support and grow along with us.

Finally, we lift up another ritual of midlife expansion that was developed by Irene Fine. This one she calls *Simḥat Ḥoḥma*—"the joy of wisdom." She describes a series of ceremonies that use different elements of Jewish culture and tradition, all focusing on the image of the

Wise Woman. She suggests that the woman whose wisdom is being celebrated and encouraged may give gifts—physical objects, blessings, teachings—to an assembly of her friends.

One thread of liturgy that runs through the *Simḥat Ḥoḥma* ritual is a song of invocation that Debbie Friedman wrote specifically for this event. Since the focus was on Women of Wisdom, Friedman went beyond the Torah's passage on God's call to Abram (Gen. 12:1) to go forth from Haran: In her rendering, God addresses Sarai—"*L'ḥi lah*"—as well as Abram—"*Leḥ l'ḥa.*" In both the feminine and masculine forms of this command, the two Hebrew words have the same two consonants. The first word means "Walk forth" and the second, "Toward yourself," and each of the words could come to mean the other, simply by transposing the vowels that in any case do not appear in the original text. "Walk forth by going more deeply into yourself—to a land that I alone, God alone, can make visible to you."

The song is a fitting close to this chapter. For it expresses both the most ancient urgings toward a Jewish midlife transformation, moving from familiar territory into unknown possibilities, and the most contemporary "midlife transformation" of Judaism itself, as women and men hear themselves together and equally called forth by God—from the familiar territory of what Judaism has been before, into unknown possibilities. Unknown—yet already deep within our own communal self.

> *L'ḥi lah*—to a land that I will show you;
> *Leḥ l'ḥa*—to a place you do not know.
> *L'ḥi lah*—On your journey I will bless you,
> And you shall be a blessing, you shall be a blessing,
> You shall be a blessing—
> *L'ḥi lah.*

∾ 10 ∾

Separation as Growth

THE TORAH'S STORY of the creation of the universe is a story of separations: light from dark, waters above from waters below, earth from ocean, female from male. Most of these separations are shown as acts of creativity—but the last of them, the Torah is quick to add, should lead to a reunion: "Therefore a man clings to his wife, and they become one flesh." (Gen. 2:24)

Yet the Torah provides for divorce as well. Without celebrating divorce, it sees that sometimes it may be necessary, and will create more good than will preserving a destructive marriage. It has been left to our own generation to explore more fully how, when the separations of divorce become necessary, to make them into a source of creative possibility.

The two of us enter this examination of Jewish divorce with our own memories and concerns. Each of our life-paths brought us through previous marriages to divorces. In choosing whether and how to give a Jewish aspect to these divorces, each of us had to make a midlife reassessment, both of our daily lives and of our Jewish commitments.

So we come to this turn of the life-path spiral bearing memories and hopes that for us make the history of Jewish divorce not "cold facts" but "hot facts." Perhaps the hottest of these facts is the degree of inequality between women and men in shaping the act of separation. It turns out that not only for us and for our generation, but for many generations past in Jewish life, even 2500 years ago, this was an issue.

Biblical Divorce

In the social system of Biblical Israel, divorce (even more than marriage) was in the hands of the husband. Some modern scholars think there was probably, as in Sumerian law, an oral declaration—"You are not my wife"—along with a reversal of the symbolic act of espousal in which the groom spread his robe above his bride—that is, a Sumerian divorce was finalized by cutting the corner of the wife's garment.

The Torah required a written certificate as well, as it commands: "A man takes a wife and possesses her. She does not find favor in his eyes because he finds *ervat davar* [now usually translated "something obnoxious"; more literally, "a matter of nakedness"] about her. So he writes her a *sefer keritut* [literally, a "document of cut-off"], hands it to her, and sends her out of his house." (Deut. 24:1) The *sefer keritut* may have included the words "She is not my wife, and I am not her husband" which Hosea (2:4) mentions.

There was no biblical provision for a wife to do likewise. There was no biblical provision that a wife must agree to the divorce, and no court was empowered to oversee its terms (except possibly to enforce a financial settlement that had been agreed before the two were married). And the husband's authority to divorce his wife was limited in only two cases:

- If he accused her of having falsely claimed to be a virgin when he married her, and then evidence was produced proving his accusation wrong, he was flogged, fined, and forbidden to divorce her for any cause thereafter. (Deut. 22:13–19)

- If a man raped a woman who was neither betrothed nor married, he had to pay a bride-price and marry her (if she agreed), and could not divorce her. (Deut. 22:28–29) (If she had been either betrothed or married, he would have been executed.)

Today, we may feel it abhorrent that a woman might have been locked into a marriage with a man who had done either of these things. But from the perspective of a society in which only a man had economic independence, a woman whose ability to contract a marriage had been fatally compromised needed protection and support— and was entitled to get them from the man who had thus damaged her. So even these limits on the husband's authority show how unequal were the man and woman in Israelite marriage and divorce.

Yet even during the biblical period, we can discern some currents in Jewish culture that began to work toward equality in divorce. In Elephantine, a Jewish military outpost on the upper Nile River, marriage contracts were written, from about the fifth century BCE on, that provided wives as well as husbands with authority to end the marriage. This permission was given financial teeth as well: The wife's dowry had to be returned, and her clothing and other possessions remained hers when she left, no matter which party initiated the divorce.

Some scholars think this step may have been encouraged by Egyptian divorce laws that were more egalitarian. But this leap toward full equality did not strike root in the centers of Jewish life.

Rabbinic Restrictions

Rabbinic tradition as expressed in the Babylonian Talmud (with an entire tractate devoted to divorce) explored and codified divorce with an overall assumption of male authority, but with considerable concern to protect women. Rabbi Eleazar said that "Whoever divorces his first wife, the Altar itself sheds tears because of him." (T. B. Gittin 90b)

The first rabbinic approach to restricting divorce was to require an elaborate document, the *get* (plural, *gittin*), that had to be written only and precisely for a particular couple on a particular date, and could therefore not be available in "boilerplate" for a husband's snap judgment. It had to be written by a skilled scribe with absolute exactitude according to a precise formula, a further safeguard against its being easily produced on a husband's whim.

And meanwhile, the Rabbis were requiring that a *k'tuba* (marriage contract) must include provisions for a serious financial settlement in case of divorce, thus further encouraging a husband to think twice before divorcing his wife.

On the reverse side of the coin, the Talmud began to provide valid grounds on which a woman could demand a divorce. "Demand" here meant that a rabbinical court would put economic or physical pressure on the husband to give a *get*, since only the husband could do so. These reasons included:

- the husband's failure, through disease, impotence, or unwillingness, to have sexual relations with his wife;
- his becoming physically repellent by contracting a loathsome disease or his taking on an occupation that made him literally stink—tanning hides, for example;
- his refusal to provide his wife with necessities, abusing her physically or verbally, or leaving for another country without her agreement.

Meanwhile, the Rabbis, after long debate, enormously broadened the grounds on which husbands might divorce their wives. The question was of course profoundly connected to how different rabbis understood the social, emotional, and spiritual meaning of marriage; but the debate took the form of interpreting *ervat davar*, the reason the

Torah gives for a husband to divorce his wife. *Erva* means "naked-ness." The House of Shammai argued that *ervat davar* means "a matter of nakedness"—sexuality—and therefore that divorce was only legit-imate in case of the wife's adultery. The House of Hillel argued that *ervat davar* meant "nakedness in something" and that "nakedness" is here only a metaphor for anything unseemly, whether sexual or not— "even if she has merely spoiled his food." A century later Rabbi Akiba argued that the Torah's proviso "If she has not found favor in his eyes" should be understood independently, so that any discomfort at all experienced by the husband could be sufficient cause for divorce. Akiba's view subsequently became the general understanding. (T. B. Gittin 90a)

As a result, men could initiate and complete a divorce for any rea-son they chose, while women had to have extremely weighty reasons before they could even ask a rabbinical court to compel a divorce. Faced with this serious inequality and the social strains it was evi-dently creating, some Jewish leaders once more revived efforts toward equality in divorce—this time at the heart of the Jewish world, not its far periphery.

After the Talmudic period, in Babylonia and in Jewish communi-ties influenced by the Geonim (leading sages) of Babylonia, there was one long-lasting effort to move within a Talmudic framework toward an almost fully egalitarian use of the *get*. The Geonim essentially ruled that any objection a woman had to continuing her marriage (not just the special reasons listed by the Talmud) required a rabbinical court to compel a husband to deliver a *get*. (Their reasoning was that other-wise, wives would go—were going—to the non-Jewish authorities to wrest a divorce from their husbands, and both respect for Jewish law and the structure of Jewish families were thus being endangered.) Al-though this still meant that wives had to go to court to get a divorce that their husbands could accomplish entirely on their own, the result was much more nearly equal.

From about 600 CE to 1200 CE, this approach flourished in what were then the major centers of Jewish life. But as these centers shifted to Europe, rabbis in Europe—both south and north, what we would call Sephardi and Ashkenazi—came to reject these Geonic precedents. So for the last eight hundred years or so, Jewish law has not treated wives and husbands as even approximately equal in matters of divorce.

But one more step toward some measure of greater equality emerged from the Ḥerem de Rabbenu Gershom of Mainz. Around the year 1000 CE, he issued two major rulings:

- He required that for a *get* to be valid, the wife must agree to receive it. (He provided an escape clause that if she refused, it could still be validated with the approval of one hundred rabbis.)
- He forbade men to have more than one wife. This ruling had major implications for divorce, since it prevented men from failing to divorce their first wives and so leaving them in limbo while marrying someone else. It increased pressure on the man to get a wife's permission for a divorce.

The first ruling—requiring a wife's consent to a divorce—was accepted everywhere in the Jewish world. The second, against polygamy, was ignored by Jews in Muslim-dominated areas, where polygamy was legal, while accepted among Jews of Christian lands, where polygamy was forbidden.

What ceremony of giving a *get* has emerged from this centuries-long legal and institutional debate?

So complex and so essential have the details of divorce become that the custom in almost all halakhic circles is to allow only rabbis specially skilled in *gittin* to oversee the process.

The husband and wife (or agents for them) appear before such a rabbi skilled in *gittin*, a highly skilled scribe, and two witnesses who are qualified to testify before a rabbinical court.

The scribe formally gives the husband specially prepared paper and a quill pen so that they become the husband's property. He then lends them to the scribe, and specifically directs the scribe to write the *get* for his wife.

The *get* must be handwritten, with no errors (any error requires starting all over again), and has to be written specifically for the sake of this particular couple, with a specific date and a specific place named along with the full names of the husband and wife.

The *get* must follow a traditional Aramaic text with no deviations. It pronounces a complete separation, including the words "You are now permitted to any man."

When the *get* is complete, the man declares that he is giving it of his own free will. The woman declares that she is receiving it of her own free will.

The two witnesses then sign it.

The man and woman again declare that they are giving and receiving the *get* voluntarily, and the man affirms that he will never question its validity.

The man picks up the *get* and drops it into the woman's hands, declaring, "This is your *get*. You are divorced from me and are permitted to [marry] any man."

She places the *get* under her arm and walks several steps away from him.

She then hands the *get* to the rabbi, who tears it in a unique and identifiable way and takes possession of it for his own archives or those of the local Jewish community or his denomination, essentially to be available if there is ever any question.

The rabbi then hands the divorced woman a certificate affirming when, where, how, and by whom the *get* was given and received.

That ends the ceremony.

It is, as befits the content, the bleakest of all Jewish ceremonies. Even a death, a funeral, calls forth a communal sharing of food; the *get* does not.

As if to embody the Torah's description of a *sefer keritut*, a "document of cut-off," and also as if to echo the tearing of a garment to mourn the dead, the *get* is actually torn. True, the tradition suggests that this is simply to make the *get* unique, like taking its fingerprint. But the emotional charge of the tearing nevertheless remains.

One looks almost in vain for any analogue to the broken glass at a Jewish wedding which is a reminder of sadness at a time of joy. Where is the reminder of joy at this time of sadness? Perhaps, perhaps, the possibility of joy is hidden in the releasing of the woman: "You are permitted to any man."

But for many women, the deepest sadness has been not simply the torn relationship but the tradition's insistence that women have only a passive role in deciding what to do about it, when, and how. Modernity has turned this feeling from the individual silent tears of individual women—who knows how many?—into a great salt wave of tidal change.

The Creative Renewal of Divorce

Modernity has had three profound impacts on Jewish patterns of divorce.

First, Modernity has made patterns of marriage much more complicated, and divorce much more likely. Modernity has meant an increase in life-span, in geographic and social mobility, even in psychological mobility: people may try out two or three countries, two or three occupations, even two or three character structures and spiritual paths, in a single lifetime. The chances that two people may find themselves still intimately connected through all these changes are many fewer than they were for their grandparents, who walked one or at most two paths over the course of their lives. At first, only one member of a couple might be going through such changes—perhaps expecting the other to learn the newest dances fast enough to keep up. But when, as became increasingly the case, both parties were hearing different drummers change their different rhythms, then dancing together for a lifetime became much harder.

Secondly, Modernity imposed a secular state's rules of marriage and divorce upon all citizens. The Jewish community's ability to keep an unbroken legal connection between marriage and divorce became much weaker. Typically, most secular Western governments left a good deal of latitude for their religious traditions to define when a marriage began, but insisted that issues of children and property made it necessary for the State to define how and when a marriage ended.

Some parts of the Jewish community (especially the Reform denomination) responded by turning all issues of divorce over to the State, and agreeing that a civil divorce was sufficient to permit the initiation of another Jewish marriage.

Another part of the community (Israeli Jews) agreed, albeit with much grumbling, to let the Orthodox Jewish rabbinate set the rules of marriage and divorce, while putting the secular state at its disposal, to enforce many of its rulings.

And still other Jews (Diaspora Orthodox and Conservative) negotiated uncomfortable waters in the hope of honoring both State and Torah. (For example, they insisted that only after a secular divorce would they grant a Jewish one, but also refused to hallow a new Jewish marriage unless any previous ones had been ended by Jewish as well as secular law.)

Finally, some newer currents of Jewish thought, Reconstructionist and renewal in bent, redefined some of the issues as more spiritual and cultural than legal, and used Jewish patterns—with important changes—because they would bring much deeper satisfaction, not because Jewish law required them. By this last standard, as Jews expressed both the emotional and spiritual need for a Jewish divorce with more depth than a day in Secular Bureaucratic Court, and at the same time rejected the traditional patterns of Jewish divorce as demeaning or discomfiting to them, these newer energies began to create new versions of the *get* as sacred process.

Each of the two of us (Arthur and Phyllis) went through a version of divorce—two different versions—that tried to respond to the needs of our selves and our partners by adapting the ancient practice of the *get*.

Arthur recalls: In 1978, as my first marriage ended, my then wife and I were committed to treating women and men as fully equal. I knew of no one who had been Jewishly divorced in an egalitarian way, but I very much wanted to find or create a Jewish approach to divorce that would be based in equality. My wife and I asked four Jewishly knowledgeable friends of ours—two men, two women; of the four, one rabbi—to take part in an egalitarian exchanging of *gittin*. We wanted one (a woman) to write the *get*, another (a man) to oversee the ceremony, and two (a man and a woman) to be the *eydim*, or witnesses.

We listened carefully to still another rabbi who leaned toward egalitarianism and was creatively inclined, but was also committed to preserving the boundaries of *C'lal Yisra-el*—"united Israel"—when it came to such matters as personal status and the validity of marriages. He urged us to have two "kosher" witnesses (that is, observant men) and a male scribe do the "official" *get* in the traditional way for on-the-record purposes; and then, if we wished, to do a separate *get* that accorded with our own values.

But we decided that this notion of an "official" *get* that was real for legal purposes and a "private" *get* that was real for emotional purposes was itself a violation of our values. So we decided to proceed as we had planned.

The traditionally concerned rabbi had one additional recommendation: That the two of us exchange letters that spoke from our own hearts about how we felt about the marriage we had shared. This advice we found very wise, and indeed the actual exchange (which we did a week or so before the exchange of *gittin*) did give the *get* ceremony a different tone and timbre.

One thing these personal letters accomplished was to bring some heartfelt content about this specific marriage into a form that without it was paradoxically both utterly universal and narrowly specific. To some couples, it is a serious frustration that the same *get* that is handwritten for only one couple in one place at one moment in time is also utterly formulaic, without variations, in its literal content. So for us it was a relief to be able to speak in our letters from our own realities.

Since 1978, some of these practices have spread more broadly in the Jewish world. The exchange of twin *gittin* has become customary in the Reconstructionist and some renewal communities. Some couples have written and exchanged personal letters as we did; others, instead of reading them, have burned these letters in each other's presence—on the theory that what is spiritually healing is saying your say, not having the other person hear it.

Phyllis recalls: My divorce came seven years after Arthur's, and by that time, the world had already changed enough that it wasn't hard to find a nearby Reconstructionist rabbi who was accustomed to writing an egalitarian *get*.

My first husband and I chose as the scribe to write our *get* the same artist who had designed our son's and daughter's Bar and Bat Mitzvah invitations. We both felt a connection to her, since she had shared other significant life-cycle moments with us. Each of us chose an *eyd*, a witness, from among our closest friends.

Having been separated seven years, and having resolved the legal issues of support for the children in civil court, we were in a peaceful place with one another. We were ready for the separation to be complete, and we had already said what we felt needed to be said to one another about appreciation and about disappointment. The ceremony was short, honest, and much more emotionally satisfying than had been our experience in civil court, in its recognition of both release and regret that is the true nature of divorce.

When I recently acted as *m'saderet gittin* (facilitator) of a *get* process for a couple of friends, the situation was more complex. The divorce decision was more recent; it was not mutual; it was laden with feelings of betrayal. Additionally, the man wanted a traditional *get*, while the woman felt that such a *get* would deny her dignity as an equal partner of the marriage and of the divorce. Though she was willing to receive such a document, she wanted and needed the emotional satisfaction of a ceremony that treated her as actively rather than passively involved and enabled her to be whole and real in her participation.

The two of them each invited an *eyd* from among their closest friends, and they chose to include their adult son as an additional witness. Because there had been little satisfying communication between the couple in their divorce process, we used the ceremony as a structure for some limited communication to unfold. I invited them to thank each other for some loving aspect of their years together; I invited them to give each other letters that the rest of us would not see or hear in which the unspoken and unheard feelings of hurt and disappointment could be received; I invited them to bless each other, and the rest of us joined in offering them blessings, as they granted each other the freedom to move on in different directions with their lives.

The ceremony, like the reality in their lives, was painful. It offered them the dignity of being true to themselves in very difficult circumstances. Each of us was touched by the rawness and by the humanness.

Rabbi Vicki Hollander has suggested that the hours before the issuance of a *get* be set aside as a day of fasting, like the time before a wedding. She herself, as she prepared for the *get*, dressed in white, as she does for Yom Kippur, and recited the confessional *Vidu-i* (recited on the eve of marriage and of death), confessing her own part in the "undoing of the marriage." She asked women friends to sit quietly with her through the ceremony as *shomrot*, like the *shomrim* that sit with a body before burial. After receiving the formal *get*, she handed her ex-husband a handwritten *get* of her own, confirming her own release and his. Returning home after the *get*, she changed into colorful clothes and ate the hardboiled eggs that symbolize death and rebirth. With her friends she walked around the block as mourners do at the end of *shiva*, symbolizing their reentry into the world.

Rabbi Nina Beth Cardin has designed a separate ritual for the woman who has just received a traditional *get*. She focuses it upon the tearing of a cloth—perhaps a pillowcase or bedsheet—reminiscent of the bed of marriage, the *k'ri-a* of a garment after a death, and the tearing of the *get* itself. In her ritual, the tearing is introduced by a passage from the Prophet Joel: *"Kiru bigdeyhem v'al l'vavḥem . . . ki YHWH ḥanun v'raḥum, ereḥ apa-yim v'rav ḥesed."*—"Rip your garments, not your heart; for God is filled with overflowing love and motherly compassion, is slow to anger, swift with loving-kindness."

Others who have been involved in the *get* process have called together groups of friends to help them move through the emotional and spiritual path of divorce. After some *get* ceremonies, women friends have met to relive and "give away" the memories of the marriage. Wrote Cindy Gabriel, a participant in two such gatherings:

> . . . Six of her close women friends were waiting. We welcomed her with hugs and tears, brought her into our circle with lighted candles. She retold the story of the *get* ceremony and how she too released him from the connection. We all talked of dreams, sang, cut up a symbolic item she had brought, fed her her favorite foods and gently rocked her in a hammock. The energy shifted from nervous anticipation to a gush of released emotions to a soothing vibration and finally to laughter. It was very healing for all of us.
>
> For another friend, we did a pre-*get* ceremony. Three of us went to a beautiful outdoor place, where the year before, among her women friends, she had realized her marriage was over. She brought photos, letters, and a few other objects that reminded her of the whole (humiliating) process she had been through the past year. She invited us there as witnesses to hear her story, which she told using the objects as a guide. We cried with her, validated her feelings, and helped her bury the objects. We finished off with hugs.

Anne Brener, who has written poignantly in *Mourning and Mitzvah* on how to respond to death, has suggested that addressing a divorce as a small death, and using such instruments of mourning as the Kaddish, makes good sense in facing the death of a relationship. Implicitly, she is pointing to the truth that the Kaddish is both an expression of mourning and an affirmation of rebirth.

All these innovations have three things in common: They move toward treating men and women as equals; they deal with divorce as not only a legal event but one that also takes place in the emotional, intellectual, and spiritual worlds; and they evoke a range of emotions, not sadness only, as welcome in this moment. These three new aspects of the *get* have one approach in common: they broaden the people, the dimensions, and the emotions of the *get*.

These three kinds of broadening are intertwined. Including women in the community of those who are empowered to take part has the effect of broadening the dimensions of divorce beyond law alone, to include feeling and intellect as well. And once the palette of emotion is opened, the spectrum of expressible emotions is broadened: sadness becomes a part, but not the whole, of the emotion that can be expected.

Rarely has it been clearer that the equality of women and men leads beyond sheer equality to the renewal of the content and process of Jewish life. For piling the silencing of women on top of the sadness of the breakup is bound to make the sadness even worse. But once women are free to make divorce happen, not merely suffer it, then they are free to explore the whole range of thoughts and feelings that emerges.

And still more: if *they* become free to cry, laugh, rage, remember, then so do their former husbands. Expanding the *get* beyond its legal dimensions helps men as well as women to reflect on the marriage just ended, its joys and suffering; to reexamine their own responsibility for being unable to fulfill the hope they held beneath the *ḥuppa*; to grow into new human beings in midlife.

In that sense, like Abram bemoaning his childlessness, both men and women can transcend the pain that has brought them to the *get*— and the pain that has demanded that they transform the *get*. They can receive a new and deeper *Brit Beyn haB'tarim*, a covenant between the sections that have been ripped apart.

Since both Western and Jewish cultures have tended to point women toward "specializing" in emotion and spirituality rather than the law, it is not so surprising that the advent of women's equality in Jewish life should bring with it a broadening of the *get* beyond its legal dimension. It was less expectable, perhaps, that even the legal aspects of the *get* would be affected by the rethinking of gender roles and sexual ethics that has had such a deep impact on many other moments of the Jewish life-cycle.

How may the legal dimension of the *get* be changing? Once parts of the Jewish community decided to broaden marriage itself to include same-sex couples, the nature of the *get* was necessarily transformed. For in most Jewish communities, even those that kept the *get* as a Jewish aspect of divorce, there has been some kind of accommodation to the secular divorce law of the State. But except in a very few jurisdictions, there is no secular divorce law for same-sex couples.

So, as we noted in our chapter on marriage and the wedding ceremony, those parts of the Jewish community may find themselves shouldering a new responsibility: Like the Jews of the Middle Ages, they may need to shape law for the Jewish people in arenas that the State has refused to touch.

So the next generations of the Jewish people, drawn and driven by Jewish visions of ethics and spirituality, may be drawn as well to a new maturity. Just as individuals who have thought they were "all grown up" have found ceremonies marking their midlife transformations necessary to help them "grow up" into another stage, so the Jewish people as a whole may be undertaking a kind of midlife transformation.

And the midlife transformation of divorce in particular may well become a midwife in this rebirthing of our people in its wholeness, as well as in the lives of individual Jews. The Holy Altar weeps at each divorce. And then the salt tears gather into an ocean that can birth new life.

Joining in the Covenant

WHEN INDIVIDUALS CHOOSE to join the Jewish people, they are transforming large parts of their life as it was shaped in childhood. The choice itself creates a "midlife," no matter what the calendar says.

In America for an entire generation, the numbers of those who are choosing to become Jews has been far higher than such numbers have been since the earliest years of Rabbinic Judaism, two millennia ago. So in an unexpected way, as this happens, the Jewish people as a body is experiencing a collective "midlife transformation." It makes sense for us to look at this moment from both perspectives.

That moment of high conversion rates so long ago came when both the internal shapes within and the external boundaries between different religious and ethnic communities were heated to the melting point by the impact of Hellenistic-Roman civilization. As the boundaries melted, the nature of Judaism and of other cultures changed, and the boundaries between them became far more permeable. After several generations, the various cultures settled into new forms, and the boundaries between them became more rigid.

So we can take these numbers in our own generation as an index to the depth of social change and the breadth of spiritual search.

Biblical Boundary-Crossing

In the Torah's stories of the earliest history of what became the People Israel, we hear three sorts of relationship: clear membership in the Abrahamic clan; clear otherness; and uncertainty.

The uncertainty began in Abraham's own household. He took Hagar as a wife, yet later sent her into a perilous wilderness. Her very name suggests the ambiguous word *geyr*—"stranger," "foreigner," "sojourner." Indeed, she is called *Hagar haMitzrit*—"Egyptian sojourner"—in what was perhaps an ironic reference to how the Israelites themselves became *geyrim b'Mitzra-yim*, "sojourners in Egypt," and must therefore learn how to treat lovingly the *geyrim* who lived later in their midst. (Perhaps we can hear the Torah-poet hinting that since they had not treated Hagar with love in the first place, the experience of *geyr*-hood in Egypt bore the karma of reaping what you sow.)

Hagar's son Ishmael was circumcised while he was still part of Abraham's household—indeed, on the same day on which Abraham himself was circumcised. Abraham agonized before deciding whether to send him into the wilderness. And even after this traumatic separation, Ishmael remained closely connected enough to join in burying his father. Yet his own future is treated by the Torah as the story of another people.

These two, at the very start, make clear how unclear the boundaries of the tribe can be. In the traditions of the peoples who see themselves as descendants of Abraham through Hagar, there never was a break: Abraham never sent Hagar away, and indeed all his life honored the son—in their tradition, Ishmael rather than Isaac—who was willing to surrender his body to the upraised knife. (Not only the knife of circumcision, but the knife of mortal sacrifice.)

In the Torah, Hagar speaks her suffering aloud. Ishmael does not. Yet their story makes clear how agonizing the choices can be for those who live "on the edge" of their own identity, and for those who struggle to define the boundaries.

From the Torah's perspective, while circumcision did not make a male unambiguously part of the clan, the absence of circumcision clearly defined him as not a member. This becomes clear in the story of the Sh'ḥemites, whose leader first—according to the storyteller—raped Jacob's daughter, Dina, and then sought to marry her. Her brothers demanded that he and all the male members of the clan be circumcised before this marriage could be celebrated. Then the sons of Jacob murdered all the men of Sh'ḥem on the third day of their circumcision, when they were most in pain. Even though the storyteller never lets us hear Dina's version of the story, the anthropology is clear enough: to be male and uncircumcised is to be an outsider. (Gen. 34)

The story of the Exodus from slavery has almost at its start and almost at its finish two assertions that circumcision was central to Israelite peoplehood. Just after God had commissioned Moses to become the liberator, the mission was nearly aborted in an eerie tale of how God threatened to kill Moses, and relented only when Moses' wife Tzipora snatched up a flintstone to circumcise their son. (Exod. 4:24–26)

And when the Exodus itself was actually under way, God explained that it must be celebrated in the future by eating a special meal of roast lamb, the Pesaḥ offering. "The whole community of Israel shall offer it." But then the Torah continues, "If a *geyr*/sojourner who sojourns with you would offer the Pesaḥ to YHWH, all his males shall be circumcised. Then he shall be as a citizen of the land. But no foreskinned [male] person shall eat of it."

What to make of these two passages? The Torah may be describing a very ancient transformative moment in the history of the people, like the two moments when first Rome and still more recently Modernity triumphed and the boundaries melted. If for the Clan of Abraham circumcision had been necessary, was it so any longer in the ancient moment of this new covenant of liberation? And the answer came: Yes. Could others join in the great celebration of the Pharaoh's overthrow? And the answer came: Yes, if they were circumcised.

Yet there is a hint in Torah that in the revolutionary moment itself, not all those who crossed the Sea and assembled at Sinai were biological descendants of Abraham and Sarah. There was an *erev rav*, says Torah, a "mixed multitude"—people who were "twilight" (*erev*), on the threshold between "in" and "out." One of them, says a *midrash*, was Pharaoh's daughter, the one who saved Moses' life, now no longer Pharaoh's daughter, "Bat-Paro," but "Bat-Yah"—God's Daughter.

When the Torah turns to the life of the People Israel as a national/cultural unit settled in the Land of Israel, it becomes clearer who the *geyrim* were: Those who lived more or less within its boundaries were not hostile, and yet did not share in all aspects of Israelite society. They were subject to many of the same laws—Shabbat, the festivals, the right to refuge if they committed manslaughter by accident, prohibitions on idol worship and child sacrifice. But *geyrim* could charge and be charged interest on loans, though Israelites could not.

The main difference between *geyrim* and full Israelites was that *geyrim* held no ancestral right to land within the Israelite boundaries. (Israelites might be temporarily landless, but as members of one of the twelve tribes had rights to and could be redeemed for a landholding out of their family history.) Thus *geyrim* were economically dependent—most were day-laborers or artisans—and the Torah repeats again and again that they must be loved and protected, since Israelites could remember what it felt like to be *geyrim* in Egypt.

The point is that at this juncture, the boundaries of peoplehood were not starkly sharp and clear. Certainly belief in YHWH, the God of Israel, and in YHWH alone was not a clear and distinctive marker for membership in the people.

We have, for example, the story of Naaman, general-in-chief of Aram (Syria), who contracted a skin disease that some Israelites claimed to know how to cure. He came for help to the Prophet Elisha, and was cured after immersing himself in the Jordan as Elisha directed. "Here!" Naaman avowed. "I take it to heart that there is no god in all the world except in Israel."

Then he took home with him the quantity of Israelite earth two mules could carry, as if perhaps to say that this God was connected with the Land of Israel alone and needed Israelite soil to be divinely effective.

And finally, he apologized in advance: "When my master [the king of Aram] goes to the Temple of Rimmon with me beside him, and I prostrate myself in Rimmon's Temple, may YHWH please forgive me." Elisha responded, "Go in peace." One can almost hear God smiling. (I Kings 5)

So was Naaman what we would call a "convert"?

The most famous biblical story of a "convert" is the tale of Ruth. She was a Moabite—from a people despised by most Israelites. She married one of the sons in an Israelite family that had migrated to Moab in flight from a famine in their home territory. After her husband's death she committed herself to accompany her widowed mother-in-law, Naomi, back to Naomi's home in the Land of Israel: "Where you go, I will go. Where you lodge, I will lodge. Your people shall be my people, and your God my God. Where you die, I will die; and there I shall be buried."

The story does not suggest that this declaration made her an Israelite. For it explains that she was welcomed to glean in the fields of a rich landholder as a *geyr*—though she calls herself a *nohria*, a word meaning a markedly more foreign person, perhaps even from a hostile nation. (Ruth 2:10) It was by marrying the landholder that she was welcomed into the community. Ultimately she had a child who became the forebear of King David. The story describes both a people and a convert who unambiguously celebrate the welcoming of an outsider.

Some modern scholars think the story was invented long after the time ascribed to Ruth, long after even the era of King David. According to this assessment, it is part of a polemic against the demand of Ezra and Nehemiah that the Jews returning from exile in Babylonia divorce their wives of non-Israelite origin.

In that case, the story of Ruth is one of the earliest expressions of a debate that still continues 2500 years later: Does it weaken or strengthen the Jewish people for people who grew up in another tradition or community to marry Jews, whether or not they formally become Jews themselves? That the Scroll of Ruth was not only defined as Holy Scripture by the Rabbis but even assigned as reading for the festival of the Giving of the Torah, Shavuot, is perhaps the best evidence that, on balance, the early rabbis leaned in the direction of inclusion.

Rabbinic Boundaries

As the structure of Jewish peoplehood shifted from a geographic-national base to one scattered through the world and defined chiefly by words of Torah, the meaning of *geyr* was remade by Rabbinic Judaism. The label *geyr tzedek*—"upright sojourner"—was used for someone who explicitly accepted Torah in a formal ceremony and became fully part of the Jewish people. *Geyr toshav*—"resident sojourner"—was used in the Talmud for a person who lived by most Jewish norms, worshipped YHWH, but had not undergone a formal transforming ceremony.

What was this defining ceremony? It began with an argument, a wrestling, with a *beyt din* (rabbinical court) made up of at least three rabbis: "Why do you wish to be a Jew, seeing that in our days the Jews are persecuted, driven, exiled?"

The candidate for conversion may answer that s/he knows of all this suffering and yet feels unworthy of the privilege of becoming a Jew. (Perhaps this person fears s/he may not have the strength to affirm God's holiness through suffering, yet feels called to try.) "Such a one we accept at once, explaining the lighter and the heavier commands, the punishments that follow on transgressions and the rewards that follow on observance." The Rabbis specified certain commandments as especially important for the prospective convert to learn. These were precepts that benefited the poor: allowing the poor to glean grain overlooked by the regular workers; devoting the produce of the corners of the fields to the poor; and tithing for the sake of the poor. (T. B. Yeb 47a) In most cases, the *beyt din* demurred three times, urging the candidate to reconsider. Yet the wrestle was to some extent a dance. "We draw close with the right hand, thrust away with the left."

While an approach based on sheer love of God and Torah brought warm acceptance, the Talmud was not so warm toward approaches motivated by some sort of self-advancement—for the sake of marrying a beloved; in hopes of preferential treatment by a powerful or wealthy Jew; from fear that natural disasters were God's warnings to convert. Yet if someone had accomplished the ceremonial conversion, such motives did not disqualify the act. (T. B. Yeb 24b)

Once the *beyt din* decided to allow the candidate to move forward, the conversion process involved several steps. While the Temple still stood, the convert brought offerings—cattle or two small birds, depending on wealth and income. (Notice the echo of Abram's offerings in the covenant between the sections, *B'rit Beyn haB'tarim.*) After the Destruction, these offerings were not replaced by a requirement of *tz'daka*. The requirements that did continue were circumcision for men and immersion in a *mikva* for both men and women.

What to do with a man who has already been circumcised, but not as part of accepting the Abrahamic covenant? The two great contending schools of Talmudic thought, the House of Shammai and the House of Hillel, disagreed. Shammai taught that a drop of blood must be drawn from the penis; Hillel argued that this was unnecessary. The teaching of Shammai prevailed, and in halakhic circles to this day *hatafat dam b'rit*, "the covenant's drop of blood," is drawn.

With full circumcision the *mohel* is required, and with the drop of blood may choose to say two blessings:

*Baruḥ ata YHWH eloheynu meleḥ ha-olam asher kidshanu
b'mitzvotav v'tzivanu lamul et hageyrim.*
Blessed is the One . . . Who has commanded us to circumcise converts. (T. B. Shabb 137b)

*Baruḥ ata YHWH eloheynu meleḥ ha-olam asher kidshanu
b'mitzvotav v'tzivanu lamul et hageyrim ul'hatif meyhem dam b'rit
she-ilmaley dam b'rit lo nitka-yemu shama-yim va-aretz, she-ne-
emar: im lo b'riti yomam valaila ḥukot shama-yim va-aretz lo samti.
Baruḥ ata YHWH koreyt hab'rit.*
Blessed is the One . . . Who has commanded us to circumcise converts, and draw from them the blood of the covenant, for without the blood of the covenant heaven and earth cannot be lifted up, as is said: "If not for my covenant, I would not keep firm by day and night the carved-out realities of heaven and of earth." [Jeremiah 33:25] Blessed is the One Who cuts the covenant.

The convert then receives a certificate attesting to completion of the *B'rit Mila*.

The final act in conversion is immersion in the *mikva*. The origins of this practice for conversion are unclear, though it is easy to see the analogy to the use of immersion for other clarifications in ancient biblical practice. In many instances described in Torah, the alternate state of being that was called *tuma* was generated by such events as childbirth, menstruation, seminal emission, or touching a corpse. A *tamey* person could not bring offerings to the Temple. (For the meaning of *tuma*, see our discussion in Chapter 3 on *mikva* after the menstrual period.) This state of *tuma* was then resolved and dissolved by immersion in a *mikva* or a natural body of running water. After the immersion, someone who had been *tamey* became *tahor*, and could once again approach the Temple.

Biblical texts never explicitly said that being a non-Jew meant being *tamey*, but the Rabbis could easily have felt that full inclusion in the covenant was analogous to approaching the Temple, and that immersion should mark the change as it had marked moving from *tamey* to *tahor*.

The *beyt din* needs to actually witness the immersion. Since the candidate must be utterly naked, however, male rabbis can directly witness only the immersion of men; for a woman they depend on the sound of splashing water and the report of a woman attendant that the candidate has fully immersed.

The immersion itself is the moment of transformation. Normally such acts require that a blessing be said before the act. But someone who is not (yet) Jewish cannot affirm that "You have made *us* holy through the *mitzvot*." So the blessing, which ends, *"v'tzivanu al ha-t'vila"* ("and has commanded us concerning immersion"), was said after the immersion instead of before.

Although halakhically only one immersion is required, the custom arose and spread everywhere to immerse three times. For the second immersion, the new Jew recites, *". . . sheheheyanu v'ki-y'manu v'higianu lazman hazeh."*—"Who has filled us with life, lifted us up, and brought us to this moment." And after the third, s/he calls out, *"Sh'ma Yisra-el YHWH eloheynu YHWH ehad!"*—which may be translated, "Hear O Israel, the Lord our God, the Lord is One!" or more recently, "Hear O Godwrestlers, the Breath of Life is our God, the Breath of Life is One!"

After the immersion—a profound plunge into the oceanic sense of God, the Womb of rebirth—new Jews harvest the fruits of this encounter by taking on new names. The "child of" aspect of their names is supplied with *ben Avraham Avinu* or *bat Avraham Avinu* ("son" or "daughter" of Abraham our Father"; in egalitarian Jewish circles today, *ben/bat Avraham v'Sarah*. They may choose an appropriate name for themselves, or in some regions men may take on *Avraham* not only as their forebear but also—since he was the first "convert" to Judaism, and so the model for all converts—as their own name: *Avraham ben Avraham*.

After the immersion, the waiting *beyt din* attests to the completion of the process with a certificate signed by its three members.

Except for the complexity of the name sometimes making clear the origins of the convert, Rabbinic Judaism has in principle avoided making a point of the convert's non-Jewish birth. Since many Jewish teachers responded to non-Jewish hostility and violence with their own hostility—even contempt—for a non-Jewish world that could elevate expulsions and pogroms into a religious precept, many Jewish authorities viewed such origins as somewhat shameful. In this atmosphere, the new Jew was not to be reminded of his or her origins, and every effort was made to cancel out memories of the convert's former life.

Renewing the Covenant

Two aspects of Modernity seem to have given energy to the great wave of conversion to Judaism. One of these is the creation of an overarching secular society that has diminished the barriers between people of different ethnic and religious communities, and encouraged contact between them. Another is the thinning-down of community and spiritual intensity that results from that same overarching secularity. People who have experienced little community or spirituality in their "homes" have felt impelled to search for it elsewhere.

Some have suggested a third explanation for the wave of conversions. This one rests on the notion that there are individual souls that cross the generations in different bodies. In the Holocaust, say some more mystically inclined Jews, millions of Jewish souls were sent into a limbo where there were millions fewer Jewish bodies in which to be reborn. So they returned as Christians, but their soul-impulse drew them toward Judaism.

For those less mystical, there may be more social-historical ways to understand this teaching: that the Holocaust opened many eyes to the ancient streak of cruel anti-Semitism that has long been embedded in certain aspects of some Christian thought, while, simultaneously, the renewal of Jewish energy that followed the Holocaust has opened the spiritual wisdom of the Jewish past and emerging present to ears that had never previously turned to hear them.

Perhaps for all these reasons, many converts to Judaism report that when they first discovered Jewish life they felt inwardly as if they had "come home"—quite aside from matters like falling in love with a Jew. The result for many has been much like one way of understanding the Voice that spoke to Abram in Haran: *"Leḥ l'ḥa!"*—"Walk toward your self! Only by going outward can you go inward."

There is a Hasidic story: Shmerl, a woodcutter in the Carpathian Mountains, wakes up three mornings in a row from the same strange dream. In the dream he sees a clearly visible bridge five hundred miles away in Poland, and under this bridge is a great buried treasure. Three times! Shmerl shrugs, puts on a heavy coat, walks the full five hundred miles to the Vistula River, and finds the bridge. Just as he locates the exact spot of his dream, two Poles saunter by. Says one, "Such a strange dream I had last night!—about a Jew named Shmerl under whose bed in his tumbledown shack is buried a great treasure." Shmerl blinks, shrugs, walks back home, digs under his bed, and behold!—a bag of gold!

In some Jewish circles, this story is said to mean, "Look, the treasure is under your own bed! Why are you searching among Buddhists, Navajos, Sufis?" But clearly also, part of the point of the story is that you will never find the treasure under your bed unless you leave home. And part of the point as well is that the Pole also had "true torah"—a wise and accurate dream.

The irony here is that the story speaks to all communities, in all directions: To Jews who learn meditation from a Buddhist, and then come—or don't come—back "home" to teach some Jewish forms of meditation. To Christians who find a home in Judaism. And to many others.

Meanwhile, the new Jews come into an ethnic faith community with some sense of learned ethnicity, but still are more tentative than many of those born into Jewish homes. In certain ways, however, this more tenuous ethnicity may be a positive advantage. Choosing Jewish foods, for example, the new Jews may be more likely to explore Jewish values than automatically to replicate Jewish practices—to ask, for example, "Is *kashrut* a compromise with vegetarianism? Then perhaps tofu and tempeh are more 'Jewish' than the Russian beef borscht and the Middle Eastern shwarma that are conspicuously labeled 'Jewish food.' " Shaping the Jewish path of prayer, they may ask not only, "What were Jews doing in the seventeenth century?" but also, "What works to put us in touch with God today?"

Such examples suggest, and many anecdotes confirm, that "Jews by choice" (as some prefer to call new converts) often outstrip born Jews in the passion and commitment they bring to Judaism. And in the presence of these "Jews by choice," many other Jews are becoming conscious of the degree to which in a free and secularized society all Jews are "Jews by choice." All who stay or become involved are freely deciding to do so, and could easily choose differently without suffering ostracism.

So Judaism itself is changing in response to these new energies from new Jews.

Converts today, like Nan Fink Gefen in *Stranger in the Midst*, report that a full range of hostility, fear, admiration, skepticism, welcome, and matter-of-fact encounter greet them as they move into different regions of Jewish life. They find the choice of Judaism involves more choices than they may have expected when they began exploring a Jewish path: changes in family relationships, changes in the way they experience world history and the morning newspaper, changes not only in who their friends are, but in the tone and form of what their friendships are.

Since many more people are now in the process of conversion at any given moment than was true in previous generations, the process itself has somewhat changed. There are far more likely to be classes with a dozen or more people in "Discovering Judaism." Often some people born into Jewish homes, as well as candidates for conversion, are learning in such classes. (Couples on the verge of marriage may learn together, for example.)

Many communities and congregations require the candidate to write a personal statement of why s/he seeks conversion—a spiritual autobiography. And some *batey din* require the candidate to sign a statement of commitment to uphold the central values and precepts of Judaism (as understood by the presiding *beyt din*).

In some communities, the traditional final meeting with the three-person *beyt din* to secure its authorization to take the final step may be partially modified as a broader community carries on a discussion not only of this particular candidate's desire to convert but of the entire meaning of Jewish identity, in which all present are explorers.

Some rabbis have added to the *beyt din*'s traditional reminder of the pain of being Jewish a sharply pointed question: "Have you taken into account that if you had taken this step just [sixty] years ago in Europe, the chances are that your choice would have sent you to a cruel and early death?"

For some Reform congregations, immersion in learning has replaced immersion in water as a ritual practice leading toward conversion. But the *mikva* for conversion is also staging a comeback, among the growing number of converts who are being guided by Conservative, Reconstructionist and tradition-oriented Reform rabbis and by renewal-oriented rabbis in all denominations and in non-denominational settings. Since most American *mikva-ot* were built by Orthodox congregations or groups, there has been increasing strain in some communities where non-Orthodox rabbis have sought to use them for conversion. In some places, there has been accommodation. In some, non-Orthodox groups have built new *mikva-ot*. In some, definitions of an acceptable *mikva* have been stretched.

At the same time, the power of Orthodox rabbinates in Israeli politics and their influence over the government's decisions on whom to recognize as Jews has impelled some Jews who do not have Orthodox views to seek conversion under Orthodox auspices, so as to hold more open the possibility of migration to Israel. When Orthodox power in Israeli politics has been most fully deployed to insist on defining conversion in any country as valid only by Orthodox norms, strong opposition has arisen among non-Orthodox Jews outside Israel. So these contradictory currents of change have themselves had an impact on Israeli politics and on those American Jewish institutions that have deep involvements in Israel.

The overtones of immersion (and for men, of *hatafat dam b'rit*, the blood drawn as a token of covenantal circumcision) are different in a culture where many, not a rare few, are experiencing it. Friends may accompany the convert to the *mikva*. Songs, chants, meditations may accompany the formal blessings. (Rabbi Jane Litman, for example, suggests taking the traditional three immersions as times to honor, heal, and let go of the past; to welcome and imagine the future; and to feel deeply the absolute moment of the present, in body, mind, and spirit.) Choosing a Hebrew name, and perhaps changing the name by which one has been known in public secular life, may become a profound exploration of one's own identity.

In the new atmosphere of celebration, more converts are wearing their choice as an important and public aspect of their Jewish identity. Some may choose to celebrate their new relationship by coming up to the Torah for the first time shortly after their conversion, or by inviting friends to take part as they affix their first *mezuza* to their doorpost. Some may take part in networks of "Jews by choice" and seek ways for the community to smooth the path of converts.

Just as the secrecy practiced by many converts during the era of Rabbinic Judaism has declined in the midst of large numbers of converts, so for some converts the desire has declined to "forget" all their previous understanding of the world. Some rabbis now counsel converts to bring with them the essence of what they found life-giving in the past, and, while abandoning the definitive practices of their previous religion, translate that life-giving core into Jewish terms and practice, while leaving behind what did not nourish them.

For some converts, the moment of transformation—as for those Jews who are shaping the first new household of their own, or are newly entering marriage—becomes a moment to choose what a "Jewish household" means to them. What kinds of food, what ritual objects, what patterns and cycles of time, what attitude toward the use and reuse of fuels and cloth and paper and all sorts of other objects, what efforts to protect the earth and heal society, will be welcome here?

So in accepting some version of the Torah covenant that binds an entire people in some way, new Jews may also find themselves thinking and writing their own individual torah-covenant, their own *k'tuba* with God and the Jewish people, to define the path they intend to walk.

In Jewish tradition, the act of conversion by an adult is one that lasts a lifetime. Unlike marriage, for this *ḥuppa* there is no *get*. No separation, no divorce. Yet the very act of conversion teaches deeply that we may need to make a "midlife" transformation. How to resolve this seeming contradiction?

Jewish wisdom itself reminds us that within the shape of Jewish life there is a spiral of continuing self-assessment and transformation. Every Shabbat, every approach of the "sabbatical month" which contains Rosh Hashanah and Yom Kippur, remind us of the need and opportunity for *t'shuva*, turning ourselves in a deeper direction. And we also learn the Shabbat of the years: the *sh'mita* year in every seven, during which we pause to renew our relationships with God, each other, and the earth. So perhaps the new *"k'tuba"* of each convert should make provision for a sabbatical reexamination. Every seventh year, a time to sit and evaluate where this path has taken her/him, and consciously decide how to make the next turning on the spiral.

PART 4

∾

Becoming Seed

❧ 12 ❧

Going to Seed

THE PLUMS, so purple that the eyes get lost within their violet shadows, are eaten by birds or gathered by humans, or rot into the ground. The peaches, so fuzzy-skinned they scratch the skin; the oranges and pomegranates, grapes and melons—all the fruitful harvest—do the same.

The landscape turns bare. Beneath the ground, invisible, the seed sets in.

Beyond the triumphant transformations of the middle of our lives, after the great harvests of our love and work, we go to seed. We take up less space, both in the gyrations of our bodies and in the housing we fold around our shoulders. We take up less space in thought and social action, in our business or profession, and even in the generosity of love. We turn inward.

Whether we can shape and celebrate this turning will make a great difference to the rest—the resting—of our lives. How can we do that, especially in a culture that rewards only work and regards resting as a waste of time?

There have begun to be some efforts to focus on what Rabbi Zalman Schachter-Shalomi calls "From Age-ing to Sage-ing." To see this time of resting as not a waste but a great deposit into the bank of seed. For—imagine instead a world in which the wisdom of many generations, stored in the seed in all its subtle variations, is burned as waste!

So the aging and their society both need to give new value to this aspect of life.

There are four moments of the inward-turning that would seem especially appropriate as focus-points for ceremony. One is retiring from a job or a career. Another is shifting to a smaller home. The third is learning to "share" the dying of the growing number of one's friends who are walking the last steps of life. The fourth is a conscious gathering to bless the next generation and plan one's own death.

The first strikes some interesting resonances with the Jubilee tradition of the Hebrew Bible. In that tradition (Lev. 25), every fiftieth year was a year of social and individual transformation. One crucial aspect of that transformation was that working paused, for a long Shabbat. Indeed, the count of fifty for the Jubilee was based in a sabbatical count of seven sevens, seven weeks of years in which each week had seven years: forty-nine years plus one.

In that year, there was no organized agriculture. No sowing, no harvesting, no pruning of the grapevines. Whatever grew could casually be plucked. Whatever had been stored before could be drawn on to meet whatever needs arose. A whole society made itself into the nomadic hunter-gatherers of its early days.

Even more astonishing, every family returned to its earliest holding. Those who had come to own more land, gave up the burden of their wealth. Those who had lost the land their family knew, gave up the burden of their poverty.

The Hebrew word for this momentous event, *Yovel*, has entered many languages not in translation but in rough transliteration—thus, "Jubilee." But some modern scholars, probing into the origins of this odd word, have concluded it was originally the term for a special note blown on the shofar (ram's horn) by shepherds—the special note to call home the flock at the end of a day of wandering in meadows, responding to the shepherd's crook, fearing wolves and lions.

"Home-bringing" is the way Everett Fox's translation of the Torah renders *yovel*.

Home-bringing. An apt metaphor for the moment of retirement.

Bar Yovel, Bat Yovel. One who has become a child of the Home-bringing.

One way to apply this fifty-year pattern might be that at the age of fifty, men and women should explore life in a mode of rest, a year off in the midst of active life, not waiting till their bodies, minds, emotions are more weary. This might indeed be a boon to all of us, and to our societies. But this seems precisely the harbinger of the kind of midlife transformation we have talked about before this, in Chapter 9. Here we are looking for a different turning on the spiral. So retirement seems more fitting to the need.

What might a *Bar/Bat Yovel* ceremony look like? The most salient ceremonial element of the Jubilee was a blast of the ram's horn. That might be followed by acts of inward turning:

- planting seeds;
- clearing out a house of unused clothing and furniture and decorations, giving these to an agency that serves the poor;
- simultaneously choosing a few precious items to be highlighted;
- choosing special teachings or objects to be given in a letter or a package, to younger members of the family, friends, co-workers, a synagogue, a museum, a library;
- writing, audiotaping, or videotaping stories of the past about family, politics, work, love; or presenting such stories that have previously been prepared;
- arranging to be interviewed by friends or by professional historians for an oral-history project.

Beyond these events, which are both "real" and "ritual," a *Bar/Bat Yovel* might want to become a mentor to some person/s two generations younger. To these "grandchildren," chosen by the body or by the heart and mind, it would be profoundly valuable to hand down skills and wisdoms of handicraft, faded songs and recipes, tools that once worked to build community.

And a *Bar/Bat Yovel* could take as teaching the *Yovel*'s effort to let the earth recover and catch its breath from the previous years of being used. The *Bar/Bat Yovel* might devote special attention to the wisdom of the seven generations past and the seven yet to come, wisdom of healing the rhythms of the earth.

"Going to Seed" might include downshifting to a smaller home. Many people move often in their lives, but many of these moves are to places with more space for bigger families. The reversal of this direction could seem saddening. But from a perspective of lightening loads and of strengthening others, it could be an act of joy as well.

To make it joyful, the shift to new quarters needs to be celebrated. Emplacing the *mezuza*, with special attention to the passage written on its scroll about "teaching it diligently to our children," can be made the focus of the ceremony. Many of the suggestions we have made above for the *Bar/Bat Yovel* transfer of memory, wisdom, beauty, could be connected to this change of homes as well as to a cessation of work. Rabbi Carey Kozberg has developed a ceremony for coming to live at a nursing home or other elder community—one that acknowledges fears of being cast off, and responds to them with prayer and song, often from the Psalms.

Third, there is the realization that a growing number of one's friends are dying. Standing alone, this knowledge might mean only more sadness, suffering. But it can become an opening toward healing of a new kind.

In most of the life-cycle practices we have described, there is an element of teaching or of learning. Yet for this moment there may be an inward-turning that is neither teaching nor learning but simply sharing, reflecting. Calm. Present.

Phyllis recalls: What is the role of those of us blessed to accompany a loved one along the path to the ultimate doorway? Not so different, in fact, from the one that has enabled us to hear and respond to the needs of a preverbal infant. Or to hear and respond to a friend or family member or lover at any other stage of life, whether joyous or painful.

That's the ability that each of us has, if we choose to use it, to get our egos, our beliefs, our fears, our need to control, out of the way so that we can be fully present with people preparing to let go of their bodies, listening deeply to where they are so that we can join with them, for a time, in that place.

Almost like entering a trance, we can make ourselves available for this merging that offers companionship to those facing death, new growth toward Mensch-hood for the witness, and deeper understanding of a crossing we will all ultimately face. For each of us, another experience of the Oneness of all life.

In the very last days of my beloved friend Shira Ruskay's twenty-six-year wrestle with cancer, she instructed those around her to stop talking with her, not to engage her, so that she would not be called back from the final journey toward death that she had begun. That instruction is important for those of us who are present near the end of the life of our loved ones: loud voices, falsely cheery conversations, conversations that ignore the presence of the dying person or the nearness of death, rob us all of the chance for encounter at this holy time.

In the last days of my friend Faye Kahn's life, literally hours before she died, I sat with her. By that time, she appeared mostly nonresponsive. Sitting close, eyes closed, hands gently touching, breathing increasingly in synch with one another, we two women could communicate, as people are often able to, without words. I heard a music and rhythm in Faye's labored breathing; as I tuned in to that rhythm and began to chant softly, Faye's breathing eased and quieted. Others entered and left the room, most of them joining in the final love song to Faye. Several hours later, Faye breathed her last breath. All who had been privileged to be with her those final days and hours knew that we had been given a rare glimpse into *olam haba*, the world that was coming.

As Shira so poignantly said, at 2 a.m. two weeks before she died, *"This* is *olam haba."* There's only this, a world that is always coming, coming, coming. There's only this, being present in the here-and-now that's always coming, present in the fullness of our beings, present with the people whom we love. Often there's more life in death than in life itself. And more love, too.

Death, like each of the liminal life moments, calls us to each other, beyond answers, beyond questions, to the place where we know beyond doubt that we are all connected for all time, at the level of soul, to the Breath-of-Life.

Finally, there is the possibility of consciously setting aside time to name the approach of one's own death and to bless the next generation. That is what Jacob did (Gen. 49) when he gathered his children at his bedside, told them how he understood their lives—praise, rebuke, insight all mixed together—and explained how he wanted his body to be dealt with. Then Jacob "drew his legs into his bed," and died. But we do not need to leave this process till the last minute—as if most us knew when the last moment would be!

Jacob's blessings have become the progenitor of Jewish "ethical wills," in which an elder distills the knowledge and wisdom of a lifetime and writes, for family and friends and possibly for a wider public, a message intended to continue. Perhaps the message is to be written now but delivered only after death. Or perhaps it is urgent to speak the truth as soon as possible.

And Jacob's clarity about where he wishes to be buried suggests taking the time to actually arrange the handling of the body.

- What about a "living will" concerning medical treatment if a sick patient is not able to make decisions?

- Should the family and the authorities be notified that organs are available for transplant, or does the person who is "becoming seed" prefer to leave a body whole for the earth? (Traditional Jewish practice would have strongly insisted on an intact body; now that organ transplants can save lives, the overriding principle of *pikuaḥ nefesh*, saving life, might balance the equation.)
- When death comes, will the body be buried? And if so, where and by whom?

In a number of Jewish communities, there are now arrangements for simple burial, in affirmation of the ancient tradition. Some funeral homes have agreed to make available simple pine coffins, at very low expense, and to make the process of decision-making clear. Far more effective to make these decisions and arrangements already known ahead of time.

All these decisions embody the values of the elder who is envisioning death.

More deeply, what about a *ḥeshbon hanefesh*, an accounting of the self? What about sitting down to cast up the acts of shattering and healing, the people loved and alienated, any injustices that remain to be made right, any loves unspoken or ill-spoken that remain to be affirmed? And not only to write down the accounting, but to act upon it?

Do we want to try to guide the process of our dying by shaping it in imagination during life? Would we like to rehearse the kind of death we'd welcome? And perhaps to imagine the journey afterwards—minimally to clarify our own philosophy of death-and-life, and maximally to influence what that journey will be like?

The ambiguity that lies at the heart of an inner contraction has been made a central myth of Kabbala, Jewish mysticism. According to some currents of Kabbala, the universe began with such an inner contraction—a *tzimtzum*. (Say the word lovingly and fully—"*tziiiiiiiiimtzoom*"—to get the feel of how something long and stretched out can become short and deep.)

The original *tzimtzum* was and is God's Own. According to this myth or metaphor, God was/is/will be All in All, utterly undifferentiated holiness. And God withdraws inward, opening up a womb-space within which there could be creation. And there is! From a thin film of Divinity left in the empty void, there grows a world. All that we know as creature and creation emerges from this act of self-contraction. From nought, Infinity!

The ambiguity of *tzimtzum* is indeed at the heart of what we face in "Going to Seed." Ought we to be sad at the contraction involved in turning from roly-poly colorful fruit into the tiniest of seeds, or joyful that our accumulated wisdom might go deep underground into another generation?

The point of celebrating this last turn on the spiral of our lives is to make it both sad and joyful. Neither emotion need be disheartening, if we make the sense of impending death into an opportunity for teaching and for the Be-ing that lies beyond even teaching.

∾ 13 ∾

The Doorway Whose Other Side We Cannot See

So NOW WE COME TO THE MOMENT OF DEATH. And we find our story of the life-path forking into two:

From one perspective, we are still following the person who has been the central focus of these pages; the one whose birth and childhood and adolescence shaped an "I," who encountered a "Thou," who harvested the fruitfulness of all of life's encounters, and who from that harvest went to seed. The person who now is dying, the person who now dies.

There is a major strand of Jewish wisdom that says we can glimpse the next step on the life-path of that person. That says our ceremonies guide the soul of one who has walked across a threshold, and who is celebrating with us as we celebrate.

From that perspective, we could apply the teachings of those who study ritual, and look to see how the rituals of death allow the soul to leave the conventional community, encounter God, become a new self, and return to the community transformed.

Another major strand of Jewish wisdom focuses on those we still can see, the mourners. In this light, we understand the rituals of grief as ways to walk these people through their own next spiral in the path of their own lives.

Perhaps we need not choose between these two perspectives.

Death in the Biblical Tradition

In the Bible, Abraham's first step in responding to the death of someone close to him was the purchase of a site for Sarah's grave, at the Cave of Maḥpeyla. (Gen. 23) His sons Isaac and Ishmael buried him there as well (Gen. 25:9), and later Isaac and Rebekah, and Leah and Jacob, were also buried there. (Gen. 49:29–33) Thus the Torah set the whole pattern and assumption of a family burial-place, and indeed of burial as the way to deal with the body. No ritual of mourning is described at that point except for the burial itself. As for the question of the continuity of identity after death, the Torah used only the phrase "He was gathered to his kinfolk." (Gen. 25:8)

When Rachel died, evidently too far from Maḥpeyla to be buried there, Jacob raised up a pillar at the place where he buried her.

We have seen that when Jacob was near death, he called his children together to give them truthful blessings—sometimes harsh—concerning how their futures would emerge from their past actions. And he left instructions to take his body back from Egypt to Maḥpeyla.

Now for the first time we hear of an emotional outburst from a mourner: Joseph "fell upon his father's face, wept over him, and kissed him." (Gen. 50:1) Then he had his father's body embalmed in the Egyptian fashion, and after a seventy-day mourning period—Joseph, remember, was viceroy of Egypt—carried the body toward Maḥpeyla. Once they had crossed the Jordan into Canaan, they paused for *shiva*—that is, a seven-day mourning—as if Joseph now felt "at home" and so could mourn in a more familial way. Leaving the multitude of courtiers behind, the family itself completed the journey to Maḥpeyla.

As for Joseph himself, on the point of death he had his family promise that in some uncertain future when "God had taken note" of them, they would carry his bones back with them to the Land. He too was embalmed. (Gen. 50:24–26)

The Torah's law codes have much less to say about the practice of burial and mourning than we might expect. We do learn that even the body of someone who has been executed is to be treated with respect, more for the sake of God and the Land than for the criminal: "You must not let his corpse remain on the stake overnight, but must bury him the same day. For an impaled body is an affront to God; you shall not defile the land." (Deut. 21:22–23)

And we learn that contact with a dead body makes anyone *tamey*, a state of uncanny intensity that, as we have already discussed, makes it impossible to have contact with the communal holiness of the Temple. An elaborate ritual of the "red cow" is set forth by Torah to end the state of *tuma*. The red cow is to be burnt with red wood (cedar), and scarlet dye was thrown into the fire; its ashes were mixed with water, and by sprinkling this water on the *tamey* person, the *tuma* was relieved. (Num. 19)

When King David faced the mortal illness of a beloved child, he wept and fasted. When the child died, he washed and changed his clothes, prayed prostrate at the Holy Shrine, and ate. When the courtiers asked why he had ceased his grieving, he answered: "While the child was still alive I thought my fasting might bring the compassion of YHWH to grant him life. But now that he is dead, can I bring him back again? I shall go to him, but he will never come back to me."

The Rhythms of Grief According to the Rabbis

Rabbinic Judaism wove the threads of time into a far more elaborate pattern of mourning. Let us follow the process from the realization of a serious illness to the years of memory long after death. In traditional Jewish communities, this process continues to be followed. In those less traditional, some aspects of it are observed more fully than some others. There have been fewer ethical objections from the Jews of Modernity to the traditional rituals of death than to many of the other life-path ceremonies.

First, as people who are sick begin to worsen, friends encourage them to say *Vidu-i*, a confession (literally, "I acknowledge"). To calm them they are reminded, "Many have said *Vidu-i* and recovered, many have not said it and died. Whoever acknowledges his sins has a share in the world to come; and the acknowledgment itself may fill you with new life." One formula:

> I acknowledge to You, YHWH my God, God of my forebears, that my healing and my death are in Your hands. May it be Your will to grant me a complete healing. But if You are determined on my death, I lovingly accept it at Your hands. May my death atone for all my misdeeds, iniquities, and transgressions of which I have been guilty against You. You Who are Parent to orphans and Protector of widows, protect my beloved family. Into Your hand I give my breath, my spirit. You have redeemed me, God of truth. *Sh'ma Yisra-el, YHWH eloheynu, YHWH eḥad.* Hear, Godwrestlers/Yisra-el: the Lord our God, the Lord is One.

Rabbinic tradition also teaches that the *Sh'ma* should be said just at the point of death. Tradition taught that Rabbi Akiba, as he was being tortured to death by the Romans, said the *Sh'ma* and smiled. His students asked whether he was immune to pain. He answered that he had always wondered how to obey one word in the passage that accompanies the *Sh'ma*—the one that commands us, "You shall love God *b'ḥol nafsheḥa*, with all your breath/soul." Now, he explained, he could do it: With his last breath and his whole soul he could love God. Thus he made his death a *midrash*, and made himself an example for Jews of the future.

There is another way to understand this teaching. The Torah teaches, and we recite in every service, that we should place the words of the *Sh'ma* at every doorway, and these words are indeed in each *mezuza*. Why there? Perhaps to remind us at precisely the threshold of what might seem two utterly different worlds—home and away, the gates between our own city and culture and the foreign world of barbarians, the threshold between sleep and waking—that what could seem two separate worlds is really One. At the threshold between life and death, between "this world (*olam hazeh*)" and "the world that's coming (*olam haba*)," this affirmation would hold a deeper meaning.

So as the end draws near, the dying person may say words that are more familiar to us from the closing service of Yom Kippur. The echo may teach us in both directions: Is dying like ending the deep struggles of Yom Kippur and entering into a calmer sea? As Yom Kippur ends, are we to remember that the Awesomeness of death still stands before us? In both moments, we affirm the Majestic God of Mystery:

YHWH meleh, YHWH malah, YHWH yimloh l'olam va-ed.
Baruh shem k'vod malhuto l'olam va-ed. (Three times.)
YHWH hu ha-elohim. (Seven times.)
YHWH reigns, YHWH has reigned, YHWH will reign forever and beyond.
Blessed be the Name of God's radiant reign, forever and beyond. (Three times.)
YHWH is God. (Seven times.)

And then the *Sh'ma*.

Meanwhile, as their illnesses become of greater concern to the community, in synagogue the names of the sick are added to prayers for healing. After the reading of the Torah, a special prayer: May the One Who blessed our forebears bless this one [with the name, in Hasidic circles often connected with the mother's rather than the father's name] with a complete healing, a healing of spirit and a healing of body, *r'fu-a shleyma, r'fu-at hanefesh ur'fu-at haguf.*

If the illness proceeds to where it seems irreversible and the patient seems within three days of death, s/he becomes understood as a *gosses*. A candle may be lit at the bedside, signaling with its flickering light the flickering of the soul. While nothing active can be done to hasten death, active means of delaying it—sounds that have kept the sick person alert, prayers that forbid entry to the Angel of Death—can be withdrawn to lessen suffering. (In our own generation, some have drawn on this permission to stop actively delaying death, to suggest that ventilators and other medical instruments might be withdrawn, in order to permit an end to suffering.)

Since Jewish tradition has placed such emphasis on the breath as the crucial element of life (from the awakening of Adam on), the cessation of breathing has traditionally been taken as the crucial sign of death. Physicians may also check heartbeat, pulse, the reflex of the eye to shining light. Once death is confirmed, those present say: *"Baruḥ dayan emet"*—"Blessed is the True Judge," a blessing without the customary invocation of God as Lord and King.

The body is left untouched for about eight minutes, and a last check for breath, by brushing a feather across the nose and lips, is done. The nearest relative closes the eyes and mouth, and the jaws may be tied together. Traditionally, the body is placed on the floor, feet toward the door, and a candle lit near the head—to give the departing soul, who may be confused about directions in a nondimensional world, guidance on the path forward. Mirrors are turned toward the wall, and water standing in basins is poured out.

From the moment of death until burial, the body is accompanied by someone saying Psalms. This practice is called *Sh'mira*, "guarding."

Soon the body is brought to a *Ḥevra kadisha*, or "holy fellowship," made up of men for a man, women for a woman, for *tahara*—purification or clarification. *Tahara*, and the whole process of traditional burial, calls for the body to be as fully integral in its physicality as possible. Autopsies have been strongly opposed except where secular law demands it—for example, to obtain evidence about possible criminal assault or a possible communicable disease that could not be procured in any other way.

The *tahara* process begins, indeed, with a plea directly to the body for forgiveness of any acts that might seem disrespectful or offensive. The body is stripped and washed for physical cleansing, in a prescribed order: head, neck, right arm, right torso, right leg, left arm, left torso, left leg, genitals, right back, left back, fingernails and toenails. As the washing proceeds, a series of verses from the Bible are recited:

The angel responded, speaking to those who stood by, 'Remove these filthy garments from him!' and then said, 'See, I have removed your transgressions from you, and clothed you in sacred robes.' (Zech. 3:4)

I will sprinkle clear water upon you, and you shall be clear. I will clear you of all your *tuma*. I will clear you from all your cycles. (Ezekiel 36:25)

Then verses on parts of the body, as each is cleansed:

His head is burnished gold, the mane of his hair black as the raven; his eyes like doves by the rivers of milk and plenty; his cheeks a bed of spices, a treasure of precious scents; his lips red lilies wet with myrrh. His arm a golden scepter with gems of topaz, his loins the ivory of thrones inlaid with sapphire, his thighs like marble pillars on pedestals of gold. Tall as Mount Lebanon, majestic as a cedar, his mouth sweet wine—he is all delight. This is my beloved, this my friend, O daughters of Jerusalem. You are a fountain in the garden, a well of living waters that stream from Lebanon. (Song 5:11–16, 4:15)

Then comes the central and indispensable part of *tahara*: "Nine *kav*" of water (about 4½ gallons) are sluiced across the body while it is held upright. The water-pouring is done so that the flow is kept continuous.

Then the body is dried and dressed in shrouds (*taḥriḥim*) following an order that tracks the description of the High Priest's clothing in the Torah: headdress, trousers, tunic, the *kittel*, and a belt. (The *kittel*, white robe, is what men have traditionally worn at their weddings and at every Yom Kippur and Pesaḥ Seder. Here woman wear them as well, and indeed are clothed as the men are, except that traditional women are unlikely to wear a *tallit*.) The slipknots that hold each garment on are tied with bows shaped like a *shin*, the Hebrew letter that is also placed on the face of a *mezuza* and denotes *Shaddai*, the Nurturing God.

Articles of clothing that are soaked or spattered with blood are placed in the coffin, since the physical integrity of the body includes its blood as well.

Finally the dead person's own *tallit* (prayer shawl) has the twisted fringe (*tzitzit*) cut from one of the four corners, and the *tallit* is placed around the body in the coffin. (In communities where secular law does not require a coffin, the body may be covered and placed upon a plank of wood.) Often, earth from the Land of Israel is placed in the coffin. The burial is scheduled for as soon as possible. Though with very great care it might be possible to shape a burial on a festival day while staying within halakhic bounds, this is rarely done.

Meanwhile, the close-in mourners—defined as parents, children, siblings, and spouse—are in a special state of almost suspended animation called *aninut* (each one an *onen*). From death till burial they are forbidden to pray, to say the *Sh'ma*, to put on *t'fillin* (leather boxes for the arm and head, bearing verses from the Torah), as they would normally do each morning, or to perform any of the other active *mitzvot* required by the Torah. No one tries to comfort them.

Most commentators have suggested that *aninut* protects the mourners from the unbearable strain of praising God while their dead yet lie before them, and protects God and the community from the blasphemy of thought and deed that might otherwise pour from hearts drenched in rage and despair.

During this time or as the funeral begins, the close-in mourners do the act of *k'ri-a*—ripping an article of clothing they are wearing. The rip is about three inches long, and visible above the heart. The same garment is worn till the end of *shiva*. Before tearing, the mourner recites an expanded version of the blessing said upon first hearing of the death: *"Baruḥ ata YHWH eloheynu meleḥ ha-olam, dayan ha-emet."*

Then the *levaya*, or funeral. (Literally, the Hebrew means "connecting" or "escorting," and it refers to escorting the body to the grave.) Family and community gather. The coffin has been closed: No chance to make the corpse into an idol or a public spectacle. The guardians who have been chanting Psalms enter with the body, ending their chants only as the prayers begin. Indeed, the service begins with Psalms.

Usually a *hesped* is then presented by a family member, a friend, or a rabbi. (But sometimes the *hesped* is reserved for a later memorial.) *Hesped* is often translated as "eulogy," and it is the word applied to a public recollection of the life of the dead. But at root it is the Hebrew for "lament," and it calls forth truth about the mourning process, not just a mechanical recitation of good deeds. In traditional communities, no *hesped* is spoken on such days of special joy as festivals, New Moons, and Hanukkah.

Finally, the prayer *Eyl Maley Raḥamim* ("God filled with compassion") would be said:

Eyl maley raḥamim shoḥen bam'romim hamtzey m'nuḥa n'ḥona taḥat kanfei hash'ḥina b'ma-alot k'doshim ut'horim k'zohar harakiya mazhirim et nishmat [the name of the deceased] *she'halaḥ l'olamo* [for a man]/*she'halḥa l'olama* [for a woman]. *B'gan eyden t'hey menuḥato (menuḥata). Ana ba-al haraḥamim, hastireyhu (histireyha) b'seter k'nafeḥa l'olamim. U'tzror bitzror haḥayim et nishmato (nishmata). YHWH hu naḥalato (naḥalata). V'yanu-aḥ (V'tanu-aḥ) b'shalom al mishkavo (mishkava), v'nomar ameyn.*

And this translation might evoke the central image of the prayer: God's Presence carrying the newly rising soul under Her wings, as the mother eagle teaches her young to fly:

God full of compassion, Who dwells on high—as the expiring soul-breath of [name] floats outward toward the hidden places of eternity, let it rise restfully, held by the wings of Your Presence, to join the holy and pure who glow as bright as the dome of Heaven. May s/he find rest in the Garden of Delight. May You, Master of Motherly Compassion, shelter him (her) forever and beyond beneath the shelter of Your wings, and bind up his (her) soul in the bond of life. May s/he, who has left her/his life-work as our inheritance, find You, Yahh, the Breath of All Life, what s/he inherits. May s/he find peace and wholeness in her/his resting-place. And let us say, Ameyn.

At the cemetery, just before or after the placement of the body in the grave, there is a recitation of *Tzidduk HaDin*. This is a collection of verses that affirm the ultimate flow and pattern of the universe, the ultimate though unfathomable justice of a universe in which death not only comes but sometimes comes cruelly. No accident that the passages start with an image of God as Rock, the unyielding granite aspect of Divinity: *"YHWH natan, YHWH lakah y'hi shem YHWH m'vorah."*—"The Rock, its works are perfect and all its ways are just." In a slightly midrashic translation, we might hear: "The Breath of Life has breathed in; the Breath of Life has breathed out. Blessed is Yahh, the name of the Breath of Life."

Pallbearers then carry the coffin to the grave. They pause seven times on this final journey, unwinding with each pause the great seven-day spiral of creation, and a phrase of Psalms is said at each pause.

Once the coffin or bier is lowered into the grave (or once the grave has been filled), the close-in mourners recite a special Kaddish that is said only at the burial itself. Unlike the familiar Mourners' Kaddish, this version does take cognizance of death. Its first paragraph, which replaces the usual one, affirms:

Yitgadal v'yitkadash sh'mey raba b'alma di hu atid l'ithadata
ul'ahaya-a meytaya ul'aska yat'hon l'hayey alma. Ul'minvey karta

di yirushleym ul'shaḥ'lala heyḥley b'gava. Ul'meker palḥana nuḥra'a
min ara v'la-atava palḥana di shmaya l'atrey v'yamliḥ kudsha b'riḥ
hu b'malḥutey v'yikarey b'ḥayeḥon uv'yomeyḥon uv'ḥayey d'ḥol beyt
Yisra-el ba-agala u'viẓman kariv v'imru ameyn.

May the Great Name become still more holy and more expansive
in a world that is moving toward a future of renewal. Then
what is dead will be filled with life, raised up forever. Then
Jerusalem will be rebuilt, the House of Holiness completed;
idolatry will be uprooted and the sacred service lifted to where
earth and heaven meet. May the Majesty of the Great Name
become fully apparent during our lifetime and the lifetime of all
Israel;—And let us say, Ameyn.

And then this Burial Kaddish continues like the usual Mourners'
Kaddish. *Eyl maley raḥamim* is said again.

Then family and friends join in covering the body with earth. Each
uses the reverse side of a shovel (indicating reluctance rather than
alacrity) to pour three spades-full of earth into the grave, and then—
rather than give it directly to someone else—replaces the shovel in the
mound of earth, ready for another to take up the task. The task is considered a valuable aspect of comforting the dead with this warm blan-
ket of earth, and freeing the living from their denial of the death, as if
to say: "Even my muscles affirm what my mind and my heart still
deny."

The close-in mourners pass between two lines of friends who
say to them, *"HaMakom y'naḥeym et'ḥem b'toḥ sh'ar avley Tẓi-on
viY'rushala-yim."*—"May the Ever-Present One comfort you among
all who mourn for Zion and Jerusalem."

The mourning family returns to the home of the person who has
died or someone close, and begins sitting the seven days of mourning—*shiva*. As they and friends arrive at the home, they pause at the
doorway to pour water over their hands, symbolically immersing to
end the state of *tuma* arising from emotional and physical contact with
death. They light a large memorial candle that will last for seven days.

During the *levaya*, friends will have prepared the "meal of consolation" for both physical and spiritual renewal. The foods include lentils and hard-boiled eggs, both symbolic of the roundness of the life-cycle. (Ancient Jewish legend taught that the famous dish of lentils with which Jacob bought the birthright from his famished elder brother, Esau, was part of the *shiva* observance for the death of their grandfather Abraham.)

Through the days of *shiva*, the close-in mourners suspend their usual lives—work, sauntering in the neighborhood, cooking, sexual relations, wearing leather shoes and fancy clothes, even studying Torah or other sacred texts. Three daily prayer services are held at home, and friends make sure a *minyan* is present so that the Mourners' Kaddish can be said at every service.

The family often sit in specially low chairs, and generally do not rise to greet anyone. Friends come to visit but wait to be greeted, rather than imposing their presence on the mourners. Many bring food so that the family does not need to attend to cooking. Upon leaving, friends say gently, *"HaMakom y'naheym et'hem b'toh sh'ar avley Tzi-on viY'rushala-yim."*—"May the Ever-Present One comfort you among all who mourn for Zion and Jerusalem."

When Shabbat comes, the public aspects of *shiva* mourning are suspended (while the private limitations like that on sex continue) and the mourners go to synagogue to join in the community's joyful renewal of life. As they enter, the congregation greets them with the same blessing of consolation. With the end of Shabbat, *shiva* resumes.

The advent of a festival such as Pesah or Rosh Hashana cancels *shiva* altogether, so long as even a few moments have been observed after the burial and before the festival begins. But if the burial occurs during the middle days of Pesah or Sukkot, the family observes the festival and then begins a regular *shiva* after the festival ends.

Shiva ends after the morning service on the seventh day, often with a walk outdoors by the close-in mourners to symbolize their return to normal life.

Then begins a period called *shloshim*, "thirty"—thirty days from the burial. (The thirtieth day means that the moon is at the same place in its cycle as it was when the body was buried.) During this time, the mourners continue to say Mourners' Kaddish. They do not cut their hair, shave, take part in social events or celebrations, wear new clothes, or take part in the festive meals that accompany such religious markers as a wedding or a *b'rit*. (But attending the ceremony itself is permissible.)

After *shloshim*, all mourning practices traditionally end, except for saying Kaddish for a parent. That continues for, typically, eleven months—at any rate, something a little less than a year. Why such an odd time? Because according to tradition, saying Kaddish helps the soul of the person who has died rise step by step from whatever punishment might have been necessary to scour its guilt away. Even the worst of sinners is thought to need only a year of such scouring. So no one would wish to say that her own parent needs a full year of saying Kaddish, and yet no one would wish to deprive a parent's soul of the needed Kaddish. So eleven months has become a reasonable ending-time.

Perhaps but not necessarily at the same time, a gravestone is erected with the name and life-dates of the person who has died. This custom dates back all the way to Mother Rachel, whose grave Jacob marked with a pillar. Often this stone is dedicated by a special gathering of mourners. The stone may be covered with a translucent cloth, and then unveiled as a memorial. The custom arose for all who visited the grave to place a stone upon it, joining their small "pillar" to the larger one. At the graves of some great seers and teachers—for example, the grave in the town of Safed of Shlomo HaLevi Alkabetz, author of the beloved hymn *L'ḥa Dodi* that welcomes Shabbat—the grave is piled heavy with pebbles.

Mourning for parents continues in a rhythm throughout the rest of one's life. Every year on the anniversary in the Jewish calendar of a parent's death—the *yohrtzeit*, to use the familiar Yiddish word that literally means "year-time"—the children light a memorial candle as the sun sets, and recite the Mourners' Kaddish in the synagogue. And where possible, they visit their parents' graves in the days before Rosh Hashana. (In strict application of *halaḥa*, only for parents is *yohrtẓeit* observed. Many now observe *yohrtẓeit* of other relatives.)

On Yom Kippur, Sh'mini Atzeret, the last day of Pesaḥ, and the second day of Shavuot, a *Yiẓkor* ("May You remember") service is held in the synagogue. Not only close family but also teachers, leaders, friends, martyrs, are all remembered on that day with the recitation of *Eyl maley raḥamim* as well as Mourners' Kaddish and other prayers, and with the lighting of memorial candles.

In the last generation, much was written about how this long process addresses the psychological and therapeutic needs of the family and friends of the dying and the dead. For it helps us move in many different gaits of hope, horror, grief, and memory—from the time when there was still hope of recovery from illness, through the intense and lonely rage and despair just after death, through the need for action in the burial, through the need for community during *shiva*, into the slowly lessening pain of the next month, the next year, and on into recurring moments of painful and joyful remembrance thereafter.

But to us this seems not merely psychotherapeutic. Indeed, for the mourners this process works like their own fourfold life-cycle ceremony: bringing them out of the ordinary community, into the sharp transformative confrontation with God involved in the *aninut* and the burial, then into a new sense of Self embodied in the *shiva*, and then slowly returning—changed—into a changed community.

As we said in the first chapter, about *B'rit Mila*, and also about such moments as becoming Bar/Bat Mitzvah and getting married, the central figure is not the only one who is moving somewhere new in the spirals of a life. At each of those stages, parents and grandparents most obviously, and others as well, are experiencing a transformation in their lives. So too at a death. But here the mourners may or may not be in some "orderly" chronological place in the life-journey. If the dead person is old enough to have adult children, as often we wish were the "normal" time of dying, then those children may well feel themselves now on "the front lines" of life and death. Before, perhaps, there had been someone a generation older who was closer to the river. Now they face a stark and awesome landscape. For them this moment bears a special weight, and they themselves are certainly in a new turn of the life-spiral.

Yet death may not follow such a "normal" chronological path. The mourners may include parents, even grandparents; a community of students, or of teachers; a whole range of people who are confronting not even necessarily the death that has just occurred but the spectre of their own.

So for all these sorts of mourners, the journey of their own lives is either narrowed or enriched by the way the traditional Jewish pattern of mourning speaks to them. If it helps them grow, helps them in the transformative moment of meeting God to take another step in their own evolution, then it will have well served them, and all reality.

The Life-Path of the Dead

As we said at the beginning of this chapter, it would be possible to focus on the dying/mourning process as the life-cycle ceremony only of the mourners whose faces we see clearly as we watch them dance their spiral on the public stage. But does that mean the "central figures" in these dramas have no script at all, because we cannot hear them voice it, see them dance it?

Jewish teaching from the past did not say so. Beginning with the mysterious story of King Saul's consultation with the ghost of the dead Prophet Samuel (I Sam. 28), becoming more and more complex through rabbinic history and more and more elaborate still in the explorations of the Kabbalists, there is a strong thread of conviction about the continuity of individual identity after death.

During the last two hundred years or so of Modernity's triumph, many Jews have shunted these teachings aside as raising questions not answerable by the evidence Modernity accepts, and therefore not even worth the questioning. Indeed, millions of Jews during the last century barely knew that there were Jewish doctrines of afterlife, and if they did know, rejected them as irrational and superstitious. For many, it was an article of faith that what survives death is only the memory of the dead and the consequences of their actions in life, for good or evil.

Yet the complex threads of Jewish beliefs about post-death continuity are so rich and strong that we cannot fully describe the fabric here. What is more, we need not, since for our generation Simcha Raphael (in *Jewish Views of the Afterlife*) has brilliantly brought those teachings together in a way that should be most helpful to those whose desire to know far outstrips their knowledge.

But there is one aspect of the question that we do want to address. That is the time just before and just after death—the time we might reasonably see as part of the life-cycle ceremony of the dead themselves.

One of the greatest of Jewish mystical texts, the thirteenth-century Zohar, asserts that thirty days before a person's death, the "image" of that person is withdrawn and rises to Heaven. Throughout the person's life, that image (presumably an aspect of the Image of God in which every human is made) has carried the flow of life and abundance from Heaven into the tangible and intangible energies that make up life. With it gone, the body slowly becomes unable to sustain itself, and the person moves into a dying state.

Until that point, all a person's actions have been entering themselves into the "book" of the universe: All such deeds have consequences, and these consequences themselves rise up to accuse or justify, to calm or torment. Now the person's inner thoughts also enter the balance of judgment. And on the day of death, a final assessment begins. Indeed, the entire life of the dying person passes in review—as if the memories buried in every brain cell are discharging all at once, and providing an ethical as well as biological accounting.

And at the same time, the dying person gets to see beyond the curtain. The *Sheḥina* Herself (God's Indwelling, feminine Presence), as well as guides who seem filled with light, dead relatives, teachers, all beckon. But so does the dark side, unless the dying person has lived in accordance with Torah.

During the period of *shiva*, says the Zohar, the soul may have intense difficulty in understanding that it has actually separated from the body. Just as the mourners are learning that the death has really occurred and are coming to terms with it, so the soul is learning that its body is gone, and that it needs to move on. As the mourners are comforting each other, the soul is learning to be comforted in its new way of existing.

It may be spun by twin catapults from one end of the universe to the other and back again, in each great circle spinning off dross from its previous life. After thirty days of this initial process—the period of *shloshim*—it will once again have a body, though an ethereal one, and now that ethereal "body" needs to be purified.

So, depending on the person's particular accumulation of *mitzvot* and misdeeds during her/his lifetime, the soul may now move slowly or quickly through the scourings and clarifications of *Gehinom*. This journey may take as long as a year, punctuated by times of calm on Shabbat.

From this process the soul emerges into a realm of blissful companionship with God in Eden, the Garden of Delight. Even here, the remembrance of *yohrtzeit* each year by those the soul has left behind may lift it to a higher rung of joy. Indeed, the custom arose of studying Mishna to help the soul's ascent, because *Mishna* is an anagram in Hebrew of *Neshama*—"life-breath" or "soul."

Ultimately, the soul may be ready for another *gilgul*—another turn of the vital wheel, another life-cycle. This recycling of souls was seen not as punishment but as an invitation to still more advancement, like an invitation to strengthen a weak muscle. The number of limbs and sinews in a human body were thought to make up part of the number of *mitzvot*, the sacred commandments. If one limb were weak, so might be the doing of its corresponding *mitzvot*. So those souls who still needed strengthening of a psychic limb might get a chance to do so in another body. Those who had in a previous lifetime achieved high levels of clarity might reenter a body in order to bring their wisdom to the human community. In this way, the dead would indeed become seed, giving new life to a later generation.

To us, what is noteworthy about this schema is that it weaves together two main dimensions of action: the ethical behavior of the newly dead person while s/he was yet alive and active in this world; and the time rhythms of death-day, *shiva*, *shloshim*, *yohrtzeit* as acted out by the mourners. Either can correct for defects in the other, and if both have been, are being, well lived, then the journey of the soul will be sweet afterlife.

This understanding of the afterlife invites the mourners not only to assist the soul in its journey but to feel themselves walking a parallel path. Each thought and feeling is transformed into its more ethereal form, and the mourner is able to glimpse another world that is experiencing much the same pain of loss, the same sweet memories, the same sorrow at missed opportunities of healing, the same excitement that all may be repaired with a second chance, the same sense of harmony in sharing wisdom.

As below, so above.

The Renewal of Mourning

As we have seen throughout this book, the impact of Modernity on Judaism during the past century has brought about many changes in life-cycle ceremonials. In the case of this final passage, however, there have so far been fewer changes.

Why might this be?

We think there are several factors at work. First of all, the generational wave that began making major changes—the wave that included efforts to make sure that women and men are treated as equals, large numbers of conversion to Judaism, and deep interest in Jewish responses to the ecological crisis—is made up of people who are mostly not yet old enough to be experiencing large numbers of deaths among them. So their exploratory energy has so far gone in other directions. Already, however, we are beginning to see new questions arising that may well lead to important changes in the liturgies of death and mourning.

Secondly, a great deal of the energy for change in observing the other life-passages has come from efforts to dissolve the traditional role distinctions between men and women (for example, the creation of *b'rit* ceremonies for baby girls, the involvement of young women in Bat Mitzvah observances identical with Bar Mitzvah observance, egalitarian weddings and divorces) or to recognize life-passages that only women experience (menarche and menopause). In regard to death and mourning, traditional ceremonials treat women and men with much more similarity than do most of the life-passage ceremonials. Such few role distinctions as have been defined—like the assumption that only sons, not daughters, could say Mourners' Kaddish—have softened and eroded much more easily than those of baby *b'rit*, or *ḥuppa*.

Yet other impacts of Modernity have nevertheless raised new questions about the ceremonials of death and mourning. And the development of what might be called "postmodern spirituality" has also raised new questions, especially about attitudes toward the nature of the soul and afterlife.

We will first take up the emerging questions about ceremony, and then look at the new questions about the soul and afterlife.

How do we address what has been the prevailing isolation of death, far more than other life-cycle events, from the ongoing life of Modernized communities? Mourning in premodern Jewish communities often involved the intimate contact of all the people in a village or a neighborhood with the presence and the practices of death. Deaths of children from smallpox, of women in childbirth, of men with cholera, peppered every household with kernels of despair. Often, villagers and neighbors expressed their grief in full-throated, whole-body clarity.

One of the practices of many Modernized communities has been to isolate death, create a whole professional and corporate structure to deal with it separately from all the processes of daily life, and put strong controls on the expression of grief. So Jews who live in Modernized communities have been likely to know less about death and about its rituals, and literally to hear less of the grief that has accompanied it, and so to have less social support to express their own feelings with strength and clarity.

Arthur recalls: I remember my grandmother wailing, shrieking openthroated at my uncle's grave—and being sternly hushed by my mother, who had tightened her mouth to swallow the pain. Two generations, two very different approaches.

So in the newer communities of Jewish practice, affected by Modernity but often uncomfortable with its controls over emotion and unhappy about its tendency to build walls around the dying and the dead, there have been efforts to learn a different sort of mourning. One remarkable book, Anne Brener's *Mourning & Mitzvah*, guides mourners step by step along the classic Jewish path—with a difference.

Brener recognizes that there are now few close-knit villages and neighborhoods in which the mourning-wisdom of the tradition can be left to bubble up in every *shiva* kitchen. Conscious intention must take the place of what in those villages were effortless responses schooled from childhood on. In many of those kitchens there was a wrinkled woman sipping boiling water with a slice of lemon—and talking. Telling. Now pages of a book must take the place of lemon slices.

Brener also recognizes that our generation has a more complex relation to emotion than either of the two exemplified by Arthur's grandmother and mother. So Brener provides "whole-self" exercises to assist mourners to fulfill each aspect and stage of mourning. These exercises encourage not repressing emotion but either vigorously and outwardly expressing it, or, alternatively, channeling it into quiet, inward explorations. Brener treats the traditional practices as pointers, recipes, toward the transcendence of denial, the recovery of memory, the expression of grief, the healing of survivors. Recipes for expression rather than repression. Yet expression in the form not always of an outward shriek but often rather, of a letter written to the friend or parent who has died, or a journaling with vivid notes of memory of a person's looks and ways of speaking—reflections rather than explosions.

The high mobility of many Modernized Jewish families now raises new questions for the mourning process. Since many families now live in several different cities, should we begin to see *shiva* as a multilocal service? Should the bereaved family sit *shiva* for several days at the home of the person who has died, and then (like Jacob's family) move to their own hometowns to sit where their own friends and community can join them?

What about those (like the intimate friends we discuss in Chapter 8) who by the traditional definitions are not "family" at all? In an era when many Jews are shaping "intentional families" and intimate friendships precisely because blood families are widely scattered, should such relationships be accepted as having the weight of family when it comes to mourning? Can more than one "family" sit *shiva* for the dead, in such a situation?

Given the Modern increase in contacts between different religious communities and the blurring of boundaries between them, what mourning practices do we owe each other? Most poignantly, how should converts to Judaism respond to the deaths of their non-Jewish parents and siblings? Should they sit *shiva*, or perhaps set aside the same seven days but observe them in a different way? Use Kaddish, or perhaps chant the Twenty-third Psalm (which is sacred in Jewish, Christian, and Muslim traditions) as an analogue to Kaddish?

Should parents' attitudes toward Judaism, and toward their child's conversion to Judaism, be taken into account in assessing whether or how much to adopt Jewish practice in mourning them? Or is the child's need to mourn paramount, and should that mourning take place, regardless, in the forms of the mourner's own life—now Jewish forms?

What about friends who are members of other faith communities?

In light of the rise in numbers of families where one spouse is Jewish and the other is not, should Jewish cemeteries—which have emphasized family burial plots like Abraham's grave in Maḥpeyla—continue to be reserved for Jews alone? How should the Jewish community deal with the death of a member of an "intermarried" family?

And what about tragic, agonizing times (like those in which the two of us are actually writing) when members of our larger family are dying at each other's hands? When some of the children of Abraham through Hagar and some of the children of Abraham through Sarah are killing each other, is it possible to mourn the dead of both branches of the family?

The last line of Mourners' Kaddish says: *"Oseh shalom bim'romav hu ya-aseh shalom aleynu v'al kol Yisra-el"*—"May the One Who makes harmony in the farthest reaches of the universe make harmonious peace for all Israel" [and, many add, *"v'al kol yoshvei teyveyl"*—"and for all those who dwell on the planet"]. Is it possible to insert *"v'al kol Yishma-el"*—"and for all Ishmael"?

Modernity's medical-scientific prowess has also raised new questions about burial. In the light of much more effective medical use of harvested organs to save the dying, how do we balance *piku-aḥ nefesh* (the rule that saving a life is paramount) and *kavod hameyt* (profound respect for the dead)? Should we waive the traditional Jewish concern for the physical integrity of the body to be buried and harvest vital organs of the dead for transplant, if the transplant might save a life? Or only if saving a life is certain? And if we do accept organ transplant, what does *tahara* then involve, in order to affirm respect for the dignity of the body? Should we modify the specific practices of *tahara* in

order to balance honor for the dead with healing for the sick? Or do
we decide that respect for the dead continues to require the protection
of the physical integrity of the corpse wherever possible, and let that
ancient respect stand as a challenge to the assumption that modern
life-saving technology should always be preferred?

*Modernity has given us much more knowledge about the causes of
death.* Modern epidemiology has let us understand how society's decisions may be responsible for many deaths that once looked like blows
of inscrutable fate: the increase in some cancers, a result of environ-
mental pollution or of the corporate marketing of addictive poisons;
the AIDS pandemic in some cultures, in part the result of official sexual puritanism combined with entrenched poverty; waves of suicides,
a result of increases in unemployment.

Do we dare say these truths aloud when we face the individual
death in all its unique effect upon family and friends? Few of us can at
such grief-stricken moments bear to take note that the behavior of the
person who has died may have had some part in causing death. But at
the level of society's choices, can we invoke the Prophets' teaching of
"Measure for measure," "What we sow is what we reap," without
blaming the person who has died?

Might mourners set aside some time to examine whether society
has acted in such a way as to speed the death they have just suffered?
If this seems more like an assault on their grief than an expression of it,
think about specifics: Would it seem outrageous for mourners of a
child who has been killed in a school shooting to mention the preva-
lence of handguns or of violence in the media as contributory causes?
In the 1980s, did it seem outrageous for those who were mourning a
death from AIDS to mention the society's homophobia and prudery as
possible reasons that adequate energy was not being put into preven-
tive efforts like the teaching of safe sex?

In other words, must grief preclude action to prevent more deaths?

Timing is a separate question. In some situations, the funeral service may be the right moment to address these questions. In others,

they might be raised at *shloshim*, thirty days later, as part of the mourners' stepping back into the world.

Parts of our culture, including some Jews, increasingly see human life not as radically cut off from the lives of other species on our planet but as part of a great continuum. So there are emerging efforts to honor and mourn the deaths of whole species and the deaths of particularly beloved animals and trees.

Finally, one emerging question arising out of a uniquely Jewish memory: In the light of the burning of millions of Jews in the Holocaust ovens, should cremation of bodies be viewed with even more horror, or with a sense that the fires have been redeemed by their victims—so that cremation should be accepted as a possible Jewish practice?

The Renewal of Death

On the surface, all these questions have addressed the ceremonial practices of the mourners. Let us now turn to the other life-path that is implicated in the mourners' journey: the life-path of the dead.

Simcha Raphael has pointed out that during the last generation, secular social scientists have been gathering reports of "near-death experiences." Some of these reports have paralleled some aspects of traditional mystical Jewish teachings about death and the "life-path" of the dead. Indeed, Raphael draws these two literatures together (and also some reports concerning the afterlife from other spiritual traditions, especially Tibetan Buddhism) into a proposed synthesis that may speak to some Jews today and tomorrow. His synthesis is a tour de force.

Meanwhile, there has also been a resurgence of Jewish interest in *gilgul n'shamot*—recycling of souls. This increased interest seems to have something to do with the aftermath of the Holocaust. Stories multiply, and circulate, of converts to Judaism who insist that they have not been "convinced" or "persuaded" or "converted" to become

Jews, but instead have felt themselves coming "home" into a comfortable fit when they discovered Jewish teachings, rituals, and people. One hypothesis that has been put forward to account for these unexpected feelings is that these people may be carrying Jewish souls that had before been carried by people who were murdered in the Holocaust. Because of the sudden massive drop in the numbers of Jews, there were too few Jewish bodies in the next generation through which these souls could return to earth. And perhaps they were so deeply marked by the circumstances of their deaths that the Jewishness of their souls was intensely reinforced at the moment of transition, with few mourners able to smooth the path as in the tradition we have already heard about. So, says this suggestion, they entered non-Jewish bodies but sought their way to Jewish circumstances where they could feel more at home.

Aside from these reports about individuals, people—Jews and people of other spiritual traditions—who have visited Auschwitz in silent meditation rather than as part of a political agenda have reported an awesome sense of the presence of hundreds of thousands of souls. To use an analogy from secular physics, it may be extremely hard to detect a stray muon, one microscopic particle whirling in a swirl of billions larger in size. Even twenty, or two thousand, such ethereal particles may evade almost all sensing mechanisms. But put six million in the same place at the same time, and they may be more detectable on sophisticated measuring instruments.

These various developments have come together to unsettle the Modernist consensus in which many Jews rejected or ignored the possibility of an afterlife. Indeed, many in the present generation—Jewish or not—are skeptical of Modernity and its science of cold facts; skeptical of the dictum that "anything that exists, exists in some amount—and can be counted." Their skepticism has grown out of experiences in arenas far beyond the question of an afterlife. They have been especially taken aback by the ease with which Modern science can be used in its analytic mode for tearing apart cultures, families, species, the web of planetary life. They have sought a more integrative, more holistic form of knowledge. So in regard to afterlife as well, such people are open to the possibility that Modernity's analytic mode may be corroding a reality of woven continuity.

Yet it is not at all clear that "postmodern" Jews will simply return to premodern pictures of the afterlife, strengthened perhaps by the studies of near-death experiences by Elisabeth Kübler-Ross and her students. Instead there are some signs of an emerging "spiritually informed skepticism," quite different both from the impassioned beliefs of Hasidic and Kabbalistic Jews and from the corrosive rejection or agnostic self-assurance of Modernity.

Indeed, one aspect of the Modern Age has stirred up the deepest earthquake beneath all the ways all cultures have sought to deal with death. It has been said that when our societies glimpsed the possibility of the death of all human beings, in nuclear fire or an ecologic whimper, this vision was a meta-death in which all the earlier meanings of death we had constructed fell to pieces. Perhaps at this moment the naked truth shone clear. Try as we may, succeed as we do, to give meaning to all the moments of the cycles of our lives, this moment slips past the boundaries of meaning.

Think of it this way: Each of the life-cycle ceremonies we have discussed has provided a sense of meaning for the changing moments of our lives. As they proceed in a path that we can see and can create and re-create, they give our lives a sense of growing meaning. They give us a handle by which to shape ourselves.

But what happens if we meet a moment that we can't get a handle on? A moment when we can only grope in shadows?

How could such a moment be part of a life-cycle that invites us to create its meaning? In the same way in which the "names" of God we call *Eyn Sof* and *Ayin* can sit uneasy among the other Names of God. *Eyn Sof* means Infinite. *Ayin* means Nothingness. All the other Names of God—*Elohim*, the Unified Creative Powers of the Universe; *Eyl Shaddai*, the Nurturing One on High; *Eyl Elyon*, the Highest in the

Heights; *Eh-yeh Asher Eh-yeh*, I Will Be Who I Am Becoming; *YHWH*, the Breath of Life Who Makes Being To Be, among others— are ways to get a handle, a candle, on what cannot be held in the hands or in the vision. But with *Eyn Sof* and *Ayin* we say: "We give up on trying to get a handle on You, I, She, He, It—Who/Which are without boundaries, without shape, without description. Yet we must cope with that Infinitude, that Emptiness, and so we give It Names." Death is the *Eyn Sof* and the *Ayin* in the cycle of our lives; it blows apart the rituals of meaning. And yet we must create its rituals of meaning.

For a generation that has both digested Modernity and decided to go beyond it, there is a Hasidic teaching that could be very fruitful in addressing the issues of death: "What is the world? The world is God, wrapped in robes of God so as to appear to be material. And we ourselves are God, wrapped in robes of God; our task is to unwrap the robes and dis-cover that we and all the world are God." This teaching affirms both a secular and a mystical understanding of the world. It suggests that one powerful way to relate with God and to understand God is to relate with and understand the world. And the other way around as well. So perhaps it offers a way toward synthesizing the Modernist view that only the memory of the dead and the consequences of their actions in life survive their deaths, and the mystical-Jewish view that the dead themselves live through life-cycles of growth and maturation.

In the world, every act of the living lives on after their deaths. Every act of compassion and cruelty, initiation and fulfillment, enlightenment and obfuscation, Doing and Being, enters into the world. Its consequences are indelible, whether or not anyone remembers to attach a name, a label, to them. All these living never die.

In the Mourners' Kaddish (as in every Kaddish), the only Name God has is *Sh'mey Raba*, the Great Name. What is the meaning of this strange name?

Imagine a Name that holds within its whirling spiral the names of all the beings in the universe. Every quark and galaxy, every symphony and law code, every leaf of grass and every redwood, every turtle, beetle, human being. There is no past or future, for all these names from past and future are present in the present, in *Sh'mey Raba*.

It is often said that the Mourners' Kaddish is not a prayer for the dead—it never mentions death—though we say it in memory of the dead. It seems to celebrate the God by Whose decree of death we are aggrieved. To some this is a puzzle.

Originally the Kaddish was used to punctuate the different sections of a prayer service. One way for us to understand our using it for mourning is that it punctuates the different sections of a life-path—the one that's visible and the one that happens beyond the doorway whose other side we cannot see.

Perhaps we can also hear the Kaddish speaking in one breath about both the living and the dead, all of whose deeds are woven inextricably into the living; those "dead" who therefore cannot die. Speaking in one breath, of all those names within the Great Name.

One *neshama*, one breath. One in-breath/out-breath. One moment of inspiring, one moment of expiring, one breath.

From this perspective, there is no doubting the reality of afterlife. The only question is whether we acknowledge as the Kaddish does— "beyond all blessings, songs, praises, and even consolations we can utter in the world"—the awesomeness of this continuity.

From this perspective came Shira Ruskay's teaching in the last days of her life that *olam hazeh*, this very world, is at every moment the world that's always coming, *olam haba*.

From this perspective come many Jews who are much more open than most Jews have been in the last two centuries to the possibility that *neshamot*, life-breaths, "souls" live on beyond the grave, nourishing new connections and new in-spiration, so that new life might actually be sprouting from a hidden Jewish seed, gone underground.

So perhaps we can see emerging a new approach to understanding death in Jewish terms:

One that sees the realm of God and the realm of earth as not so distinct.

Sees this world and the coming world, *olam hazeh* and *olam haba*, as not so distinct.

Sees the seed in the earth and the seed in the womb as not so distinct.

Sees the end of this book and its beginning as not so distinct.

The Education of a Mensch

WHAT TO DO when your own life-cycle reaches a turning that feels important to you?

First ask yourself where you think this fits in your four-step life-dance. Are you giving birth to a new aspect of your own identity, seeking to encounter another, harvesting your life-experience, or summing it up by seeding for the future? There may well be aspects of all four; how do they color your own perception of your moment?

And then you might explore two different possibilities:

If this is one of the moments on the spiral that the tradition has recognized for generations or centuries, then fill the old forms with new meaning.

If it is a moment you see as momentous but the ancients did not, then construct a ritual that meets your needs—and that may well draw on Jewish teachings in new and unexpected ways, or may even not draw on them in any explicit way at all.

How do you walk either of these two life-paths?

To begin with enlivening the old: Look deeply at the traditional form. Soak yourself in the description we have provided of it in this book, and at the resources for each ceremony that we mention in the essay that follows this one, "Go and Study."

Ask yourself one crucial question: Why did they—the Rabbis, the rebels, the feminists, whoever—shape the ceremony this way? What was going on beneath the service? To welcome a newborn, why snip the foreskin? To celebrate a marriage, why say seven blessings?

If you put yourself in the position of the original liturgist, you may come to feel the passion, the joy, the suffering, that underlie great ritual. You may or may not experience the same emotion, the same thought, the same body tremor, as did the ritual's creator. But if you unpeel your own response and find it full of life, it will not matter whether it is the same one as stirred a poet two thousand years ago. Does it stir you now? That is the question. For it is your life-cycle you are wheeling into.

And even as you use the forms, ancient or new, that you have found already crafted, you may want to clarify your own *kavanot*, your own intentions and understandings of the ceremony. What *for you* is the meaning of your *ḥuppa*, whence comes the cloth you are using for its roof? In *your* midlife transformation ceremony, your own Covenant between the Parts, what is the past work you are cutting open to reexamine, what is the new task you are stretching to accomplish? As you do this, you may find that some other passage, some other poem, some other song or artful instrument, wells up in you. Try it out, to see whether it blends into the larger ceremony. If it does, use it.

Indeed, before the moment itself comes, practice the whole ceremony you are planning. Practice not in order to get it better but to get it deeper. Deeper inside yourself. And listen to your own responses. What feels fake? Drop it. What feels more true than you could have imagined? Deepen it still more.

Ask yourself how to apply the four-step dance that we have pointed toward:

- What act, what statement, will for you bespeak leaving your accustomed role in your accustomed community? Is it literally walking out of the circle of your friends to a separate place? Is it dressing in some distinctive clothing? Singing a new song?

- What will it mean to you to encounter the Mystery, to open yourself to the unexpected Other? Is it to read a Psalm, a poem, to retell a dream you had, to chant in a new language or an old one? Is it to embrace an ancient tree, to lay a cornerstone, to break down a wall, to tear a cloth, to eat a pomegranate?

- What can you do to express a transformed Self? Write a page of diary, teach a word of Torah, unveil a painting of your own, dance a new dance, give a gift of money or a beloved object to some group that is newly a part of your life?

- How can you reenter your community in a new relationship with it? Do its members give you blessings? Do you walk to sit in a different chair? Are you invested with a new title?

If you are facing a moment in your life that has no "official" ceremony to accompany and mark it, your task is similar but perhaps a little harder.

Think deeply about the transition you are marking.

A new job? Perhaps look into biblical stories of work—when Moses became a shepherd, when David became a therapeutic guitarist to the king, when Shifra took up midwifery. What are the tools of your new craft? Can you use them as symbols of the change? Can you anoint them, make them holy? Can you write a code of ethics you intend to guide your work by, or ask your community to join in writing it? Can you draw on models that have appeared in Jewish history, like the Maimonidean code for physicians?

An important birthday? What are the Jewish teachings about reaching this age? What stories in the Bible or the Talmud, in Hasidic memories or Zionist histories, mention people who have reached this age? What are your own hopes, your fears? Can you unveil the memories you have captured in photographs or sound recordings, can you express your hopes and fears in language, music, dance? Can a friend, a parent, tell the story of what this birthday meant to her? Is there an act of *tikkun*, of healing in the world, that you have longed to do but felt unready? Could this birthday become the time of readiness, and could the act of *tikkun* mark the moment?

Whatever the moment that calls out to you in your own journey, marking it with awareness and joy can enrich your own life and that of your community. A series of such moments, if you can see them as jewels strung on the spiral of your life, can become the education of a *Mensch*.

And if your moment of awareness stirs a whole community of friends and family to weave such moments in their many lives together? Such a weaving can help enrich the Jewish people in taking up its own share in the sacred task of healing and hallowing the world. Giving a clearer shape to your own future can help to give a more decent shape to the future of the planet.

Go and Study

During the past generation, many books and articles have both reported and encouraged the flowering of new Jewish life-cycle ritual. Some of these have focused on one part of the life-cycle; some have addressed the different moments in the cycle, through a series of articles by different authors. There have also been several useful handbooks for various ceremonies. We have divided these books into those that traverse the cycle and those that focus on specific parts of it.

THE JEWISH CYCLE AS A WHOLE

See especially Rela M. Geffen, ed., *Celebration & Renewal: Rites of Passage in Judaism* (Jewish Publication Society, 1993), and Debra Orenstein, ed., *Lifecycles: Jewish Women on Life Passages & Personal Milestones* (Jewish Lights, 1994), for insightful and knowledgeable essays on different aspects of the life-cycle.

Richard Siegel, Michael Strassfeld, and Sharon Strassfeld, eds., *The Jewish Catalog* (Jewish Publication Society, 1973); Sharon Strassfeld and Michael Strassfeld, eds., *The Second Jewish Catalog* (Jewish Publication Society, 1976), remain useful in the life-cycle events they describe, including the pioneer work of Shoshana and Mel Silberman on weaning.

Mark X. Jacobs breaks new ground and heals old earth in his pamphlet on *Caring for the Cycle of Life: Creating Environmentally Sound Life-Cycle Celebrations* (Coalition on the Environment and Jewish Life, 1998).

Though they do not focus on life-cycle ceremonies, Zalman Schachter-Shalomi, *Paradigm Shift* (Jason Aronson, 1993); Shohama Harris Wiener and Jonathan Omer-Man, eds., *Worlds of Jewish Prayer* (Jason Aronson, 1988); Jonathan Omer-Man and Shohama Wiener, eds., *The 58th Century* (Jason Aronson, 1991); and Ellen M. Umansky and Dianne Ashton, eds., *Four Centuries of Jewish Women's Spirituality: A Sourcebook* (Beacon Press, 1992), have some material on them and a great deal that is useful in thinking about them. (*Worlds of Jewish Prayer* includes an early covenanting ceremony for girls by Daniel Siegel and Hanna Tiferet Siegel. It has been considerably developed since; call them at 617/363-0371.)

Two rabbi's manuals—Perry Raphael Rank and Gordon M. Freeman, eds., *Rabbi's Manual* (Rabbinical Assembly, 1998), and Seth Daniel Riemer et al., eds., *Rabbi's Manual* (Reconstructionist Rabbinical Association, 1997)—are excellent guides to old and new liturgies. Remember that you do not have to be a rabbi to buy and use these manuals.

For a sense of life-cycle ceremonies in many diverse Jewish communities over the centuries, it is useful to consult Herbert C. Dobrinsky, *A Treasury of Sephardic Laws and Customs* (Yeshiva University Press, 1986); Julian Morgenstern, *Rites of Birth, Marriage, Death and Kindred Occasions Among the Semites* (Hebrew Union College Press, 1966); Hayyim Schauss, *The Lifetime of a Jew: Throughout the Ages of Jewish History* (Union of American Hebrew Congregations, 1960); and Susan Starr Sered, *Women as Ritual Experts: The Religious*

Lives of Elderly Jewish Women in Jerusalem (Oxford University Press, 1992).

In regard to each of the major stages of the life-cycle, we have found the following most useful:

CHILDHOOD

As we said in the text, Nina Beth Cardin, *Tears of Sorrow, Seeds of Hope: A Jewish Spiritual Companion for Infertility and Pregnancy Loss* (Jewish Lights, 1999), is a major contribution to the content of new ritual in this important arena, and to the process of creating new ritual in any area. We found very helpful, in their remarkably different ways: Anita Diamant, *The New Jewish Baby Book: Names, Ceremonies & Customs—A Guide for Today's Families* (Jewish Lights, 1993); Tikva Frymer-Kensky, *Motherprayer: The Pregnant Woman's Spiritual Companion* (Riverhead Books, 1995); Paysach J. Krohn, *Bris Milah, Circumcision—The Covenant of Abraham: A Compendium of Laws, Rituals, and Customs from Birth to Bris, Anthologized from Talmudic and Traditional Sources* (Mesorah Publications, Ltd., 1985); Howard Eilberg-Schwartz, *The Savage in Judaism* (Indiana University Press, 1990), for its chapter on circumcision; and Debra Nussbaum, ed., *Welcoming Your New Jewish Daughter* (Jewish Lights, 2001). In the last-named, see especially Alana Suskin's ceremony of *Brit Melakh*—the Covenant of Salt.

ADOLESCENCE

Two very helpful books about becoming Bar/Bat Mitzvah are Jeffrey K. Salkin, *Putting God on the Guest List: How to Reclaim the Spiritual Meaning of Your Child's Bar or Bat Mitzvah* (Jewish Lights, 1992), and Judith Davis, *Whose Bar/Bat Mitzvah Is This, Anyway?: A Guide for Parents Through a Family Rite of Passage* (St. Martin's Griffin, 1998). Information on the history of Bat Mitzvah celebrations came via email from Howard Tzvi Adelman, Janet Rosenbaum, and L. M. Berkowitz.

The information on the menstruation/*mikva* practices of Ethiopian Jews in Israel came (via email) from Yardena Cope-Yossef of Matan—the Women's Institute for Torah Studies.

MARRIAGE

Rachel Adler, *Engendering Judaism: An Inclusive Theology and Ethics* (Jewish Publication Society, 1998) is a major examination of the theology and practice of traditional Jewish marriage, and of alternatives.

Two important works on the changes created by gay and lesbian Jews are Rebecca Alpert, *Like Bread on the Seder Plate: Jewish Lesbians and the Transformation of Tradition* (Columbia University Press, 1997); and Christie Balka and Andy Rose, *Twice Blessed: On Being Lesbian, Gay, and Jewish* (Beacon Press, 1989). For the practice of gay/lesbian weddings, see the Spring 2000 special issue of *New Menorah* (the journal of ALEPH: Alliance for Jewish Renewal) on "Same-Sex Jewish Marriage in Our Generation"; and a handbook for preparing for gay/lesbian marriages, available from ALEPH at 7000 Lincoln Drive, Philadelphia, PA 19119.

Anita Diamant, *The New Jewish Wedding* (Summit Books, 1985), broke important ground in putting the spiritual as well as practical aspect of weddings back in couples' hands, and remains useful.

Paul Cowan with Rachel Cowan, *Mixed Blessings: Marriage Between Jews and Christians* (Doubleday, 1987); and Azriela Jaffe, *Two Jews Can Still Be a Mixed Marriage: Reconciling Differences over Judaism in Your Marriage* (Career Press, 2000), both give a cogent look at how to deal with religious and spiritual differences within a marriage.

Yitzhak Buxbaum, *An Open Heart: The Mystic Path of Loving People* (Jewish Spirit Booklet Series, 1997); David M. Feldman, *Marital Relations, Birth Control and Abortion in Jewish Law* (Schocken Books, 1974); and Aryeh Kaplan, *Made in Heaven: A Jewish Wedding Guide* (Moznaim, 1983), all present more traditional/spiritual understandings of marriage.

The "Parenting and Partnering" issue of *The Reconstructionist* (vol. 64, no. 2, Spring 2000), and Gershon Winkler with Lakme Batya Elior, *The Place Where You Are Standing Is Holy: A Jewish Theology on Human Relationships* (Jason Aronson, Inc., 1994), explore the questions of marriage and weddings from spiritually mature and creative perspectives.

MIDLIFE

Two pamphlets by Irene Fine broke early ground in this area: *Midlife and Its Rite of Passage Ceremony—with a Midlife Celebration by Bonnie Feinman* (Women's Institute for Continuing Jewish Education, San Diego, 1983); and *Midlife: A Rite of Passage; The Wise Woman: A Celebration* (Women's Institute for Continuing Jewish Education, San Diego, 1988).

Susan Berrin, ed., *A Heart of Wisdom: Making the Jewish Journey from Midlife Through the Elder Years* (Jewish Lights, 1997), is a fine collection on this segment of the life-cycle.

Nan Fink [Gefen], *Stranger in the Midst: A Memoir of Spiritual Discovery* (Basic Books, 1997), richly explores the process of conversion to Judaism.

Elise Edelson Katch, *The Get: A Spiritual Memoir of Divorce* (Simcha Press, 2001), is a powerful evocation of the journey of a Jewish divorce.

Zalman Schachter-Shalomi and Ronald S. Miller, *From Age-ing to Sage-ing* (Warner Books, 1995), draws deeply on Jewish experience and spirituality, as well as on other traditions and modern social science, to open up spiritual perspectives on late midlife.

DEATH

For us, two books in this area were transformative: Anne Brener, *Mourning & Mitzvah: A Guided Journal for Walking the Mourner's Path Through Grief to Healing* (Jewish Lights, 1993); and Simcha Paull Raphael, *Jewish Views of the Afterlife* (Jason Aronson, 1994).

For the Zohar's view of the journey of the soul, see Fischel Lachower and Isaiah Tishby, *The Wisdom of the Zohar* (Littman Library/Oxford University Press, 1989).

Jack Reimer and Nathaniel Stampfer, eds., *A Treasury of Jewish Ethical Wills* (Schocken, 1983), and *So That Your Values Live On: Ethical Wills and How to Prepare Them* (Jewish Lights, 1991), are useful guides to planting seeds for the future.

Maurice Lamm, *The Jewish Way in Death and Mourning* (Jonathan David, 1969), is an unusually helpful guide to traditional practice and ethics of mourning. It is honorably complemented by Jack Riemer, *Jewish Reflections on Death* (Schocken, 1974).

For personal search and growth in the wake of a death, see E. M. Broner, *Mornings and Mourning* (HarperCollins, 1994), Leon Wieseltier, *Kaddish* (Knopf, 1998), and Leonard Fein, *Against the Dying of the Light* (Jewish Lights, 2001).

Sidney Greenberg and Jonathan D. Levine, eds., *A Minyan of Comfort: Worship, Study, and Reflection for the House of Mourning* (Prayer Book Press/Media Judaica, 1996), and Nessa Rapoport, *A Woman's Book of Grieving* (William Morrow, 1994), are utterly different, both helpful, approaches to prayer in time of mourning.

In regard to simplicity in funerals, see www.Jewish-funerals.org, the Web site of the Jewish Funeral Practices Committee of Greater Washington.

THEORY OF RITUAL

For an understanding of life-cycle rituals, it is still helpful to begin with Arnold van Gennep, *The Rites of Passage* (orig. 1909; University of Chicago Press, 1960). We also found Ronald L. Grimes, *Deeply into the Bone: Re-Inventing Rites of Passage* (University of California Press, 2000); Catherine Bell, *Ritual Perspective and Dimensions* (Oxford University Press, 1997); Catherine Bell, *Ritual Theory, Ritual Practice* (Oxford University Press, 1992); and Victor Tumer, *The Ritual Process: Structure and Anti-Structure* (Aldine De Gruyter, 1969), major reexaminations of these ceremonies.

Three books by Arthur Waskow suggest ways of addressing Judaism and life that could seed new thought on the life-cycle: *Seasons of Our Joy* (Beacon, 1990); *Down-to-Earth Judaism: Food, Money, Sex, & the Rest of Life* (William Morrow, 1995); and *Godwrestling—Round 2* (Jewish Lights, 1996).

Our Thanks

In working on this book, in thinking about the renewal of Judaism, and in exploring our lives, we have drawn especially on deep conversations that we have had—sometimes one of us, sometimes both—with a number of our intimate friends. We are listing them here in the order in which these conversations entered deeply into our own life-cycles:

Rabbi Max Ticktin, Esther Ticktin, Rabbi Zalman Schachter-Shalomi, Shira Greenberg Ruskay *z'l*, Barbara Breitman; a men's group that included Jeffrey Dekro, Rabbi Mordechai Liebling, Rabbi Jeff Roth, and Rabbi Brian Walt; Howard Waskow, Grey Wolfe, Rabbi Shefa Gold, Bahira Sugarman, Rabbi Shaya Isenberg, Shoshana Cooper, Rabbi David Cooper, and Billee Laskin.

And we have learned enormously from the thoughts and actions of our children: Morissa Sher, Joshua Sher, Shoshana Elkin Waskow and Michael Slater, and David Waskow and Ketura Persellin.

Leon Oboler did important work for The Shalom Center, freeing some of Arthur's attention, while we were working on this book.

The birthing of this book occurred through fits and hiccups. We owe special thanks to Sydelle Kramer, our agent, and Linda Rosenberg and Elisheva Urbas, our editors at Farrar, Straus and Giroux, for their midwifery. Urbas, who originally commissioned the book, late in its gestation also provided a thorough, intelligent, and detailed sonogram.

And most of all, we thank each other for the dance, sometimes close, sometimes distant, sometimes joyous, sometimes painful, that is our life together.

POB & AOW

The Authors

In 1979 Phyllis Ocean Berman founded (with Anne Lelan Nguyen), and has since been Director (with Leslie Robbins) of, the Riverside Language Program—a unique intensive school (located in New York City) for teaching the English language and American culture to newly arrived adult immigrants and refugees from all around the world. Out of her work with immigrants she coauthored with David Blot a book of stories of immigrants' lives, *Getting into It*, and has written several articles on the impact of American public policy on immigrants and refugees.

Berman is also Director of the Summer Program of the Elat Chayyim retreat center, and a Jewish-renewal liturgist, prayer leader, Torah-teacher, and storyteller. Her articles on new ceremonies for women and new *midrash* have appeared in *Moment*, *Worlds of Jewish Prayer*, *Tikkun*, and *Good Housekeeping*. She has been ordained an *Eyshet Ḥazon* (Woman of Vision) by the Jewish-renewal community and is now studying for the rabbinate. She is the coauthor of *Tales of*

Tikkun: New Jewish Stories to Heal the Wounded World (Jason Aronson, 1996).

Since 1969, Rabbi Arthur Ocean Waskow has been one of the leading creators of theory, practice, and institutions for the movement for Jewish renewal. He is a Pathfinder of ALEPH: Alliance for Jewish Renewal. He founded and directs The Shalom Center, a division of ALEPH that draws on Jewish thought and practice to seek peace, pursue justice, heal the earth, and build community. Web site www.shalomcir.org.

Among his seminal works in Jewish renewal are *The Freedom Seder*; *Godwrestling*; *Seasons of Our Joy*; *Down-to-Earth Judaism: Food, Money, Sex, and the Rest of Life*; and *Godwrestling—Round Two* (recipient of the Benjamin Franklin Award in 1996). He is also co-editor of *Trees, Earth, & Torah: A Tu B'Shvat Anthology* (Jewish Publication Society, 1999) and the editor of *Torah of the Earth: Exploring 4,000 Years of Ecology in Jewish Thought* (Jewish Lights, 2000).

In 1996, Waskow was named by the United Nations a "Wisdom Keeper"—one among forty religious and intellectual leaders from around the world who met in connection with the Habitat II conference in Istanbul. In 2001 he was given the Abraham Joshua Heschel Award by the Jewish Peace Fellowship. Waskow taught at the Reconstructionist Rabbinical College from 1982 to 1989, and has taught as a visiting professor in the religion departments of Swarthmore College, Temple University, Drew University, and Vassar College. In 1998, he convened a multireligious group on Overwork & Free Time in American society (www.FreeOurTime.org) and in 2002, a multireligious project, "Eleven Days in September: Remembrance, Reflection, and Renewal."

With his children David and Shoshana, he wrote a book of midrashic tales of the Creation for children and adults, *Before There Was a Before*. Together with his brother, Howard, he wrote *Becoming Brothers*. It is a "wrestle in two voices," a joint autobiography focused on the conflicts and interactions between the two brothers.

From 1959 to 1982, as legislative assistant for a US. congressman, then as a cofounding Fellow of the Institute for Policy Studies, and then as a Colleague of the Public Resource Center, Waskow worked on public-policy issues regarding nuclear strategy, disarmament, race relations, the Vietnam War, community-based approaches to renewable energy, and violence and nonviolence in American social change.

Waskow and Berman decided to share "Ocean" as a middle name when they got married. They live in Mount Airy, a politically progressive and spiritually creative multiracial neighborhood of Philadelphia nestled among trees, a river, and the Weavers Way food coop. As this book goes to press, they have two children each, two children-in-law, and two grandchildren.

Index